Sustaining Family Enterprise

Meeting the Challenges of Continuity, Control and Competitiveness

Consulting Editor **Richard L Narva**

Consulting editor
Richard L Narva

Managing director
Sian O'Neill

***Sustaining Family Enterprise: Meeting the Challenges of Continuity, Control and Competitiveness*
is published by**
Globe Law and Business Ltd
3 Mylor Close
Horsell
Woking
Surrey GU21 4DD
Tel: +44 20 3745 4770
www.globelawandbusiness.com

Printed and bound by Gomer Press

Sustaining Family Enterprise: Meeting the Challenges of Continuity, Control and Competitiveness
ISBN 9781911078142

Table of contents

Preface

Richard L Narva
Narva & Company LLC

In a 2008 article on family controlled media companies in *Portfolio* magazine, Professor Jonathan Knee, the then director of the Media Project of Columbia University in the United States, wrote:[1]

> *[T]he prime determinant of how long a family dynasty will endure is how well its business is run. Nothing is more likely to spur a family insurrection and provoke demands to sell than the perception that the business is not being managed efficiently. Those who romanticize family ownership are often the same people who encourage policies that will almost certainly accelerate its disintegration.*

I think Professor Knee was on to something very important at a time when virtually all the writing on family business was about 'succession' – ie, how the older generation owners of a family firm pass control to their progeny. And to gauge by the number of pages of articles and books about family business that are focused on succession, it would seem the view of most experts was (and remains) that succession is the primary issue in a family business. I do not agree.

Should 'success' not 'succession' be the primary focus of families that control operating companies? In my view, the answer is clearly, "Yes, but …."

Yes, because without a successful business there is nothing for the family to lose when succession goes awry except a chance to sell the company at a steep discount (known as the 'family discord discount') or, worse, an unforeseen visit to a bankruptcy court. For a full discussion of the utility of focusing on success rather than succession, see the essay entitled "Entrepreneurship in family firms: reassessing the fascination with success, failure and succession" by Jennifer Halyk.[2]

But great family enterprises are never just about business success; nor is continued family control solely dependent on profits distributed to shareholders. Rather, unless the core values on which the family controlled enterprise was founded – and which undergird all decision-making by both managers and owners – are honoured regularly and with deep understanding, great family controlled companies inevitably decline to the level of their merely good competitors, and worse. Adherence to core values was the single distinguishing characteristic that Jim Collins and Jerry Porras, authors of the classic business book, *Built to Last*,[3] found to be the

1 *Portfolio* magazine, Portfolio Publications, 2008.

2 In Richard L Narva (consulting editor), *Family Enterprises: How to Build Growth, Family Control and Family Harmony*, Globe Law and Business, 2015 (see www.globelawandbusiness.com/FEH).

3 Jim Collins and Jerry Porras, *Built to Last: Successful Habits of Visionary Companies*, Random House, 2005 (first published by HarperCollins in 1994).

sole distinguishing characteristic that truly great companies demonstrated when their merely good competitors did not. And what is true about great publicly traded companies is also true for great family controlled enterprises.

Collins and Porras were not writing explicitly about family controlled companies (although at least half of the truly great companies they profiled were either still family controlled or had been for at least two generations). Nonetheless, what they found in their six-year-long research study is, in my experience working with more than 400 family controlled companies over more than 30 years, profoundly true of such firms. Without regular reference to their core values, family controlled firms can rarely achieve or sustain greatness. In this respect, family firms are indistinguishable from more widely owned companies. What distinguishes the family controlled enterprise from other business entities is the source of their corporate culture, which is first and foremost the culture of the founding family.

But while fealty to business ideals rooted in the culture of the founding family is necessary for greatness, it is not sufficient. Great ideas that are not explained well – often both to members of the controlling family as they come to maturity and to employees – lose their potency to inspire great performance. Moreover, unlike companies with broad public ownership, the core values of business-owning families may include not only 'wheat' – such as commitment to quality, a focus on employee well-being, and a deep desire to serve the needs of their customers – but also the 'chaff' of an excessive sense of privacy and habitually poor communication about emotionally powerful issues. Such unhelpful cultural norms, when found rooted in the culture of the founding family, can preclude the kind of communication in family controlled companies about core values that all great companies require in order to thrive.

The core values of great companies, whether family controlled or publicly traded, must be articulated clearly and repeated frequently – although one need not (as one of my clients did) carve them into the granite lintels over the front entrance of the corporate headquarters. There are in fact numerous other ways to ensure that core values endure.[4]

This book is an endeavour to collect the wisdom of many leading stakeholders in family firms about how to leverage the single most powerful competitive asset of family controlled enterprises, namely their culture, to ensure continuity of competitiveness, family control and family harmony. Keeping in mind Peter Drucker's oft-cited caution about too much focus on applying the left side of the brain to business, expressed as "Culture eats strategy for breakfast", the express intent of this volume is to assist stakeholders in family firms in benefiting from leverage of both their strategy and their culture – an objective that requires all hands, as we shall see, to be fluent both in the language of business and the particular dialect of the family controlled enterprise to which they dedicate their endeavours.

---

4 See, for example, my article, "Heritage and Tradition in Family Business: How Family-Controlled Enterprises Connect the Experience of their Past to the Promise of their Future", available at http://narvaandcompany.com/heritage-and-tradition-in-family-business/.

Managing intergenerational expectations, responsibilities and relationships in a family enterprise

Emily F Abrams
Narva & Company LLC
Louis Turchetta
Strategic Psychological Services

We were never given a choice about working in the business. Our parents simply expected it of us and only one of our brothers rebelled. Sure, it would be nice if our own kids were interested in the business, but we want them to make their own choices. We really just want them to be happy. (Second-generation family shareholder)

1. Introduction

Planning for the entrance of the next generation to the business is still relatively informal in most family enterprises. Parents are rarely able to take an objective approach to the subject of their children's strengths and limitations, much less receive honest feedback on their performance once they have been employed in the business. And unfortunately the damage of bringing a son or daughter into the company unprepared for the level of contributions expected of them is vastly underestimated.

These days, when a depth of organisational structure has been established and a layer of talented non-family management is contributing sophisticated strength to the performance of family controlled growth companies, shareholders who cherish the dream of a next generation of family management must utilise a process of bringing in new family members with deliberate, thoughtful planning. They must take great care to avoid creating resentment among non-family employees, maintain a high level of motivation among its non-family leadership and ensure that each new family employee meets an expected business performance standard or receives appropriate business support in the form of coaching or mentoring – it is never appropriate to afford a family employee special treatment simply because of family status. Indeed, bringing family members into a company of significant size without adequate preparation, maturity and a well-developed work ethic can not only introduce undue stress to the family but also have a profoundly negative impact on the enterprise itself that can be felt for years.

This chapter addresses the realities that parents face as they raise children in a world of increasing material consumption and changing values. We share some hard truths about how to help children counteract these social realities to become responsible adults and potential family employees with the opportunity to bring real value to the enterprise their family controls. We have learned many important lessons from dedicated parents we have advised in the past and from conscientious members of the next generation we have mentored, as they grapple with the thorny issues of parent–child relationships against the backdrop of the family controlled enterprise.

The biggest challenge for the current generation, in our experience, has been the transmission of a healthy work ethic to children whose aspirations include attaining early in their careers lifestyles akin to the level their parents achieved after a lifetime of work. Through our work with families aiming to prepare their companies and families for bringing in its first next-generation member, we have substantial evidence of the success that can be achieved through the strategies and protocols we describe later in this chapter. These procedures have also proved successful with families deeply discouraged by the poor results of earlier efforts to bring one or more of their children into the business without adequate preparation. Damage from earlier attempts to bring the next generation into the enterprise without benefit of skilled advice can be repaired slowly by developing a comprehensive plan and renewed preparation by the family under the guidance of a multidisciplinary advisory team.

While it is still relatively rare for families to seek professional advice well in advance of bringing in the very first member of the next generation, the number of forward-thinking family companies is growing. Driven by a desire to protect their business's hard-won success, fuelled by horror stories from other companies and often still smarting from their own premature recruitment to the business, senior generations are turning to business advisers to assist their preparation of formal next-generation guidelines for entry. Preparing both the company and future family employees for productive roles and the values that the family respects is a practice that requires deliberate planning, combining the art and science of proven parenting practices with regular mentoring support for the younger generation as soon as they enter the family firm.

2. Early preparation is essential

Long before parents even begin thinking about whether their children might enter the business at some time in the future, there are steps they can take to guide them towards a responsible, competent and confident adulthood.

Parents today feel an enormous sense of responsibility for their children's happiness. Some also feel a sense of guilt for not spending enough time with their children, especially in the early years. It is not uncommon for parents who want their offspring to have a better life than they did themselves to try to compensate by giving them too much and expecting too little of them. In *Choking on the Silver Spoon*,[1] Gary Buffone explains that children who are overindulged can become

1 Gary Buffone, *Choking on the Silver Spoon: keeping your kids healthy, wealthy, and wise in a land of plenty*, Simplon Press, 2003.

underachievers lacking motivation, ambition and drive. They can have a low frustration tolerance and be unable to go without or to delay gratification; often, they expect rewards without effort. Children who are given everything without having to earn it are being trained to expect everything for nothing. As Rudolph Dreikurs, the psychiatrist, educator and author of many parenting books, has cautioned: "Never do for a child what he can do for himself."[2] Individuals, in fact, thrive on overcoming obstacles and successfully completing goals – a lesson that parents can help children learn early in life.

In a family enterprise, parents can also view development of the next generation from the perspective of family systems theory. Family systems literature discusses the concept of stages of family development. One of the later stages in this framework is the 'launching pad' stage, during which children prepare to leave home and successfully transition to independent adulthood. Even so, too many parents attempt to hold on to their children to avoid what can be termed a healthy loss. Sometimes, they will not expect anything from their offspring and allow them to live in their home unproductively. At other times, business-owning parents may pressure their children into taking jobs for which they are not suited or create positions that the business does not need in order to keep their children near home.

Family members should be aware of the effect of keeping families together beyond the launching pad stage, especially under one roof, because the temptation not to alter the habitual patterns of familial interactions is powerful. For example, parents can continue to treat their sons or daughters as young and incapable, and their children can continue to play out adolescent rebellion, balking at the authority of the parent. Such interactions can be unpleasant for both generations when experienced at home. When these family dramas are acted out in the venue of the family controlled company, the credibility of both the parents as leaders and their children as future leaders can be compromised.

3. Parenting myths

Helping children develop a sense of responsibility and accountability rather than one of entitlement has become increasingly challenging for parents. Unfortunately, the role of parenting comes with no training apart from observing the parenting styles of one's own parents or those of other people. Moreover, there are no specific skills laid down and no licence is required for the job. Parenting can be considered akin to allowing an individual who has had surgery or watched surgical procedures on television to operate on someone else.

Here are two common misconceptions about parenting:

- *Myth one: Permissive parenting is not pampering* – Many parents do not set limits and pamper their children by doing things for them. Pampering is actually a form of disrespect. The key to providing children with the skills they need to make it in the world is not to make their lives easy. Children need to experience failure, frustration and disappointment and learn to get past these difficulties. While parents should provide encouragement during

2 Rudolph Dreikurs and Vicki Soltz, *Children: The Challenge*, Plume, 1991.

their children's challenges, they should not seek to take the challenges away.

- *Myth two: Children can be forced to obey* – Some authoritative parents believe they can bully their children into complying with their expectations by criticising, threatening and nagging them, and by becoming overly involved in areas that are clearly the child's responsibility. However, this approach hinders rather than promotes responsibility.

4. Roadmap for inspiring a healthy work ethic

There are a number of ways in which parents (and others) can inspire a healthy work ethic in members of a younger generation. One such method is to develop a parenting model based on mutual respect. With this more democratic approach, parents still provide guidance and discipline, but they do so in a respectful manner, modelling the behaviour they expect of their children.

Parents should focus early on encouragement and effective communication, on allowing children to take on appropriate responsibilities, and on firm but loving discipline. More specifically:

- *Providing encouragement* – One of the most powerful interventions a parent can use is encouragement, which consists of highlighting a child's assets in order to build self-esteem and helping their children focus on possibilities and solutions. Often, this requires a parent to 'separate the deed from the doer' when a child is frequently misbehaving. For example, if a child gets bad grades because he or she does not do homework, a parent can explain that he or she knows the child likes to be successful (relating some historical event that represents the child's desire to succeed, such as how hard the child worked to improve a tennis swing) and that, once the child figures out how important school is, the child's performance will improve.
- *Effective communication* – An incredibly important skill for effective parenting is communication. Parents must listen to the verbal and non-verbal language of children. Effective communicators, whether in the family or in the business, listen and try to understand the other person's point of view and share their understanding before introducing their own ideas. When confrontation is necessary, it is done skilfully and assertively rather than aggressively and angrily.
- *Appropriate responsibility* – One of the primary ways to encourage responsibility and self-sufficiency is to give children choices, where appropriate, and let them experience the consequences of their actions. For example, a parent may give a child an allowance and let them budget the money. While some portion of the money should go towards savings and some portion towards charity, the child would have the rest to spend as they choose. If the child decides to spend all the money on a video game and doesn't have money to go out with friends, the child will have to miss that chance to go out. The parent should not criticise the child's decision-making nor, tempting as it may be, bail the child out in such circumstances, which would rob the child of an important lesson.
- *Discipline, not punishment* – While effective parents may not be happy with a

child's misbehaviour, a mild emotional response allows them to take a matter-of-fact approach. The preferred method of discipline among effective parents is to use logical or natural consequences instead of punishment. With the logical consequence approach, a child is given a choice: for example, if the child returns home past curfew hour, he/she would be told that the next occurrence of coming in past curfew would result in not being allowed to go out the following night; the child can choose the consequence, or choose to avoid it by coming in on time. A natural consequence, on the other hand, typically requires no intervention from parents: for instance, if a teen decides to go out without gloves or a warm coat, the natural consequence of being cold should be sufficient to help the child learn more appropriate clothing choices.

5. Business decisions for business, not family reasons

One reality that business families must face is that not every child in the family is suited for work in the business the family controls. Doing the right thing for both the child and the enterprise sometimes means that parents need to guide their child in a direction better suited to that person's strengths and personality. When children who by nature or competence are poorly matched for available career positions in the company persist in the desire to be employed there, the company's needs should weigh more heavily on the decision maker than the desire of the child. Creating jobs for children that are unnecessary for the company creates a drain on the business, a strain on family and non-family managers, and a morale problem for company employees generally.

This recommendation applies to career positions. Availability of summer, interim, or other non-career positions need not be viewed with the same level of stringency.

6. Preparation and support for the entrance of the next generation

Here are the six formal steps that families should take to prepare for the entrance of the next generation into the family enterprise.

6.1 Create a family vision and next-generation employment philosophy

Draft a statement defining the family's philosophy toward family employment at the company. It can be a statement of any length, but it should be created as a guideline not only for the immediately anticipated members of the next generation who might join the company, but as a policy for future generations as well. It should include a statement defining who a 'family member' is in the context of eligibility for employment at the company – for instance, do spouses qualify as family members for the purposes of employment at the company?

Ultimately, this statement of the family's philosophy should become part of the constituent documents that guide and support the family's culture and core values in the business enterprise.

6.2 Create a policy for family member entrance qualifications and criteria

Early in the preparation process, create a formal policy of entrance qualifications and specific criteria for all future family employment at the company. Be sure to include in this policy:

- the required level of education;
- the number of full-time-equivalent years that a family member must work for another company before earning the right to work in the family controlled company;
- protocols for compensation, evaluation and termination; and
- mentoring support during the first few years on the job.

6.3 **Collaborate with established human resources processes**

It is important to work in close collaboration with the company's head of human resources to identify the family candidate's appropriate point of entry, which should be consistent with the needs of the company and commensurate with a position that is a suitable match for the incoming family member's education, experience, skills and desired level of involvement at the company. In addition, there should be support for the human resources function in establishing a carefully structured plan of training and professional development for the family member's initial position at the company, for evaluation of performance, and for any developmental changes in the role.

6.4 **Establish clear boundaries between next-generation employees and their parents**

Parents should interact minimally with their children during the working day and treat them as they would any other employee. Parents need to give their children the space to develop friendships among their fellow employees. They should also protect their time together outside the company in order to preserve harmonious family relationships.

6.5 **Provide mentoring support**

Mentoring is a key component of this comprehensive plan. Initiate a mentoring process that is individually tailored to support the success of each new next-generation member. It should provide non-judgemental advice and support as well as honest feedback for the new family employee about meeting the expectations of the job.

Sessions should be regularly scheduled, over a period of at least two years, for confidential conversations with an outside adviser who understands the culture of the company and ideally is part of the family's trusted advisory team. In addition, an internal mentor (usually a member of the company's management team) should be provided. This internal mentor can be changed over time to provide regular guidance for the new family member in adjusting to the demands of the job and the culture of the company.

6.6 **Preparation for the management team**

When the time is appropriate, communicate regularly with the management team about the integration of the next-generation member into management in order to maintain confidence that their own roles are respected and remain critical to the success of the business. Ask for the team's input as to whom they would recommend on the management team to mentor the new next-generation member once that member has become a manager. Ideally, the mentor would not be a family member nor someone on the new family member's team.

Management should be encouraged to treat the new family employee as they would any other employee and provide honest feedback to senior management regarding the new family employee's skills and performance.

7. Tips for new family employees

Here are some clear rules as expressed by a successful family employee whom we have mentored for the past three years. He has offered the following insights to share with those just beginning the journey:

- Don't try to come into the company too early – you might not have the maturity level or the work might be too difficult for you to succeed.
- Act like a regular employee.
- Pay your dues: don't expect anything to be handed to you.
- Don't try to use your name to your personal advantage over non-family employees.
- Don't put non-family supervisors in a difficult position by asking a parent in the company to override an action or decision the supervisor has made.
- Try to take the same steps that every other employee must undertake in order to advance in the job.
- Go to your parents as a last resort, not to pull rank.
- Be ready to put your head down and work hard for no more money than anyone else would make in the same job.
- Meet with your external and internal mentors religiously – you need them all. They're behind the process for your success and it will make a big difference. Knowing you have someone to talk to about situations that come up at work is critical. They can provide the needed perspective and understanding of the bigger picture to help you work through the issues, navigate the bumps, and even sometimes be talked off the threshold of giving up and going to work elsewhere.
- Find out what it means to be a great employee at the company. Ask your mentor what the traits and skills of elite performers are, and strive to rise to that level.
- Remember that the extra benefits of being a family member should come from the family source, not the business enterprise.

8. Conclusion

Family enterprises can offer great opportunities for the next generation to develop and succeed in contributing to the success of the company. But being born into a family shareholder group is not sufficient to ensure a child will integrate into the business seamlessly. Rather, preparation is critical to ensuring a family member's competence. Without it, the results can be disastrous for both the organisation and familial relationships.

To prepare children adequately to take on the responsibilities expected at the company, parents must learn how to be effective at instilling responsibility. The earlier that families begin the process, the greater the chance they will succeed in helping their children develop a sense of confidence, a healthy work ethic and an understanding of the responsibilities that come with a job at a company representing the family's legacy. In addition to preparing their children, parents must also understand and prepare family managers and non-family leadership as well. By following a methodical approach, the ideal outcome will be a competent next-generation employee who is excited about working in the family enterprise, is welcomed appropriately by non-family managers, contributes to the company's success and is appreciated by other employees.

How the next generation is prepared for entrance and mentored during and after the process of entering the company are key determining factors in whether the enterprise continues to be family-managed in the future, or controlled by the family but led by skilled non-family professionals – or even whether the family owners sell the enterprise. Unless the entrance of the next generation is approached with thorough and deliberate preparation by both the family and senior managers of the company, and working at the company is considered a privilege to be earned by the younger generation rather than an easier path to the lifestyle to which they may have become accustomed, issues will arise despite the best intentions of all parties.

Family values: the soul of family business

Thomas Hubler
Hubler for Business Families Inc

1. Introduction

The primary pathway to understanding a family firm is recognising the centrality of the family's history and values. The heart and soul of a family business are its values, which underlie the corporate culture of the enterprise and create the essence of a family business's unique competitive strengths. It is this 'secret sauce' element that distinguishes it from competitors and can makes it a special place to work.

In my 30-plus years of working with family businesses, I have learned that these values emerge from multiple sources. The sources include family history, religious values, hardship and adversity, and the value of hard work and determination. This chapter will focus how all the stakeholders of a family controlled business enterprise identify and nurture the values that are so essential to family business success.

In the discussion that follows, I provide a description and examples of what I do to promote the kind of dialogue that develops family values, comprising the following:

- the emergence of sharing family values;
- the creation and nurture of a common family vision based on family values, and the development of the emotional equity of the family;
- family so-called 'kything' and a reciprocal commitment to each other's success;
- introduction of a model for collaborative communication;
- regular and periodic family meetings to promote family dialogue and values;
- solidification of the moral infrastructure; and
- ethical norms based on family values.

The discussion that follows is not meant to be an academic exposition, but a description of how I see the guidelines and values applied in family businesses.

2. The soul of a family

The most perplexing question in the context of family businesses has to do with the nature of a family's 'soul'. From my perspective, this 'soul' is what drives all of what happens in family businesses, and it is the indefinable essence of a family's spirit, being and values. It is an issue that can and should be of profound importance to the largest and the smallest of family controlled enterprises. Here is what the chairman of Ford Motor Company said on the subject in *The New York Times*:[1]

I don't know if a company can have a soul, but I like to think it can. And if it can, I'd

1 M Sherrill, "The Buddha of Detroit", *The New York Times Magazine*, 26 November 2000.

like our soul to be an old soul – and everything that implies. I'd like to talk about things like values and soul. These things aren't transient. These are things you build forever.

'Soul' is not something that can be measured or quantified, but it is easily recognisable by both its presence and absence. The soul of family business is not easily defined. Set out next are attempts to reflect its nature.

David Whyte, in his book entitled *The Heart Aroused,*[2] quotes James Hillman and his definition of soul, saying: "Its meaning is best given by its context ... words long associated with the soul amplify it further: mind, spirit, heart, life, warmth, humanness, personality, individuality, intentionality, essence, innermost purpose, emotional quality, virtue, morality, sin, wisdom, death." The soul, according to David Whyte, "has to be imagined as ... given by God and thus, divine".[3] The result: it is important for families to be vigilant and receptive when the soul comes knocking, with its implied sense of virtue and conscience.

It is important to understand that the soul will emerge, but families must be receptive, vigilant and accommodating when the family's soul cautiously presents itself. The recognition of the soul is not an automatic process; it requires the family to quieten itself so as to be able to recognise the soul when it emerges. One of the primary ways in which a clinically trained adviser to family firms can intervene effectively is to assist the members of a business-controlling family to create enough quiet in the family for family members to recognise their soul when it presents itself. At the same time, managers of the family business can focus all their energies on enhancing business competitiveness.

Clearly, the family soul is shy, reticent and easily spooked. At the same time, it is persevering and can be relentless with its message. What we need to understand is creating an environment where the soul's message can be savoured and brought into the presence of family consciousness. The soul's presence, according to David Whyte,[4] is "the palatable presence of some sacred otherness in our labors". It does not make any difference whether you call that otherness God, the universe, destiny, life or love; for me it is the source of moral consciousness and creates the family point of view and family values.

3. The primacy of family values

The manifestation of the soul in family business, from my perspective, emerges as a result of discussion of family values. These values are those that the family wants to see perpetuated in the company, and they serve as a rich source for family creativity, ethics and moral stance. In my experience, and in the consultation process we use, the family is asked, "What are the family values that you would like to see perpetuated in the company?" As a result of this question a rich family discussion can occur where family values are discussed and prioritised. The discussion is often enlightening for family members as they begin to verbalise and connect emotionally in a conscious way around their common family values.

---

2 David Whyte, *The Heart Aroused*, Bantam Doubleday Dell Publishing Group, 1994, p14.
3 *Ibid.*
4 David Whyte, *The Heart Aroused*, Bantam Doubleday Dell Publishing Group, 1994, p15.

For me, these values are utilised in the creation of what I describe as a 'common family vision', which becomes the moral compass for the family as it creates the ethical climate for its family business and the foundation for the evolution of the family point of view. This family point of view is the gyroscope that guides managers, directors and owners as they build a corporate culture, develop corporate strategies and execute their business plans.

4. The common family vision

The common family vision in the context of our work with family businesses is a vision that arises from articulation of the family's values. It is used as a superordinate goal to unite the family around its values and its soulfulness. The common family vision, alongside uniting the family, also inspires family members to both collectively and individually be able to manifest the vision in all aspects of their work and personal lives.

In order for the common family vision to have a significant impact on the evolution of the family's conscience and the creation of a family point of view, it needs to be something that, in my experience, is nurtured and recited on a daily basis. The benefits of a common family vision and its value to the family may then be accomplished as a group or by an individual family member. The individual or family can measure their performance and whether they are behaving consistently with their common vision. The daily recitation and repetitive nature embodies the spirit of the common vision and its values. The repetition is similar to that of high-performance athletes when their activities become second nature because of the multiple repetitions they perform. The same is true in families when they recite the common vision so that it becomes an embodiment of their soul.

Two examples illustrate the creation of a common family vision. First, we have the Danz family (fictitious name), a family consisting of a father, mother and two sons, all of whom work in their small family business. The older son and father, although working side by side, have not spoken to each other in four years. At their initial family meeting they were able to put aside their differences and made a contribution to the common good, and participated with other members of the family to create the Danz common family vision:

In our family and business, we promote respect, honesty and fairness, and encourage an environment that is loyal and unified. At the heart of our vision is our commitment to generosity, quality and an appreciation of one other's gifts. As a hard-working and dedicated family, we communicate and celebrate our spirituality.

As a conservative, traditional Catholic family, the Danz family's vision represents their soulfulness in coming together as a family to begin the dialogue where their family point of view will emerge.

Another example is the Sweeney family (again, a fictitious name), which is a family of two parents with four adult children. Together, they own the family business; but only the oldest son and the father work in the business. The son and his father were having difficulties in terms of the son's emerging role as a leader. In addition, the parents were concerned that the financial blessings that were coming the way of the adult children would in fact corrupt them and possibly have a negative impact on their grandchildren. The Sweeney common family vision is thus:

Our family circle is an unbreakable bond of support, belief in each other, and unconditional love. It inspires us to live our lives with humility, integrity and philanthropy. We manifest this through our families, our foundation, and our business.

Again, the soulfulness of the family emerges in their common vision and becomes an inspiration to them as to how to lead their lives as a family, as well as their business and community involvement.

Another aspect of the common vision and building the emotional equity of the family is the 'prayer for loving-kindness'. This is a ritual that we create for families, which includes the recitation of the common vision, as well as the family prayer for loving-kindness. The prayer is:

May our family be filled with loving-kindness
May our family be well
May our family be peaceful and at ease
May our family be happy.

The goal of the prayer for loving-kindness is to assist the family in beginning to program their subconscious about what they want. Again, the idea is to recite the prayer on a daily basis so that it becomes a continuum or embodiment of the family's soulfulness and virtues. It becomes an inspiration to use the common vision as a resource to unite the family.

In my experience with family businesses, families are always trying to create unity in their families. The traditional methods for creating unity include compromise and giving things up; in contrast, I encourage families to set aside these notions and to understand that no individual in a family is always going to get 100% of what he or she wants. Instead, family members should focus on doing what they can to make a contribution to the common good. Hopefully, the contribution will come out of their love, generosity, sense of abundance and trust that if they make a contribution now, other family members will do the same thing when they are called upon to do so. A family member's understanding that they are furthering the common good makes it easier for them to make a contribution, as opposed to compromising and giving things up.

Another facet of the common vision that supports the development and nurture of soul in the family business is the concept of BOSS. The BOSS acronym was developed by Sherod Miller for his work entitled *Collaborative Team Skills*,[5] which is a communication and management-of-differences programme that assists families in business to create a dialogue that allows their family point of view to emerge. Basically, my interpretation of the BOSS concept is as follows:

- *B is for business:* The business and what the business needs must be defined in order to continue to be successful.
- *O is for others:* What do you want for the others in the family in relation to what they want for themselves? For me, the O is the most important part of the concept. Each member of the family needs to understand that there is a

5 Sherod Miller, *Collaborative Team Skills*, Interpersonal Communication Programs Inc, 2005 (first published 1994).

commitment by the whole family to help each other achieve what they want for themselves. This is a critical concept in family-owned businesses, where it is not unusual for family members to think that no one cares about what they want. Dads are prone to secretly hide resentment and bitterness toward their adult children and to operate under an assumption that "the kids just don't care about what I want". By the same token, the adult children often mistakenly believe that their parents are not committed to their dreams of running a company. Only through a process of discovery, where family members share what they want for themselves and for the family, is each member of the family able to understand what the other family members want.

- *S is for self:* What do you want for yourself? From my perspective it is important to articulate what it is that you want for yourself – but you can't have a team or a family business if people only think about what they want for themselves. As a result, the expression of what you want for yourself needs to be made in the context of a superordinate goal, or what I have called the common family vision: it is in the context of the common family vision that individual wants for the self are expressed. Expression of one's own wants must also be made with a commitment to a win–win situation, where the family synergistically creates a new solution that centralises the best of their ideas.
- *S is for stakeholders:* What do you want for the other stakeholders, which I define as the family as a whole, the employees, the customers, the vendors, the board of directors and, sometimes, even the community.

The goal of the BOSS concept is to create win–win solutions that honour the family's common vision, in order to help promote the emergence of a common family point of view.

Another aspect of the creation of a cohesive team that allows for the emergence of soul is a synonym for the O part of BOSS, which Mihaly Csikszentmihalyi refers to as 'psychic energy'. He develops the concept of the autotelic personality, which he subsequently titled 'flow'. In his book, *Finding Flow,*[6] Csikszentmihalyi investigates and develops an understanding about what gives people understanding in their lives. He indicates that there are three things that create meaning in people's lives: work, active leisure time, and relationships. When Csikszentmihalyi talks about relationships, he is referring to family relationships. And when he talks about family relationships, he is not talking about families of business or families of wealth but referring to typical families and their need to build their emotional equity. I believe that in families of business and wealth there is a greater risk of harm to the relationships, because business and financial differences often erode family relationships.

What Csikszentmihalyi had to say supports the notion of reciprocal commitment

---

6 Mihaly Csikszentmihalyi, *Finding Flow: The Psychology of Engagement With Everyday Life,* Basic Books, 1997.

to each other's success, which is the O part of BOSS. In *Finding Flow* he said: "A group of people is kept together by two kinds of energy: material energy provided by food, warmth, physical care and money; and the psychic energy of people investing attention in each other's goals."[7] Essentially, Csikszentmihalyi states that it is critical to invest in the emotional equity of the family by paying attention to each other's goals and investing what he terms physic energy into the family. At the same time he says: "Now that the integrity of the family has become a matter of personal choice, it cannot survive except for the regular infusion of psychic energy."[8]

Finally, Csikszentmihalyi writes about the idea of a 'joint goal', or what I would call a common family vision, when he says: "Only when there is harmony between the goals of participants, when everyone is investing psychic energy into a joint goal, does being together become enjoyable."[9] Basically, psychic energy is just another way of understanding the reciprocal commitment to each other's success: when you put psychic energy into the development of relationships in family business, as well as the family as a whole, it promotes the common good, and the emergence of a family point of view, through the promotion and embodiment of the common family vision.

The third form of promotion of a reciprocal commitment has to do with the concept of 'kything', a term discussed by Gail Straub in her book, *Rhythm of Compassion*.[10] Kything is another synonym for psychic energy and the O part in BOSS. Kything is a Scottish word that means 'connecting at a spiritual level'. Kything is not psychological, it is spiritual – to kyth is to present your soul to another. The idea is that kything happens through communion, the evolutionary step in making the communion conscious or purposeful.

In the Danz family, mentioned above, each member of the family has an individual vision so that each becomes a vision-driven person as opposed to being problem focused. The idea is to put your spiritual energy into the well-being of another. M Scott Peck, in his book *The Road Less Travelled*,[11] called this concept 'love'. The idea is for each family person to recite on a daily basis his or her own individual vision for what he or she is committed to and trying to do in their lives – both in and out of the family business. In addition, each person kyths to the other members of the family that which they want.

The common family vision is the embodiment of the soul of the family business. As well as the prayer for loving-kindness, the individual vision and kything prepare the soil, and it is the preparation of the soil that allows the spiritual seeds – the family's soul – to emerge in the concept of dialogue and the formation of the family point of view.

5. Collaborative team skills

For dialogue to emerge, I encourage family members to develop their collaborative team skills,[12] which consist of four components: talking skills; listening skills;

7 *Op cit*, p110.
8 *Op cit*, p111.
9 *Op cit*, p113.
10 Gail Straub, *Rhythm of Compassion: Caring for Self Connecting With Society*, Empowerment Institute, 2008.
11 M Scott Peck, *A Road Less Travelled: A New Psychology of Love, Traditional Values, and Spiritual Growth*, Arrow New-Age, 1990 (first published 1978).

communications styles; and mapping an issue- or problem-solving map. Families sometimes resist implementing these fundamental skills but I suggest to them that even the New York Yankees go to spring training every year to brush up on the fundamentals. The talking and listening skills and communication styles are easily understandable and become a rich resource to the family in their ongoing dialogue. This applies to both the family and the family business as they sort out various issues. The benefit of using collaborative team skills is having the whole family on an even playing field – all having the same model for communication and dialogue, as well as the same ground rules that will guide them to an effective discussion of the issues. The approach is in a simple format that makes it easy to introduce to family businesses.

The collaborative team skills approach not only supports the development of effective dialogue in the family business, but also supports the cross-cultural notions of Angeles Arrien (1993) in *The Four-fold Way.*[13] The third of Arrien's concepts – the way of the visionary – is to be able to speak your truth without judgement, criticism or blame. The idea is to be able to talk about reality and be able to "say it is so when it is so". In her seminars on her book, Arrien discusses the three cross-cultural rules that allow families to avoid conflict. They include:

- say what you mean;
- do what you say; and
- say it is so when it is so.

When it comes to saying it is so when it is so, Arrien operates on the 'rule of three'. The first rule is to say it within 24 hours; then if that is not possible, within three days; and then within an absolute maximum of one week.

Basically, the collaborative team skills approach allows families to have the kinds of dialogue necessary to support their family values. The purpose of Rule Three is to not let issues linger – it is not unusual in the context of families and family businesses for family members to avoid talking about something because they are fearful that if they do, it will upset family relationships. In public presentations, I often refer to this dynamic as 'Hubler's Speck of Duty Theory' – a famous theory taught in all of the business schools across the country! Unfortunately, in reality no one has ever heard of the theory, but the rule operates where family members are reluctant to talk about a business or financial issue in their family business because if they do it will upset the family getting together for a holiday – eg, Thanksgiving or Christmas. As a result, they create the very thing they are trying to avoid: an unhappy family. Utilising Rule Three makes it possible for family members to discuss issues in a timely and current fashion.

In family firms and in families, in order to create balance between the family and the business you need to have three separate types of meetings. These comprise family meetings, business meetings, and shareholder and board meetings:

---

12 See note 5 above for Miller's book on this topic.

13 Angeles Arrien, *The Four-fold Way: Walking the Paths of the Warrior, Teacher, Healer and Visionary*, HarperCollins, 2013.

- *Family meetings* – Family shareholder control groups should begin, first, with family meetings, so that the family can discuss the expectations and operations of the company and the family's approach to it. It is also a way to manage the boundary between business and family. Everyone in the family is invited to family meetings, even those who may not be working in the company but are affected by its decisions. A lot can be accomplished in these meetings to bring understanding, healing and power to individuals, as well as the entire family. Family meetings are one of the ways to create structure, formality and balance between the family and business systems. Family meetings are also the place where family members formulate their expectations for the company and communicate them to the board.
- *Business meetings* – These meetings are where the executive, managers and employees implement the policies and strategies that the board has created, themselves based upon the family's expectations for the business enterprise. Only company employees attend these meetings.
- *Shareholder and board meetings* – These meetings are attended by the owners of the company in the first instance and by the directors – ie, those elected by the shareholders to monitor and discuss the company's performance and hold managers accountable for their performance. For these processes (known generally as 'corporate governance') to function effectively, the family firm must first create specific, measurable processes and goals. In addition, the members of the board must have permission to discuss robustly and transparently the real business issues facing the enterprise in order for the corporate governance to have a real impact on the business. Only board members and guests whom the directors invite for a specific purpose attend these meetings.

So you can see that family meetings are at the heart of what continues within the business. They are the foundation for the core values that underlie the corporate culture of the family firm as well as the management and governance of the business. Set out in Tables 1–3 is a summary of what family meetings are all about. I encourage anyone who has a family business to use this template as an opportunity to begin meaningful communications and to catch little irritations before they become big fights. Doing so will permit the family that controls the company to set its course, develop its strategies and execute its plan on the most solid foundation possible.

It is in the context of these discussions that the family point of view emerges and their unique family resources develop to create the leverage and business advantage that allow family businesses to be successful. It is the 'secret sauce' – a unique set of spiritual principles that formulate the family's edge and give them their specialness in a way that affects their performance in the marketplace. Family businesses that continue to develop their soulfulness and that are committed not only to the development of the emotional equity of the family but of each other can anticipate strong dialogue and family resources that will abundantly and positively affect their firm's performance.

Table 1: Functions of family meetings

• Creating balance between the family and business system	• Opportunities to build the emotional equity of the company
• Creating a common vision to unite the family	• Shareholder education
• Family unity	• Celebration and renewal of family rituals
• Transparency	• Creation of a family participation plan/code of conduct (family employment policy)
• Creation of expectations for the performance of the company (return on investment)	• Succession planning discussions
• Communication	• Estate planning discussions
• Management of differences	• Wealth preparation planning and philanthropy discussions

Table 2: Benefits of family meetings

• Family harmony	• As a family, living in gratitude
• Business success	• Identifying family values regarding wealth, philanthropy and service
• Transparency	• Successful succession planning
• Successful adult children	• Having a strong sense of (spiritual) purpose

Table 3: Family skills

• Talking skills (sharing)	• Management of differences (problem solving)
• Listening skills (understanding)	• Forgiveness (reconciliation)

Culture and ethnicity in family enterprises

Everett Moitoza
Moitoza Consulting

1. Introduction

If the heart of a family enterprise is the family, then culture is one of the fundamental windows through which the founding family will perceive and operate in the business world. Culture represents the family's values, beliefs, perspectives, ideas, assumptions and, yes, behaviours. It organises the family's way of life – both at home and, by extension, at its enterprise.

Ethnicity relates to large national groups of people (Irish, Japanese, Portuguese etc) who have certain shared values, collective historical experiences, and racial, cultural, religious, language or other traits in common. Ethnicity is a major factor in determining identity – both as a family and as an individual.

Taken together, culture and ethnicity form a strong pattern of assumptions and behaviours for families that extends directly to how they will run their family enterprise. As we will see in this chapter, there is no reliable or stereotypical approach or solution to the cultural and ethnic variables that arise in the course of an adviser working with a family enterprise. The one principle to be remembered by both advisers to family enterprises and members of families who control business enterprises is that culture and ethnicity are primary realities to be considered when designing and implementing business strategies and policies. While there are other excellent studies and writings on the corporate culture of family businesses,[1] this chapter looks at the culture and ethnicity of the families who control family firms, their particular culture-based values, and the connections between the culture of their business and the culture and ethnicity of the founding/controlling family.

The chapter will endeavour to guide the reader through the common pathways that virtually all ethnic and cultural groups demand of outside advisers, non-family managers and independent directors who wish to assist or advise the enterprise and its family shareholder control group.

2. The many influences of culture and ethnicity

Culture has a main bearing on everything that people do, feel, think and perceive. Culture directly effects how things in the family, community and business are experienced and done. It is the repository of the family's assumptions, values, beliefs and ideas.

1 See DR Denison, C Lief, and JL Ward, "Culture in family-owned enterprises: Recognising and leveraging unique strengths", *Family Business Review*, 17(1), 61–70; and WG Dyer Jr, *Cultural change in family firms*. San Francisco, CA: Jossey-Bass, 1986.

One simple specific example of how culture effects business has been experienced by anyone who travels outside the United States to visit or live in other countries. For example, an everyday activity when travelling in South America is bartering in business, which is not only the norm but expected. This 'rule' affects purchases at both the wholesale and retail levels in Hispanic cultures. Bartering is a respectful process in which the seller and buyer engage, and is an honourable activity. By contrast, in most Anglo-Saxon businesses the prices of goods and services are set and it can therefore seem rude to bargain for every item.

Another aspect of culture is the corporate culture of a family enterprise. Corporate cultures, as we will see, are often direct translations of the family and its ethnicity and culture upon the enterprise. No family business is immune to its cultural and ethnic antecedents. Decision-making, hierarchies, processes, systems, structures, communication, tone, timelines, hiring practices, financial management, marketing, public relations, brand development/management, ownership and conflict management are among the many indices that can be directly affected by the culture and ethnicity of a family enterprise's founder, owner(s) and family.

Nevertheless, culture is fluid. It changes over time and adjusts to both internal events and conditions within the family, as well as external events within the society, economy, industry and marketplace. In these ways generational differences among family members can produce acculturation and values differences that can be profound. This acculturation occurs most frequently when the successor generation is more acculturated into the host culture (especially the social and business cultures) than the generation of the founder of the business. Thus, two concurrent differences in culture can be evidenced within a family controlled enterprise: differences in cultural outlook between generations in the family business; and those that arise from the founding generation's cultural clashes with the host culture.

Moreover, core values within and between generational members of a family shareholder control group are always subject to change. While such values of truth, honesty, generosity, respect, security, loyalty and honour may remain central, the expressions of these core values may take on more contemporary interpretations and definition as competitive and other factors impacting the enterprise controlled by the family vary. Never is the scope of possible changes in how these values are expressed more clearly shown than in the behaviours regarding leadership within the family and the family enterprise. From classic top-down authoritarianism to a democratic/participative organisational style – the values of the family, which are so impacted by culture, become more responsive in this context to changes within the family and the family enterprise than perhaps at any other time.

Family harmony, especially at times of succession, becomes paramount among family shareholders within most ethnic groups. Although the cultural ideal for most families is family harmony, unity and support, many family shareholder control groups chronically find relationships – both across the family and within the enterprise – strained and often at cross purposes. For many family enterprises, anticipated transition of power from one generation to the next often overturns the delicate equilibrium that endures as the preferred alternative to open conflict and precipitates the overt struggle between parents, their adult children and their spouses.

A third area of cultural challenge to the family enterprise is that of change – not only as it exists in the family but also, more importantly, as it exists in the enterprise in the form of change management. The family enterprise is a living system. And like all living systems, it must master change or die. Cultural values that support deep immutable traditions, such as the rule of primogeniture (requiring the firstborn male to inherit the business), are rigid examples of a controlling family's cultural tradition that can clash with obvious business requirements such as competence as the deciding criterion in succession planning and in selection of leadership and ownership.

The ability of the family to manage these culturally determined constraints becomes paramount. Managing acculturation of the family, as well as for the family enterprise, is a major factor in whether any change management process succeeds. Families that can manage their cultural beliefs and practices along the life cycles of both the family and the family enterprise, will be those who have the greatest chance for continuity and success. The ability of family enterprises to master change while retaining and maintaining the family's cultural essence remains the challenge to the family, the enterprise and its professional advisers. Utilising certain tools to understand the family's cultural and ethnic core in managing the fundamental changes associated with succession and its many challenges remains central to the process of working with the family enterprise to guide them successfully through the predictably turbulent transitions that all family controlled enterprises will face.

3. Available tools for assessing cultural variables in the family enterprise

Perhaps the oldest assessment instrument used in determining cultural distinctiveness is the Kluckhohn–Strodtbeck Values Inventory.[2] Its premise is that it is possible to distinguish cultures based on how they address five common human concerns. The creators of this values inventory did not propose that these were the only five concerns that were material. Rather, they proposed that they were useful in understanding cultural differences. This inventory has later been broadened to include corporate cultures, as well as ethnic ones;[3] it has also been used for conflict resolution.[4] Indeed, the term 'values orientation' used in this inventory would today be referred to as 'core values'.

The Kluckhohn–Strodtbeck instrument focuses on the assumptions that:

- there are a limited number of common human problems for which all people in all places must find some solution;
- although there is variability in solutions of all the problems, the number of such solutions is neither limitless nor random but is definitely variable within a range of possible solutions; and

---

2 See FR Kluckhohn and FL Strodtbeck, *Variations in value orientations*. Evanston, IL: Row, Peterson, 1961.

3 See RT Carter, "Perspectives on addressing cultural issues in organizations", in RT Carter (ed), *Addressing cultural issues in organizations: Beyond the corporate context*, Thousand Oaks, CA: Sage Publications, 2000, pp3–18; and TJ Gallagher, "Building institutional capacity to address cultural differences", in RT Carter (ed), *Addressing cultural issues in organizations: Beyond the corporate context*, Thousand Oaks, CA: Sage Publications, 2000, pp229–240.

4 TJ Gallagher, "Value orientations and conflict resolution: Using the Kluckhohn Value Orientations Model", in KW Russo (ed), *Finding the middle ground: Insight and applications of the Value Orientations Method*, Yarmouth, ME: Intercultural Press, 2000, pp185–194.

- all alternatives of all solutions are present in all societies at all times but are differentially preferred.

Kluckhohn and Strodtbeck describe the five value orientations as driving preferences that certain cultural and ethnic groups express when managing various issues, problems, situations, perspectives and choices in life. Knowing the individual and the group's values orientation (ie, the core values of a family enterprise) can provide priceless information when working with a family, an individual and, in our case, a family enterprise.

These five value orientations – or core values – are described below. Whether it is succession planning, intrafamily/intergenerational conflict management, business growth, risk–benefit analysis, strategic planning, executive selection, board of directors/adviser selection or communications management, Kluckhohn and Strodtbeck propose that assessing, understanding and utilising a values-based approach can provide a baseline tool for approaching growth, development and change in the family enterprise. Knowing the family and their enterprise's values adds a powerful pathway to more accurately and completely link the family enterprise system with its members as well as its non-family employees. Change occurs most easily and quickly when resistance is low. Understanding the cultural values of a family and its enterprise can rapidly identify not only the levers of change but, more importantly, also the levers of resistance.

Set out below is a condensed description of how the Kluckhohn–Strodtbeck Values Inventory can be used and adapted in assessing the values of and between generations of ethnic families in a family enterprise. (When using the term 'ethnic', all cultures are being referred to, including that of white Anglo-Saxon Protestants.) Two methods may, in my opinion, be used. One method can simply be that of using the original values orientation assessment instrument that was developed and pioneered by Kluckhohn and Strodtbeck. This instrument has 22 situations, which together determine an individual's attitude towards each of the values orientations; it also has significant established measures of reliability and validity. A second method comprises the adapted assessment survey by Lane and Hills,[5] which can be administered by presenting to each member of the family working in or owning the business 25 short situations that represent the possible values that are associated with each of them. This instrument has been verified with significant trials for reliability and validity, and four of the five items from the instrument are reproduced with permission in section 3.1 below to illustrate the format employed. The example questions for 'Activity' are omitted.

---

5 See Michael D Hills, "Values in the South Pacific", paper presented at the Annual Conference of the New Zealand Psychological Society in Auckland, New Zealand, 1977; MD Hills and E Goneyali, "Values in Fijian families", monograph, Hamilton, New Zealand: University of Waikato, Department of Psychology, 1980; Michael D Hills, "Kluckhohn and Strodtbeck's Values Orientation Theory", *Online Readings in Psychology and Culture* 4(4), 2002, available at http:/dx.doi.org/10.9707/2307-0919.1040; and RH Lane, "Polynesia and Europe meet: A new heritage", unpublished master's thesis, University of Waikato Psychology Department, Hamilton, New Zealand, 1976.

3.1 Four sample items measuring Kluckhohn and Strodtbeck's values orientations

Preliminary explanation:

I will ask you 25 questions. There are three possible answers to each question. Please listen carefully to each question and then each of the three suggested answers to that question. I can play them again if you would like to listen to them again. We do not want your name.

There are no right or wrong answers to these questions – we want to know how you feel about them. Take as much time as you need to answer them.

Value 1 (Relational):

Here is the first question:

When our group sends a delegate to a meeting, I think it best:

a) to let everyone discuss it until everyone agrees on the person; [collateral]

b) to let the important leaders decide – they have more experience than us; [lineal]

c) for a vote to be taken and the one with the most votes goes, even if some people disagree. [individualistic]

Now please tell me the answer which comes closest to the way you feel. 1.______

Now tell me the answer which is your second choice. 2.______

Value 2 (Humanity and Nature):

Here's the next one:

When I get sick I believe that:

a) doctors will be able to find a way to cure it; [mastery over nature]

b) I should live properly so I don't get sick; [harmony with nature]

c) I cannot do much about it and just have to accept it. [subjugation to nature]

Now please tell me the answer which comes closest to the way you feel. 1._____

Now tell me the answer which is your second choice. 2._____

Value 3 (Human Nature):

Here's the third question:

Most people, when they can do something wrong and get away with it, will:

a) usually do it; [people are evil]

b) sometimes do it; [people are a mixture of good and evil]

c) hardly ever do it. [people are good]

Now please tell me the answer which comes closest to the way you feel. 1._____

Now tell me the answer which is your second choice. 2._____

Value 4 (Time):

The fourth question is as follows:

When I send money for use overseas, I think it should be spent to:

a) make a better life for the future; [future]

b) make a better life now; [present]

c) keep the old ways and customs alive. [past]

Now please tell me the answer which comes closest to the way you feel. 1._____

Now tell me the answer which is your second choice. 2._____

The responses from the family members or non-family executives are then tabulated and represent the individual's values orientation. As noted above, each individual would have a rank order of their three values responses for each question. Together they would be added to comprise a values orientation profile from a first-, second- and third-order position for each of the five orientations.

3.2 Five common human orientations and three possible values responses

In Kluckhohn and Strodtbeck's scheme, a basic outline of possibilities is expressed as set out in Table 1. An expanded outline of the orientations and their values responses, along with annotations as to what each orientation and its corresponding value response(s) mean, can be found in Table 3 within section 4.1 below.

Table 1: Example concerns/orientations and related values responses (basic)

Concerns/orientations	Possible values responses		
Human nature: What is the basic nature of people?	Evil	Mixed	Good
Man–Nature relationship: What is the most correct relationship to Nature?	Subjugated to Nature	Harmony with Nature	Mastery over Nature
Time sense: How should we best think about time?	Past	Present	Future
Activity: What is the best mode of activity?	Being	Becoming	Doing
Relational: What is the best form of social organisation?	Hierarchical	Collateral	Individual

4. The utility of a family enterprise values profile

Table 2 presents the universally considered American middle-class values orientation, as compared with substantial data that represents the profiles of both Italian and Irish cultural values.[6] These value orientations can, by extension, assist in predicting how individuals in a family business think, act and feel about the family, the enterprise and the world around them. The value orientations are operative in any culture and organisation. They can identify, in many ways, the main impediments to change in a family enterprise.

6 Reprinted with the permission of Guilford Press from J Spiegel, "An ecological model of ethnic families", in M McGoldrick, JK Pearce and J Giordano (eds), *Ethnicity and Family Therapy*, New York, NY: Guildford Press, 1982, pp31–51.

The ordering of values from first to third place, as in the Time value (American value of Future > Present > Past; Italian and Irish Time Values of Present > Past > Future), presents potentially distinct values orientations. For instance, if a founder/owner father holds a Present>Past>Future hierarchy ("Don't worry about tomorrow. Be here now.") and his daughter/successor holds a Future>Present>Past hierarchy ("We need to plan for tomorrow now."), then the age-old family business statement from parent to adult child of 'someday all of this will be yours' rings hollow for years as the parent focuses on maintaining the *status quo* and the successor focuses on the future in order to get the planning, structure and processes in place and to begin actively preparing for this succession event. Knowledge and insight by founders/owners and successors of this simple time perspective and how it impacts succession planning can provide poignant and effective breakthroughs.

Table 2: Values typically seen in American middle-class, Italian and Irish ethnic groups

Value/ethnic group	**American middle class**	**Italian**	**Irish**
Basic nature of mankind	Mixed>Evil> Good	Mixed>Evil> Good	Evil>Mixed> Good
Man–Nature relationship	Dominant> Subjugated> Harmony	Subjugated> Harmony> Dominant	Subjugated> Harmony> Dominant
Time sense	Future>Present> Past	Present>Past> Future	Present>Past> Future
Activity	Doing>Being> Becoming	Being>Becoming> Doing	Being>Becoming> Doing
Relational	Individual> Collateral>Lineal	Collateral>Lineal> Individual	Lineal>Collateral> Individual

The above description of these three ethnicities could easily be used to stereotype a family culture or family business. My experience has been that, even within each ethnic family enterprise I have worked with that self-identified as with American, Italian or Irish (or whatever family enterprise culture presented) cultural values, there have existed many more variations from these stereotypical profiles than those portrayed in this table. My experience has shown me that each and every family enterprise has its own family, ethnic and cultural values profile. They have all reached some degree of acculturation while holding some degree of their original ethnic values, beliefs and ideas.

When looking to understand and advise a family enterprise and the family shareholder group that controls it, the professional adviser is well advised to plan a values profile assessment on each and every individual who either works in or has ownership of the family enterprise, as well as their spouses. When such an assessment is done, the trusted adviser has a tremendous view into the values of both the founder/ownership generation and the successor generation. These cross-generational profiles are priceless tools for identifying fundamental values differences within the family's culture, between generations and with their stereotypical legacy culture. Less importantly, I will often compare them with the normative American middle-class values, looking for significant departures or similarities. These comparisons can assist in determining where the family enterprise is with respect to its divergence from certain employees.

4.1 Five common human concerns and three possible values responses

Table 3 presents brief definitions of the three possible values responses associated with each of five concerns/orientations.[7]

Table 3: Example concerns/orientations and related values responses (expanded)

Concerns/ orientations	Possible values responses		
Human nature: What is the basic nature of people?	Evil. Most people can't be trusted. People are basically bad and need to be controlled.	Mixed. There are both evil people and good people in the world, and you have to check people out to find out which they are. People can be changed with the right guidance.	Good. Most people are basically pretty good at heart; they are born good.

continued on next page

7 See TJ Gallagher, "The value orientations method: A tool to help understand cultural differences", *Journal of Extension*, 39(6), 2001; and LR Kohls, Developing intercultural awareness, Washington, DC: Sietar, 1981. Table contents reproduced with permission.

Concerns/ orientations	**Possible values responses**		
Man–Nature relationship: What is the most correct relationship to Nature?	Subjugated to Nature. People really can't change Nature. Life is largely determined by external forces, such as fate and genetics. What happens was meant to happen.	Harmony with Nature. Man should, in every way, live in harmony with Nature.	Mastery over Nature. The great human challenge is to conquer and control Nature. Everything in the world can be overcome by humankind with technology and effort – eg, placing a man on the Moon.
Time sense: How should we best think about time?	Past. People should learn from history, draw the values they live by from history, and strive to continue past traditions and beliefs into the future.	Present. The present moment is everything. Let's make the most of it. Don't worry about tomorrow: enjoy today.	Future. Planning and goal setting make it possible for people to accomplish miracles, to change and grow. A little sacrifice today will bring a better tomorrow.
Activity: What is the best mode of activity?	Being. It's enough to just "be". It's not necessary to accomplish great things in life in order to feel your life has been worthwhile.	Becoming. The main purpose for being placed on Earth is for one's own inner development.	Doing. If people work hard and apply themselves fully, their efforts will be rewarded. What a person accomplishes is a measure of his or her worth.

continued on next page

Concerns/ orientations	Possible values responses		
Relational: What is the best form of social organisation?	Hierarchical. There is a natural order to relationships. Some people are born to lead; others are followers. Decisions should be made by those in charge.	Collateral. The best way to be organised is as a group, where everyone shares in the decision process. It is important not to make important decisions alone.	Individual. All people should have equal rights, and each should have complete control over their own destiny. When we have to make a decision as a group, it should be on the basis of 'one person, one vote'.

4.2 Specific implications of each orientation, with its possible values responses, within a family enterprise

Each of the concerns/orientations taken as examples in Tables 1–3, together with their possible values responses, are explained further here.

(a) Human nature

Using this orientation, family members and their enterprise employees are being assessed as to their views about the basic nature of people – for instance, are they trustworthy; do they see the best in an individual and treat them with respect; are family members and employees seen as wanting the best for the entity; can individuals be expected to 'do the right thing' when no one is looking? This human nature orientation acts – especially for founders/owners in family enterprises – as the basic foundation for their decision-making regarding control, delegation, trust and change.

The three possible responses in this context are as follows:

- *Evil:* When the family's responses show a basic human-nature value of 'evil', trust factors (within both the family and the organisation) will be affected significantly. Trusting the successor generation will be impacted, as well as transitions of any type. Change management initiatives will not be trusted to anyone but the founder/owner(s). The expectation is that the founder/owner(s) must watch everyone closely; individuals are not to act independently. Hierarchical management structures and processes will usually be emphasised, where 'top down' decision-making will likely become the rule with little dissention allowed.

  Accessing and developing trust within this value orientation is difficult for all who try to access and impact the system for consulting of any type (other than when, or if, the family enterprise is in extreme danger of collapse – due to either a family or business crisis).

Cultures that may exhibit more of this value than others are those with significant beliefs that are grounded in religious doctrine that people are essentially born evil ('original sin').

- *Mixed:* In this value position, people are essentially good, but corruptible. So ambition, greed, power, opportunity and achievement can taint the basic core of human goodness. Individuals are seen from this values vantage point as a product of their upbringing and initial conditions. Education, community and parents are seen as contributing forces that shape the individual. Everyone therefore needs assessment and scrutiny as to whether they are good or evil – people need to be vetted and prove their motives, worth and morals. 'Trust with verification' becomes the watchword for this value assessment.

  Family enterprises with this value position are frequently open to intervention and change, but only after careful trust is developed with an intervener or adviser. In these settings (as compared with cultures in which humankind is considered evil) it is far more likely that democratic organisational structures can become a central value as trust and performance develop over time.
- *Good:* Family enterprises with this value often hold a *laissez faire* management attitude and style. Trust abounds toward family business members, employees and their motives. Caution in over-trusting or undermanaging in the organisation can be problematic.

  While easily able to enter a family enterprise, a consultant working in an enterprise with this cultural foundation may have a significantly difficult time implementing real change because the structures, processes, procedures and systems may be minimal and ineffective. Greater scrutiny and assessment of the succession process here is often in order. Decisions regarding successor evaluation and/or promotion criteria and decisions may be vague or imprecisely connected with competence, experience and performance.

(b) *Man–Nature relationship*

Here, we are assessing the family members' and enterprises' relationship to natural or supernatural forces in the world. The basic issue relates to the individual's thinking about how power in the universe and on Earth is felt, and how that norm is incorporated into the culture of the family enterprise. Is Nature more powerful and more of a determinant of how life will be than what an individual can control? In family enterprises, is the legacy of the family part of that powerful natural force that the family believes destines them to business success, or something that overrides ability and leaves the business in ruins? Here are the options:

- *Subjugated to Nature:* Family businesses with this value believe that there is nothing much any person can really do to change the natural course of events – ie, life, relationships and business are generally determined by external forces such as 'fate'. What will be, will be; and there isn't much anyone can do except to accept the natural fate. "If it's meant to be, it's meant to be" is the general thinking.

The impact on a family business with this value is generally inactivity, passivity and reactivity. While few family businesses hold this value, it can arise in various degrees. An example of this premise is a situation where the founder/owner states that he or she is not willing to do any succession planning: "My family can figure this out after I'm dead." The passivity, delay and avoidance of conflict all work to generate a fate that is difficult for outside professional advisers to override.

- *Harmony with Nature:* From this viewpoint, humankind should, in every way, live in harmony with Nature. This value is often ethnically expressed with both Native American and Asian family enterprises. Family enterprises that express this value often live with respect for the concept of 'balance' in one's life and in the universe. This holds for work–life balance as well as that of being environmentally and ecologically sensitive to one's footprint in the world. Working with, as opposed to powering over, the competitive forces in business becomes one of the fundamental beliefs of these businesses. Conversely, these family enterprises may err in the direction of keeping situations balanced to the point that everyone is compensated to the same degree or that the *status quo* is a comfortable, balanced position to be in. Growth, while desired, may not be behaviourally driven as a core value even when business conditions clearly indicate that this is the only pathway to a thriving future.
- *Mastery over Nature:* In these systems the core premise is that hard work, talent and perseverance can conquer all. Technology, tools and personal will and desire can ultimately overcome all the challenges that are presented by Nature. Defending against floods, predicting earthquakes and boring roads through mountains for transportation efficiency are all examples of the value choice of humankind over Nature. In business, the belief that a person or group can control international market forces or the utility of drilling for oil in the Arctic are two extreme expressions of this value.

(c) ***Time sense***

Essentially, this core value is all about how people see time in their life. Do they focus on the past, the present or the future? Clearly, the family and its members' time orientation will have very significant implications for how the company is managed, as well as in how it will transition during succession events. Research with different cultures has depicted American culture as future oriented, Italian and Irish cultures as present oriented and Asian cultures as past oriented. However, I would caution all those working in such cultures to resist this stereotyping and use the values instrument on a case-by-case basis with their family enterprise clients. Both intergenerational and cross-generational differences can present family- and individual-specific profiles that defy cultural generalisation.

In the Past value position, people and systems work on preserving and maintaining traditional activities and beliefs: "If it was good enough for my father, it's good enough for me." In the Present value position, the focus is on now, where the motivation is to take old, traditional activities and ideas and modernise them to present standards. In the Future value position, the focus is on what is to come – on future planning and innovation to meet the expected demands of a changed and changing future. In more detail, the responses represent the following:

- *Past:* Reverence for times gone by, tradition and history are the hallmarks of this orientation. Family legacy, especially the family enterprise legacy, remains the central feature of this time value. Change comes slowly and with great struggle against the legacy issues that underpin the entire family and its enterprise. Professional advisers may be maintained well beyond their committed or talented years. Maintaining and sustaining the family enterprise systems, structures, personnel, processes and product/service offerings can hamper business growth, as well as the timely selection of successors and senior management. In order to institute change in this value orientation, professional advisers need to leverage, relate and develop all change activities with relevance and reverence to the family and its business beliefs and traditions. Speed of change must be calibrated to the family system's maximum acceptable tolerance.
- *Present:* This value position can be one of those more easily managed for change if it is paired with a significant second value position that is future oriented. In the Present time position, family enterprises may remain static with the success that they have attained and not want to plan for future innovations that may be becoming visible and necessary, both in the business and in the family. Strategic planning can be difficult to institute, because the persons in control – both owners and executives – are likely to prefer to focus on today's environment and events. Their relationships can be taxed and overshadowed by current conflicts or struggles. A hallmark characteristic of the Present value position is that change frequently occurs reactively as opposed to proactively, and this reaction is often precipitated by some external event. The old saying that describes this situation best might be "If it ain't broke, don't fix it."
- *Future:* The quintessential change-hardy time value is Future. This is marked by planning, prospective analysis, future modelling and a driven desire to replace outdated models of working and being with new ones. "Change!" is the mantra of the future-time-oriented family business, and constant change is the desired action pattern. Often, this position is mostly held by the younger members of the family enterprise, with the elder generation holding to present or past value orientations.

Investing in strategic planning, identifying vital future capital expenses, maintaining state-of-the-art technology and hiring at the top talent level are all characteristics of these family enterprises. When the intergenerational time values described above occur, the professional adviser's task is to develop a change rate that respects the values of the different generations.

(d) Activity

Here we are measuring the preferred way in which people interact and behave in interpersonal relationships. In the Being value orientation, the focus is our motivation to experience things or activities that are personally important and enriching to us as opposed to others; it is not important to achieve great things. The Becoming value orientation is similar to the Being orientation but has a motivation to develop and grow in abilities which are valued by us, although not necessarily by others – the purpose of life is for one's own inner development. Conversely, the Doing value orientation is all about the Protestant work ethic where "if you work hard and apply yourself fully, you will be rewarded with success – both personally and in business". In the Doing orientation, a person's worth is measured by what he or she accomplishes – for instance, striving for upward mobility/success (as is seen in the United States). The three orientations can be explained more fully thus:

- *Being:* This value position is relatively rare in a family business, which tends to be more Doing alongside being lineal/hierarchical/paternalistic in its values and structure. In the Being value, individuals are seen as primarily concerned with their own individual expression of feelings and development as opposed to those of the whole family enterprise. This value in offspring can lead to significant issues with the founding/ownership generation, who see this value position as self-centred and not valuing being a team player. In a Being culture, the ability to serve up both family enterprise achievement and self-actualising goals optimises the success for both the enterprise and the individual. This value can frequently be seen to varying degrees in certain southern European countries as well as in South American and Caribbean islands.
- *Becoming:* Like the Being value, the Becoming value is about what, who and how the person is, in contrast to what they are accomplishing. Again, this is not a common value orientation within family enterprises. Nevertheless, it can frequently be seen (to varying degrees) in family enterprises in certain southern European countries and in South American and Caribbean islands, among others.
- *Doing:* This value position perfectly represents the American achievement ideal. Competition, achievement, social contacts and networking with the activity designed for material gain are the main focus points of this value orientation. Individuals in family enterprises with this orientation hold the business in first place in their discussions, thoughts, ideas, feelings and activities. This is what is spoken about in many moments of free time and during out-of-hours leisure and family-based get-togethers. Work is primary and all else is secondary. In contrast with this value position, family enterprises that do not have Doing as their first value position may work extremely hard but they are not inclined to bring that work home, preferring a separation or boundary between work and home. Issues of work–life balance and accusations of people not working enough or not working to their potential will be primary concerns and complaints in the Doing value orientation.

(e) ***Relational***

The relational orientation is looking to determine the best form of social organisation for individuals and their enterprises. Should it be structured as hierarchical, collateral or individualistic? Here are some guidelines:

- *Hierarchical/lineal:* Most family enterprises are overwhelmingly hierarchical in structure, with the founder/owners making the decisions of what to do, when to do it and (in many cases) how to do it.[8] It may sometimes contain a collateral component for certain decisions, but in the end it will be the owner's decision on how to proceed. The chain of command is clear and relatively rigid, based on ultimate ownership of the entity by the family. Flexibility and information transfer from the lower echelons in the organisation is a particularly important variable. Hierarchical systems that can seek, receive and use information from subordinate tiers of the enterprise are those more change-hardy and often display significant longevity.
- *Collateral:* This value position is an index of democratic structure in the family enterprise. In a purely collateral system, everyone has the same power and stature. Decisions are made by consensus and the founder/owners will work to steer the consensus in their predetermined direction. Working together, rather than working individually for the group/enterprise or for individual rewards, is the central value within a collateral orientation.
- *Individualistic:* In this type of system, everyone should have equal rights. Everyone should have and enjoy complete control over what happens to them. Everyone has the same single vote and no one's vote is greater than anyone else's. This works well when the enterprise is very small and the work processes or products are extremely independent from one another. But in such settings, adhesion within the family and the enterprise is usually weak, as diffusion from individually focused needs, desires and drives can weaken the enterprise's focus and energy. Family members can even disrupt the enterprise's mission by making decisions independently of others.

5. A family enterprise case study

5.1 Background to the family

Frank C is a 62-year-old first-generation Portuguese (Azores) American, who was born in the United States and is now the founder, owner and chief executive officer (CEO) of a 110-employee industrial/commercial cleaning company that he began after finishing high school 40 years ago.[9] His first language is Portuguese, although he speaks fluent English without a hint of a Portuguese accent. Maria, his wife of 39 years, has worked beside him in starting the business and now, at the age of 57, oversees the seven administrative office staff.

Frank and Maria have five adult children. While all five have worked part time in the business during junior high and high school, only the three oldest now work

---

8 See, for example, the chapter entitled "Understanding Paternalistic Leadership in Family Enterprises", in Richard L Narva (ed), *Family Enterprises: How to Build Growth, Family Control and Family Harmony*, Globe Law and Business, 2015 (see www.globelawandbusiness.com/FEH).

9 All names and particulars in this case study have been altered to protect the anonymity of the family and business on which it is based.

in the business: Joseph, aged 38, who is director of operations; Isabel, 36, chief financial officer; and John, 29, director of sales and marketing. The other children (Barbara, 26, and Elizabeth, 24, are married and work as nurse/administrators in healthcare. There are several cousins, nieces and nephews of Frank and Maria who hold clerical or blue-collar positions at the company. Joseph has a high school diploma and joined the company full time upon graduation. Isabel attended a two-year community college to study business administration and has taken classes in finance at the local university. John graduated from a state college with a Bachelor of Science in business with a marketing major.

5.2 Family and enterprise issues

This is a case that presented the full panoply of family enterprise issues regarding ownership and management transition. The list of issues that lurked just below the surface of day-to-day operations, but which were not addressed for many years, included the following:

- management succession;
- ownership transition from Frank to the next generation;
- the future roles and responsibilities for the three children working in the business;
- strategic planning regarding growth or stable management of the business over the next five to 10 years;
- conflict/leadership issues on the day-to-day management of the company between John and Joseph;
- the institution of capital budgets;
- determining who will manage, own and govern this business in the future; and
- estate planning issues, such as equalising family wealth between those working in the business and those who do not.

All of the issues listed above had been simmering within the family for several years, but Frank was not moved to change his strict leadership, management and control of the company. He loved running the company he founded, and he enjoyed having total control over all significant decisions. He believed that he had provided "incredible jobs, compensation and opportunity" for his three children in the company and also for all his employees. He had no hobbies, very few friends and his social life consisted of being with his family on holidays and going out to dinner once a week with Maria. The family members were extremely well connected – both at the sibling and extended-family level that included their spouses and children. All family members lived within 20 miles of one another. Remarkably, there were no intra-family conflicts of any real or lasting significance.

Then, Frank had a heart attack and quintuple bypass surgery. He wasn't surprised. In fact, he almost seemed relieved by it when he said: "I was wondering when this was going to happen." He was 50 lbs overweight and smoked five or more cigars a day. While a very successful businessman, he was fatalistic and frequently expected the worst in any situation. This hyper-vigilance actually worked at times, as he was able to see opportunities and danger at critical times when building his business. Nevertheless, he was a very cautious man who at times could be extraordinarily superstitious. Indeed, he would reluctantly confess (then immediately deny it) that at times he had a nagging belief in witches, curses and 'the evil eye'.

Some months after the heart attack and surgery, his wife and children were all able to request, and have him reluctantly accept, retention of a trusted family business adviser with whom the family control group would work on family enterprise issues of succession and strategic planning. An initial family enterprise assessment consultation was set up with the express purpose of beginning planning for succession and addressing the issues outlined above.

5.3 Assessment process

The assessment consisted of the following:

- extended, structured, individual interviews lasting one to two hours with all family members to discuss family, business issues, practices, strengths, weaknesses, relationships etc;
- administration of the Strodtbeck–Kluckhohn Values Orientation instrument with all family members who worked in the business;
- administration of the Myers–Briggs Temperament Inventory with family business members and key non-family members;
- administration of the Moitoza Family Business Inventory with family business members; and
- administration of an informal Team Test with family business members.

While all this information was taken together to form a comprehensive picture and report of the enterprise, the focus for the purposes of this case study will be purely on the role that the Kluckhohn–Strodtbeck Values Orientation instrument played in the process.

Set out in Table 4 are the values orientations for family members working in the business.

5.4 Assessment analysis

The results of the assessment can be analysed according to the five values specified in Table 4.

(a) Basic nature of humankind

Frank's assessment showed him in the Evil position and clearly feeling like his heart attack was punishment for 'sins' he was committing, such as smoking, binge eating and (later confessed) gambling. It was relatively easy to help his family see that Frank was very much wanting to do penance for his behaviour and that both the surgery and his new-found openness to discussing succession issues was an expression of that desire.

Maria, Joseph, Isabel and John were very understanding of Frank's value structure. While their first position of Good led their values and their Evil value was in the third position, their Mixed value saw that individuals can be corruptible. The

Table 4: Values orientations for family members working in the business

Values/family members	Frank	Maria and Joseph	Isabel and John
Basic nature of humankind	Evil>Mixed> Good	Good>Mixed> Evil	Good>Mixed> Evil
Humankind in relation to Nature	Subjugated> Harmony> Mastery	Subjugated> Harmony> Mastery	Mastery> Harmony> Subjugated
Time sense	Present>Future> Past	Present>Future> Past	Future>Present> Past
Activity	Doing>Being> Becoming	Doing>Being> Becoming	Doing>Being> Becoming
Relational	Lineal>Collateral> Individual	Lineal>Individual> Collateral	Lineal>Collateral> Individual

Evil value orientation of Frank's was often a part of the consultation process as he frequently referred to the topics of 'original sin', witches and the basically negative and impulsive nature of children. Culturally, he was able to connect these concepts with his immigrant mother and father's teachings and superstitions, as well as a rigid and dogmatic Catholic upbringing. With insight and discussions regarding his negative view of the nature of humankind, Frank was able to trust more the abilities of his children in truly managing and governing the family business.

(b) ***Humankind in relation to Nature***

Here again, Frank's value orientation was that of Subjugated to Nature – ie, there isn't much you can do about what happens, as Nature will have its way and you are subject to its forces and whims. These are primarily the values of rural agrarian and maritime cultures and economies, namely whatever happens is meant to happen and you have little power over it. Control is a relative illusion; luck and fate determine what happens. Frank believed these statements. While he admitted hard work and good fortune helped his business to succeed, he chalked it up, more or less, to being lucky. Given that particular core belief, he felt that at any moment it could all vanish if he did not pay strict attention to, and manage, every aspect of the business. Failure always lurked in the shadows for Frank.

This view was also validated and held by both his wife and oldest son Joseph. The belief that nothing is secure held true with them as well, and such a deeply held value significantly affected their risk and growth opportunities in the business. Conversely, the youngest and most educated siblings, Isabel and John, found these beliefs (which they grew up with both at home and in the business) "ignorant and maddening". Their value of Mastery over Nature held that anything could be accomplished if you had the right tools, education, brains and motivation. Historically, their tolerance of their parents' and Joseph's views had worn thin – and their intolerance created a disrespect and conflict with them that constrained almost all productive business discussions regarding growth and the future.

(c) *Time sense*

Here again, Frank, Maria and Joseph all indicated a Present time orientation, while Isabel and John adhered to Future. Most rural agrarian/maritime cultures hold present time values. It is about today, as tomorrow is quite unknown. Live for today and hope for tomorrow.

Conflict regarding succession planning and strategic planning among Frank, Maria and Joseph on the one side and Isabel and Joseph on the other had been on hold for the past three years. With Frank's medical crisis, he and Maria and Joseph felt a newly found motivation to begin preparing and managing the business for succession, strategic and estate issues facing both the enterprise and the family. The sudden change in reality presented by Frank's coronary crisis drew those in the family who had adhered to a Present time orientation towards a Future orientation held by the youngest two offspring.

This Time orientation difference is, perhaps, the most important value difference that can exist within a family enterprise. When Present time is foremost, very little impetus exists for proactive change in the system because an individual looks only at what is happening now. If no problems are seen or identified, little is activated on future changes that may be needed. If no other values measure is introduced by an outsider (such as the trusted adviser in this case), this Time orientation should at least be attempted.

(d) *Activity*

The work ethic in this family and family enterprise is 100% consistent, with Doing the value held by all. And all family members active in the company have shown equivalent industry in working in the business, accomplishing their day-to-day assignments in their jobs. No jealousies exist between the siblings, but differences of how to work 'smarter' rather than harder are known to occur occasionally between Joseph and his younger brother John. Mostly, these differences involved utilisation of recent technology tools and processes.

(e) *Relational*

As with the Activity value described in section 5.4(d) above, the family members, remarkably, held almost identical values. In fact, the Lineal value position occurs most frequently in family businesses generally. In this case, the founder/owner Frank was being held hostage by some of his other more powerful and debilitating values, namely those of the orientations of evil humankind, being subjugated to Nature, and focusing on the present. Together with a lineal approach to structure, these four culturally determined and expressed values all unconsciously conspired to impact this most successful family enterprise at its critical juncture – ie, identifying a succession process to follow the leadership of a founder diminished by health issues. Frank was not wanting to hear about succession and planning during his recuperation and rehabilitation from the cardiac event. He believed unconsciously that, given his Present and Subjugated to Nature values, he would die and everyone would figure out what best to do at that time. He did not want to think about it now, as he figured it would not make much of a difference.

Utilising the Kluckhohn–Strodtbeck Values Inventory, the consultant was able to engage the family in general, and Frank in particular, regarding the several cultural, familial and business issues that had impacted all the family members, leading to development of a succession plan appropriate for this enterprise.

6. Conclusion

Culture, ethnicity and the values associated with them are strong predictors of where, how, with whom and when to intervene as a professional adviser with a family enterprise and the family that controls it. Challenges of communication, strategic planning, conflict management, change management and generational succession reveal themselves as very significant within a family enterprise. Gaining a clear grasp of the core values of the enterprise and the family that controls it correlates positively with any adviser's chances of success in guiding a family enterprise through a change process.

Harmonious relations are often the key to successful outcomes in family business consulting. Thus, understanding the cultural values associated with and among the family business founder/owner, his or her offspring and the host culture can make all the difference in helping the enterprise and the family meet its challenges.

Crossing cultural boundaries: the duties of Chinese successors to their family controlled enterprises

Anna Xia
Market Ignition Group & Advisory LLC

1. Introduction

Most Western readers of this chapter are unlikely to recognise the educational path and career training of a young woman named Ocean, who lives and works in a suburb of Boston. However, any understanding of the duties of Chinese successors to leadership of business enterprises controlled by their families must begin with a review of how preparation of successors to business founders occurs in Chinese families.

Ocean is the president and chief executive officer (CEO) of the international division of her family controlled enterprise (FCE). Headquartered in Jiangsu province in the People's Republic of China, the FCE was founded in 1989 by Ocean's grandfather and father. It is a large packaging and container manufacturer, with sales offices in multiple large cities in China and a United States-based after-sale service office in Massachusetts, which was established by Ocean in 2013.

In her early thirties, Ocean is the only child of the founder and CEO of the FCE, Mr G. When she was 15 years old, she was sent by Mr and Mrs G to attend a boarding school in the United Kingdom. After that, she studied law and business in a UK university before completing her master's degree in marketing and strategy at the same university. Her parents chose the subjects and sequence of her studies; in their view, this decision was to help build a solid foundation for Ocean when the time comes for her to take over the family business. After receiving her master's degree, Ocean went back to her home town in China and joined the family enterprise as a special assistant to her father.

Her first assignment working for the family enterprise was to open a sales office in Guangzhou. After a quick orientation to the company's products and operations, she went to Guangzhou. In less than 18 months, she had opened the company's sales office there and had it running smoothly. Shortly after that, she opened the company's Shanghai office. Three years into her role, she was tasked to open the company's first office in the United States. Now, two-and-a-half years later, after the US sales office has grown from one person (Ocean herself) to more than 10 people, it now also handles after-sale services for all products sold in the US as well as a new online sales function.

When asked about her family business succession plan, Ocean said that her father had put a lot of thought into the plan since the company's beginning. Because her cousin, the only child of her aunt who owned a minority stake in the business, was not interested in joining the family firm and also because Mr G had no interest in taking the company into public ownership or employing a professional CEO to run the business, Ocean became the founder's only choice to succeed him as CEO. With Ocean's education and master's degree, and her success in the management assignments she had been given, her father hoped that Ocean would be able to prove to his long-time lieutenants in the company that she had the ability to take over in a few years. Additionally, it was his plan to appoint Ocean to manage the company's operations in the US market – its most important market outside China.

What are the reasons behind the management succession plan and the steps that Mr G undertook to groom Ocean as his successor? What are the challenges and opportunities facing so many FCEs in China that are undergoing the reality of generational succession now, or will do in the next decade? Are there any differences among Chinese living in the People's Republic of China as opposed to other countries, given that the Chinese business diaspora is spread across much of the world? These and other questions will be discussed in the remainder of this chapter.

2. General characteristics of Chinese-owned family businesses

Family controlled enterprises are the foundation of the economies of China and other countries in East Asia. In China, it is estimated there are about six million FCEs – a number that is much higher than in the US. In a 2014 survey conducted by PwC, 84% of the surveyed family businesses from China reported growth in the past 12 months, compared with 65% from overall respondents.

There are two types of Chinese-owned family businesses operating within and/or outside the People's Republic of China (PRC). One type is owned by overseas Chinese, living primarily in Taiwan, Hong Kong, Singapore, Thailand, Malaysia and Indonesia. Many of these FCEs have been highly successful family businesses for many years, continuing well into four generations of family control. For example, in Southeast Asia, Chinese family-owned businesses currently control more than 70% of the region's corporate wealth even though they represent less than 10% of the population. Many of these firms invest internationally and a significant portion go into mainland China, with both Hong Kong and Taiwan leading the flow of investments. Key characteristics of this 'overseas' type of Chinese-owned family business is the emphasis on Confucian values and top-down patriarchal authority, as well as institutional structures. (The importance of traditional Confucian values to the Chinese corporate culture and to the overall success of these companies will be discussed later in this chapter.) In addition, many small-to-medium family-owned businesses use distinctive types of human and social capital, including reliance on networks and family relationships. These intangible assets are highly specific to each individual family.

A second type of Chinese family business is owned and developed by Chinese entrepreneurs based in mainland China. Since China's economic reforms began in 1981, China's private sector has grown tremendously. More than 80% of China's private enterprises are family businesses, in which individuals or families own a controlling stake of more than 50%. In 2010, Chinese official statistics indicated that the country had close to 40 million private businesses that account for 60% of China's gross domestic product (GDP). This is a significant achievement, given that just a few decades ago the number of private businesses was almost zero, when private business was outlawed in the country. Although these businesses have characteristics similar to their overseas counterparts, such as an emphasis on Confucianist values, top-down authority and reliance on relationship (in Chinese: *guanxi*), they also have some unique characteristics.

Primary among those characteristics is the connection between family-owned businesses and the influence of the national government. No influence may be more powerful than the impact of the 'one child only' government policy on most of these families, which means that they only have one successor if they want a direct bloodline descendant to succeed them as the leader of the family firm.[1] Another element that is unique to FCEs in mainland China is that most of the family firms are first-generation firms with a short history, lacking a well-developed corporate culture. Therefore, there may not be well-established business methods for the families to preserve their values, culture, heritage and legacy.

3. Chinese culture in business

As one of the world's greatest civilisations, China has a distinctive culture. While it is a diverse country with more than 200 dialects and many geographical differences, there is a common written language. More than 90% of the population belongs to a single ethnic group, known as Mandarin or Han. The building block of Chinese culture is Confucianism – with more than 2,500 years of history, Confucianism governs Chinese beliefs and behaviours. The four core values of Confucianism are face (*mianzi*), hierarchy, group orientation, and relationship.

Chinese individuals continue to hold these core values very tightly. Even when they emigrate from China and become citizens of other countries, most still believe themselves to be Chinese, even after living outside China for many generations. They place great emphasis on the group to which an individual belongs, rather than the individual himself or herself. Chinese culture emphasises that individual goals should be subordinated to the goals of the country, the community and the family. The Western concept of individualism is viewed as somewhat selfish and potentially disruptive. 'Saving face' and 'giving face' are not only about preserving one's dignity, but also about preserving the dignity and reputation of others.

Family is the foundation of Chinese society, including Chinese business. In Chinese culture, family comes before business. For family businesses, the Chinese tend to see their business duties more as responsibilities to the family. A typical Chinese family-owned business is often composed of a founder (usually the family patriarch or matriarch), other family members holding key positions in the business,

---

1 In October 2015 the PRC government announced an ending of this policy as a response to an ageing Chinese population, whereby two children would in future be allowed. The change in law came into effect on 1 January 2016.

and many tenured workers who have been working for the family firm for a long time. Even when a Chinese business becomes a publicly held corporation, it is often family controlled.

The family members generally take a hands-on approach in the affairs of the business. Business decisions are usually made informally and often occur at family events such as dinners. The head of the family has the final word on important decisions. He or she may have advisers who are family members or close friends. Such individuals may hold a relatively low position in the company, but can go directly to the head of the company without going through the standard chain of command.

Because of the cultural primacy of family, Chinese family business owners are generally reluctant to bring outsiders into the company, and a majority of them want the next generation to take control of the business once they relinquish control. Many Chinese who control businesses don't necessarily trust outside professional management. As the well-known proverb says: "Blood is thicker than water."

4. Mainland Chinese family-owned enterprises

In a similar fashion to Western FCEs, as Chinese family businesses expand from their entrepreneurial beginnings they face unique performance and governance challenges when navigating today's highly competitive environment. Primary among these challenges are developing the next generation and managing succession planning, governance, and preserving the company's culture and values from one generation to the next. This is in part because of culture, history and the uncertain regulatory and legal landscape of China.

Under the government of the Republic of China (1911–1949), family-owned businesses were the largest commercial enterprises of China. Many businessmen started off as agents for foreign companies but were nonetheless considered patriotic because they competed successfully against foreigners, especially the Japanese in the textile industry, the most important industrial and export sector of the era. Chinese industrialists benefited from numerous nationwide boycotts of foreign goods during this period – sometimes referred to as the 'golden age of the Chinese bourgeoisie'. After 1945, though, many family businesses fled mainland China and settled in Hong Kong, Taiwan and other parts of the world. Most of those who were left behind were prosecuted during various socio-political movements,[2] such as the Great Leap Forward and the Cultural Revolution.

Modern mainland China FCEs started three decades ago following mainland China's market reforms. The reforms started from the city of Shenzhen as a pilot policy programme and gradually spread to the east coast and south of China, to areas such as the Yangtze Delta and Pearl Delta regions, and including cities such as Shanghai, Ningbo, Wuxi, Wenzhou and Guangzhou. The textile industry was reborn and bloomed. After 1998, China privatised real estate. Many of the earliest private companies have expanded into other sectors, especially in property investment and

2 See Antoaneta Becker, *The Role of Family Businesses in China*, Europe China Research and Advice Network (ECRAN), September 2011.

development; and the property boom has helped these businesses, with profits in the range of 300–600%, at least prior to 2015.[3] Nowadays many of them are keen to expand their business globally, although few have so far been successful.

Most of the first-generation entrepreneurs of the current period of China's foray into permitting a private sector grew up in China's Great Leap Forward and Chairman Mao's Cultural Revolution in the 1960s and 1970s, when there was a shortage of just about everything, including food and education. The subsequent successes of these businesspeople largely depended on their drive, instincts and entrepreneurship. In relation to their second-generation successors, close to 90% have university degrees and more than 50% have studied overseas, including at many leading institutions, such as Harvard, Wharton and the London School and Economics.[4]

With their vastly different upbringings, many of the second-generation successors often clash with their parents over the management of their companies. The children are eager to introduce Western management systems and philosophies to their family businesses, sometimes against the wish of their parents. Because these family businesses have grown rapidly, some of them become public companies in just 20–30 years. Nonetheless, many founders believe Western practices are incompatible with the reality of doing business in China. Thus, they view their children's efforts to modernise their businesses with suspicion.

The second-generation successors within these new PRC-domiciled FCEs also have a very different value system from their parents. They grew up with affluence and they dislike dealing with government officials, which is deemed to be a necessary practice in the Chinese business world. Could there be a greater contrast than to the life of their parents' generation, whose impoverished existence after banishment to the countryside – irrespective of their prior education or achievements – depended on the often random decisions of government officials major and minor?

Kelly Zong, the only child and heiress to the multi-billion-dollar Wahaha fortune, recently publicly criticised China's social problems during a conversation with the UK Guardian newspaper: "I think we lost our soul. In the US, they have beliefs: Christianity and Catholicism. China has Buddhism, but I don't think people really believe it in their hearts." Two days after the interview was published, her father, Zong Qinhong, who is one of China's richest and most powerful businessmen, sharply criticised his daughter in the Chinese media and said that Kelly Zong was influenced by foreign culture when she was young and did not fully understand the present situation in China.

5. The issue of succession in mainland-Chinese family controlled enterprises

In family enterprises, leadership transition usually entails an iterative process where

---

3 See Kaiji Chen and Yi Wen, "The Great Housing Boom of China", Federal Reserve Bank of St Louis research paper, September 2015.

4 See Peter Cai, "Why Family Business Succession is China's Biggest Threat", available at www.CampdenFB.com, November 2014.

the senior owner/manager generation selects, grooms and transfers the mantle of the family legacy and control of its business to a rising generation. For FCEs in mainland China, the rising generation is usually an only child, which means the main challenge is how to groom that only child and transfer authority to the second generation. As described in section 4 above, another challenge is the cultural difference between the first-generation entrepreneurs and their children.

Currently, first-generation entrepreneurs belonging to the founding cohort of mainland China's private sector are fast approaching retirement age. They are therefore, as a group, all facing a looming ownership transition and related management succession challenges. It is estimated that there are about three million family mainland-Chinese businesses currently facing these issues or going to facing them in the next five to 10 years. Based on published data from Family Firm Institute, worldwide – and despite the preference of the majority of family business owners to see their business transferred to the next generation – about 70% of FCEs will not survive into the second generation and 90% will not make it to the third generation. In China, a survey by Forbes China found that 65.8% of business owners in the country hope for second-generation family members to take control of their businesses.

The succession crisis is unfolding at a time when China's manufacturing and infrastructure sectors are under tremendous pressure to move away from their labour-intensive production model, which is unsustainable because of steadily increasing wages and a slowdown of infrastructure development, such as housing construction.

One of the primary challenges to mainland Chinese FCEs is that there is no history or tradition of management succession planning among them. Very few examples of successful transitions exist and this deficit contributes to the lack of succession plans, or even the absence of recognising the need for one. According to a PwC survey, 22% of family businesses in China have some sort of succession plan, but fewer than 10% of FCEs have robust and documented succession plans.[5] There is a Chinese saying, "The son takes on from the father," which expresses the traditional Chinese view that succession should come naturally, without the need to formalise it. However, because of the influence of Western culture and education, some of the heirs/heiresses to mainland-Chinese FCEs are not interested in taking over the family business. A few years ago, in Suzhou, one putative younger-generation successor cut his four fingers off his left hand to declare that he did not want to take over the family business.

Many first-generation Chinese entrepreneurs are finally becoming aware of this crisis. In various ways, they are developing and grooming their children to make sure the second generation will be able to take over their family business when they decide to retire. In 2013, Wang Jianlin (CEO and founder of Wanda Holding, and the richest Chinese in mainland China) talked to the media jokingly that he was going to give his son, Wang Sicong, RMB5 billion (equivalent to US$80 million) 20 times. Even if Wang Sicong failed 20 times, he still could come to work for Wanda. And

---

5 *Family Business Survey 2014*, PwC, 2014.

today, using the US$80 million his father provided first time around, his son established Pusi Investment Holding and invested in a number of companies, including new businesses in energy, hardware, e-commerce, healthcare and even funeral services. Five of them were later subject to initial public offerings, and one of those five has already generated a fivefold return on Wang Sicong's investment.[6]

In addition to Wang Sicong, the children of Duan Yongji (founder of Sitong Group), Wang Zhongjun (founder of Hua Yi Brothers) and Liu Chuanzhi (founder/chairman of Lenovo Corporation) have all established their own companies. These companies can either be part of the FCE or a stand-alone company. These founders and others see this type of family entrepreneurship as an effective way to break through the commonly held view that wealth does not survive beyond three generations. This optimistic view is predicated upon the idea that when they join to the company their children will learn and gain the fundamental business skills that are needed to run the FCEs.

From these examples, one can see that to address the increasing succession crisis in mainland China the founders need to develop the next generation, manage ownership and leadership transitions actively and intentionally, have a strong management team and establish an effective model of corporate governance.

6. The issue of succession in overseas Chinese-owned enterprises

Primogeniture, the right of succession belonging to the firstborn child, especially the eldest son, has a long history in China. In large overseas Chinese FCEs, families generally follow the doctrine of primogeniture. This tradition has helped preserve family wealth and pre-empt conflict. However, in the last 30 years and influenced by Western culture and education, overseas FCEs have been adopting equality and democracy in place of primogeniture. Succession planning becomes more complex, however, and may potentially trigger family disputes.

As the first generation, a founder exclusively owns the Chinese family business. The founder employs sons, daughters and close relatives, and the business relies on the founder and traditional family values to deal with business affairs, as well as any opportunistic behaviour. For example, the founder of Cheung Kong Holdings, Sir Ka-shing Li, is a charismatic entrepreneur. Starting from nothing, he was able to seize the right opportunities and establish his business empire during Hong Kong's industrialisation. Such leadership persuades employees to align themselves with the goals of the business and believe they are part of the family.

Because of traditional Chinese family values, the founder will use family rules to handle problems. This will enable the founder to save face, build relationships and decrease any legal costs; he manages his business like he manages his family. The founder will have a strong sense of responsibility towards employees, both from an economic and a moral perspective, because he believes his workers are part of his family. Therefore, corporate governance is effectively carried out in a first-generation business through family rules with a set of traditional Chinese values.

For succession purposes, Chinese founders follow Chinese family traditions, but

6 See "王健林□王思□的5□投白花：投出5家上市公司", available at tech.qq.com, 6 August 2015.

at the same time they do not want to see their own business fail. Traditional Chinese ownership practices help to buttress the future of the FCE. The founder's estate is usually passed on to the heirs in more or less equal shares. The founder typically expects all the children, but especially the sons, to work in harmony for the sake of the firm. This more-or-less equal inheritance system, with the eldest son serving as the chairman of the board to lead the company, can serve in an informal way as the functional equivalent of corporate governance.

Because of the decline of traditional Chinese culture among the current generation and the rising influence from Western values without traditional family rule as an enforcement mechanism, each offspring tends nowadays to be free to promote his or her own welfare, and disputes in business management move from discussions inside the family to legal settlements outside the family. Thus, absent intentional planning of a more formal corporate governance model, this diminution of traditional Chinese cooperation among successor owners of Chinese FCEs can leave the enterprise without an effective system for resolution of disputes among the owners.

One of the famous cases illustrating this point is the dispute within Yung Kee Holding LLC. Kam senior was the founder of a famous roasted goose restaurant in Hong Kong. He expanded his original restaurant to a number of restaurants based upon a regimen of hard work, skill and intelligence. After Kam senior's death in 2004, his vast estate was shared among his three wives and their children. The third wife and her children received Yung Kee, the famous restaurant, valued at about US$200 million. Each of her two eldest sons (respectively Kinsen and Ronald) got a 35% share, while the third wife, third son and a young daughter received 10% each. This effectively meant that the ownership of Yung Kee was changed from sole ownership to collective ownership. Between 2007 and 2010, the three minority stakeholders transferred their shares to the two brothers, with Kinsen owning 45% and Ronald 55%, which coincided with intense infighting in the Kam family. Power struggles erupted because Kinsen, the oldest son, wanted to manage Yung Kee in the traditional family way and Ronald (not surprisingly) wanted to manage it in his own way. Kinsen appointed his own son as one of three directors, alongside the two brothers and excluded Ronald from management of the family firm. The dispute between the brothers eventually went to court. Kinsen died before the Hong Kong High Court was able to rule on the case. In 2015, Hong Kong's highest court ruled that Yung Kee had 28 days to achieve a final resolution of its long-running disputes or the business would be put up for auction.

In addition to the Yung Kee dispute, there have been a number of other high-profile cases of succession disputes, including Sun Hung Kai Properties. The senior Mr Sun put the family business into a trust and set it up as being perpetual under his will, as an endeavour to keep the enterprise under perpetual family control. Similar disputes arose involving the FCEs of self-made gambling and property billionaire Henry Fok and legendary Taiwanese entrepreneur Wang Yong-Ching, the founder of Formosa Plastics group. He died in 2008 with no will and left behind a wife and two other women who were mothers to his nine children. In 2011 his eldest son, Winston Wong, filed three lawsuits against his half-siblings in three jurisdictions: Hong Kong, Taiwan and the US.

To avoid some of the succession issues that his fellow entrepreneurs and their FCEs faced, Li Ka-shing announced a succession plan in 2012 that allowed his eldest son, Victor Li Tzar-kuoi, to take the helm of the family property group, which was restructured as CK Hutchison and Cheung Kong Property Holdings. For his younger son, Richard Li Tzar-Kai, Li senior said he would provide full financial support for him to develop other businesses that would not conflict with his flagship companies so there would be a clean split of wealth between the two brothers.

From these examples, one can see that the focus of overseas Chinese FCE succession is the implementation and enforcement of a system of governance that identifies shared values, consolidates family interests and resolves conflicts. It should also provide exit strategies for the family business. The succession plan needs to set up the right ownership structure that balances both the founder's preference for keeping the business as a whole and the family members' wish to receive a fair share of their inheritance. But however elegant the models may be that founders design for cooperation among sibling co-owners, it is not enough. The successors of FCEs may share the values of founders, but may still not be a seasoned business professional. Therefore, it is essential to have a strong management team and establish an effective model of corporate governance.

7. Example of a successful multigenerational Chinese family controlled enterprise

Lee Kum Kee Corporation was established in 1888 when its founder, Mr Lee Kum Sheung, invented oyster sauce in Nanshui, Guangdong Province. With more than 120 years in business, Lee Kum Kee has become a household name as an ethnic Chinese enterprise as well as an international brand and symbol of quality and trust. As a century-old ethnic enterprise, Lee Kum Kee substantiates its core value of "considering others' interests" in every aspect of its business operations. Lee Kum Kee has also lived by the principles of "pragmatism, integrity and constant entrepreneurship".[7]

Headquartered in Hong Kong and with a global presence, Lee Kum Kee has five production centres based in Xinhui, Huangpu, Hong Kong, Malaysia and Los Angeles. Currently, the company is managed by its fourth generation and is grooming its fifth generation for leadership. It has successfully broken the family business 'three-generation curse'.

What is Lee Kum Kee's secret weapon to ensure this success? According to Sammy Lee, its fourth-generation leader, the secret is simply to build and sustain the correct family culture and succession plan. But it is crucial to note that in the contemporary business world a family member working for a family controlled enterprise plays four concurrent roles: family member, stakeholder, board member and manager. The largest problem for many family-owned businesses is the pathway from that to a family controlled enterprise – ie, an enterprise where these four roles are clearly differentiated as opposed to merged into the behaviour of a single leader wielding all of the power of the family and its cultural heritage of ownership, of management

7 See the firm's corporate overview, available at http://eu.lkk.com/en-GB/AboutLKK/OverView.

and of governance. To avoid these issues and a lack of clarity in the four roles and their respective places in a family controlled enterprise, Lee Kum Kee implemented the programme described in the remainder of section 7.

7.1 Core values

The core values of the Lee Kum Kee (LKK) Corporation are threefold:

- be empathetic;
- pay attention to others' feelings before one's own; and
- put country, community and family ahead of the individual.

In the 1980s, Lee Kum Kee's patent was infringed in Malaysia. After years of court battles, the corporation won the case. Not only did the infringing factory pay damages, but so did the 18 supermarkets that purchased and resold the products manufactured by the party found to have infringed on LKK's patents. Considering various factors, Lee Kum Kee did not require the supermarkets to pay the fines assessed by the court; rather, it asked them to sell LKK's own version of the products. The company decided that the imputed cost of marketing the products compensated for non-payment of the fines. The owners of these supermarkets were so touched that they sold many LKK products in Malaysia, thus ensuring a successful entry by the company into the Malaysian market.

7.2 Family governance

The controlling family established a committee of family members to ensure good family communications. There are currently seven members on the committee, including the chairman of the Lee Kum Kee Group, his wife and five children. The committee meets once every three months, and every meeting lasts four days. The content of the meeting is not business, but instead is family focused, including discussion of the family constitution, values and next-generation development.

7.3 Special rules for the successors

To become a successor to the current Lee Kum Kee Group leaders, the next generation needs to obey three special rules: not to marry late, not to divorce, and not to engage in illicit affairs. The last two are considered particularly important.

Members of the fifth generation who want to join Lee Kum Kee need to graduate from college, work for another company for three years before joining the enterprise, start from an entry-level position and work their way up to a leadership role in the company.

Because of these deliberate efforts, Lee Kum Kee is continuously expanding and growing very profitability as a family controlled enterprise.

8. Conclusion

China has become the world's second-largest economy. Chinese family-owned businesses are an integral part of most economies in China and many Far Eastern countries. Because most of the family firms are first-generation enterprises, China faces a serious challenge as its first generation of entrepreneurs struggles to sustain continuity of family control, continuity of competitiveness and continuity of family harmony into the next generation. There is enormous discontinuity between the scope of this challenge to the private sector of mainland Chinese business and the paucity of successful models, openness to continuity planning, and public recognition of the enormous challenge to the health of the private sector in China.

Overseas Chinese family-owned businesses face different challenges from domestic family businesses. All overseas family firms that heretofore have relied on traditional Confucian cultural norms premised upon and contributing to family harmony are being vitiated by Western influences, and by competition from non-Chinese-controlled companies with whom they compete more and more. Overseas Chinese family-owned businesses must both plan to become and move toward becoming FCEs. This means separating out the four functions that family members of family shareholder controlling groups plan in the life of a family firm, and make real the shift from a family firm where all power is controlled by one family member wielding both historic Chinese cultural norms and sole ownership power as the leader to the firm. Such firms need to plan for family business management succession, engage family members and support the future success of the business and family. A customised process that applies to the family business individually and brings together the family members is required to develop this workable plan.

Equally important, planning for this transition needs to take into consideration both traditional Chinese values and modern business thinking. The plan needs to include values, vision, strategy, investment and governance, and to consider the broader aspect of family governance, ownership structure and corporate governance in order to align family and business actions. Because a failed succession can result in the loss of a family's values and culture as well as the family's fortune, many Chinese family business founders need to become more proactive in establishing a well-developed and well-documented plan to move from being a traditional Chinese family-owned business to being a competitive family controlled enterprise, and to groom their next generation to lead it.

Ushering out a family business founder who doesn't want to leave

Christian W Dame
Interim Executive Solutions LLC

1. Introduction

At long last, the moment of truth. After months of earning trust, I was about to conclude the essential leadership succession meeting with the father/founder of a successful medium-sized business. Next up was turning over the management reigns plus the business chequebook to the troika of daughters we had been grooming to assume leadership. I turned to him and spoke: "You know Peter, someday when you die these three will inherit the business and they need to the chance to learn now, before that happens." Peter looked me straight in the eye and announced: "You mean IF I die."

Resistance to passing the leadership, and ownership, of a family controlled enterprise is seldom as stark as this example, but all too often it is very real. It's real for a variety of reasons. There can be valid business reasons: the upcoming management team – family members or others – may be weak or appear to the founder to be unready. There may be actual or perceived economic storm clouds on the horizon, threatening smooth business operations. Or family relations with key successor actors may be strained – and often as not, by the very circumstances of yielding leadership to the younger generation.

But there are often non-business reasons centred on the figure of the founder. This shouldn't surprise anyone. After all, who has been at the centre of the action from the time the doors of the business opened? Who has made the saving call time after time, crisis after crisis, in order to grow the business? Who carries battle scars, accumulated painfully year after year, business cycle after business cycle? And who is the wise man or woman that the firm's partners, bankers, suppliers, customers and even job-seeking family members call first? It's the founder, of course. It will always be so … until it isn't.

This is a how-to chapter. It's about how to have that uncomfortable conversation that everyone wants to avoid: the talk about stepping down because it's time to go. And it's about making that transition a success – for the family, for the business and most especially for the founder.

So when is it truly time to go?

For guidance, we might quote John Silber, former President of Boston University, who, in a phrase that did much to cost him a close election to the position of Governor of Massachusetts, famously said: "When you've had a long life and you're ripe, then it's time to go."

But whether you agree or disagree with President Silber, such pithy wisdom merely re-centres the evaluation criterion onto the definition of 'ripe'. Most founders would agree that they've had a long (and successful) life as a business supremo, but few would agree to being characterised as ripe. Yet perhaps 'ripe' isn't a bad analogy. When fruit is ripe, it's both most attractive and close to its end state. Fruit beyond its prime is seldom attractive to anyone.

So I would argue the case that arranging the departure of the successful family business founder is in fact related to ripeness. Gracefully ceding the field at the height of a founder's powers, with colleagues' approbations still ringing in the ears, is the gold standard for family business leadership succession. All too often, however, that isn't the reality in enterprises controlled by families – and perhaps understandably so. The successful family business is directly connected to the founder's strong ego. And people with strong egos have a difficult time letting go – of power, of making important decisions, of being defined by the family business, of orchestrating the swirl of day-to-day business activity that more likely than not defines his or her life, of being the head of the family, and of the public mantle of being a 'wise' person.

Yet, those same character traits – strengths that have made the family business leader a proven business success – are also the levers by which a trusted adviser can counsel and ultimately convince the founder that it is indeed time to go and, more to the point, that leaving at a time and in a manner of one's choosing is the pinnacle of a successful family business career.

2. Setting the stage

Long before the R-word (as in retirement) conversation takes place, all the stakeholders in the family business system have work to do.

First, someone in the family or business must discuss directly with the reluctant founder that business conditions (hopefully excellent and improving, but possibly negative and deteriorating), or family considerations (such as the founder's health or the health of a loved one) have evolved to the point where the founder must accept, as his strongest supporters and respected colleagues already do, that the time has come to plan for the next incumbent. That is to say, the first step in a successful transition process is decoupling initiating contemplation of transition from developing an actual plan and implementing it. This multi-step process is in the interests of the business, for the founder personally, and the strategy likeliest to protect his/her legacy as founder and patron of the business. In the conversation, which raises the issue of contemplating a transition plan (but not its implementation), emphasis should be placed on recognising the achievements of the founder and ensuring the continued success of the business.

There is never a perfect time to have such a conversation, but most would agree that the time to have it is before the ripe fruit falls from the tree and the business founder is publicly observed to fail in some way. In other words, it is best to initiate this conversation at a time when business is good, not bad, and the founder is strong, not under attack. Given the premise of this chapter is that the founder is reluctant to leave, few such reluctant founders are likely to be in a flexible, creative mood about the future when performance of their business is eroding and/or serious external or competitive challenges to its performances are waxing. In such adverse business situations it is likely that all personnel, not just the founder, will likely dig in and attempt to fight for the continued viability of the business, whatever the family, business, financial and personal cost to their reputation.

Before the time arrives where the objective choice is to save the business or to manage the transition from founder to successor for the benefit of all stakeholders in the enterprise, thoughtful family members or business associates can take action. Sometimes an understanding family friend or respected business colleague can be recruited to approach the founder privately and enquire about his/her plans for the next stage of the business. (We shall hereafter refer to this intervenor as 'the trusted adviser'.) That intervenor can suggest that perhaps an objective family business professional might bring different perspectives to the discussion. The trusted adviser might also provide helpful insights, based on wide-ranging experience, which could aid the founder's thinking about next steps, timing, leadership succession models, and the types of interesting mentoring and leadership outlets that might lie ahead for the founder, beyond direct business leadership.

3. Having THE conversation

The chances are slim that a reluctant founder will either engage a counsellor personally or respond positively to pressure from family members or business associates and unilaterally commence succession planning. Direct confrontation by family members is likely to bring denial, delay, destructive behaviour and defeat.

Instead, the wise family that controls a business enterprise creates an opportune time, place, and representative to open the conversation, in a non-threatening way, about the uncomfortable subject on everybody's mind, including probably the reluctant founder. And that would be letting go – of power, of decision-making, of personal attention and of physical reward. In family controlled enterprises, such letting-go usually involves three stages: trust, transparency and time. The trusted adviser's role, when he or she is introduced, is to work with the founder directly using these three elements, together with family members and business associates accepted by the reluctant founder, to begin to formulate a succession plan.

That plan begins with trust. The trusted adviser begins the succession conversation with the founder by bringing out confidence-building measures centred on three things: the goals of the founder, the needs of the business and the needs of the family system. (This last is beyond the author's expertise. It argues for a conjunctive engagement by a family business psychology professional.)

Even a reluctant founder wants the best for his/her public legacy, for the continued prosperity of the business into which they have invested much more than money and, of course, for his/her family. Sadly for many founders, family system considerations have been a secondary or tertiary consideration, but it remains a powerful human emotion that can be tapped. These ego-related considerations are the levers that the trusted adviser will engage, with support and understanding from sympatric family members and family business associates, in order to convince the reluctant founder that transition time has finally arrived. The experienced trusted adviser will necessarily weigh the ever-present professional advancement ambitions of business-involved family members and non-family business associates against the long-term best interests of the business. The medium-term interests of transferring the founder to a new role in the enterprise, or even retiring the founder in a manner that shows respect and takes advantage of the founder's legacy, and doing so in the best interests of the family system, must also be considered.

Often, the path chosen by the trusted adviser includes recommending the retention of a battle-hardened professional adviser who is experienced in advising family controlled enterprises and their stakeholders on leadership transition conversations. In discussions with the reluctant founder over what will likely be a period of months, the professional adviser (backed up by continued engagement of the trusted adviser with the founder) will focus on:

- identifying and grooming a management successor;
- a defined period of mentorship of that successor by the founder;
- exploring a new and expanded community role for the founder, based on sharing his/her wisdom and expertise;
- identifying a definitive end date for transfer of the business leadership (and sometimes the business ownership); and
- ensuring the founder understands the role mapped out for him/her once the transfer has occurred.

In my opinion, this last consideration is the key to a successful transfer.

As stated above, I believe every strong, accomplished family business founder – even a reluctant one – wants to leave behind a lasting, publicly recognised legacy contribution to society. They want to see not only that their personal historical investment in blood, sweat and tears in their business areas has been recognised by the outside world through continued business success after they depart the scene but also, more importantly, that the continued success of the business after they depart demonstrates conclusively that their many years of business leadership was a positive contribution to making the world a better for place for us all.

4. Walking the walk as well as talking the talk

After the reluctant founder has agreed to consider a transition, there remains a challenge about how to structure the process so as to keep even grudging progress alive. There are likely to be three founder concerns that will face the trusted adviser as the transition plan comes to fruition.

The first and most obvious concern is who is taking the founder's place as business leader. There are numerous answers to this concern: capable family members, trusted non-family associates or even a proven outsider. Each of these must be judged against the particular needs of the business and vetted by the founder, other family members active in the business, and the trusted adviser or other trusted counsellors. Where an existing corporate governance process exists at the time the transition process is initiated, the members of the board of directors or the advisers serving on a council of advisers should be engaged from the very beginning in the implementation of the succession plan. At some point, the best choice acceptable to the reluctant founder will become clear. Care must be taken to ensure that the vetting process is time limited, with clear criteria, a decision deadline, and a clearly delineated handover process.

The second concern is likely to be even more of a deal breaker for the reluctant founder, and it comes in various forms. How can the founder who has invested years in making the business successful be assured that the business will continue that success after he/she departs? How can that maturity, wisdom and business experience be replaced? How can the founder's financial security be protected? Of course, the founder's wisdom can't be replaced on a one-for-one basis by any successor; nor can a successor guarantee the founder's financial security. But those needs can in fact be addressed in a different manner. One technique is to institute an advisory board. The advisory board is just that – advisory, without legal authority or fiduciary responsibilities.

Much has been written on the subject of how to create effective corporate governance in family controlled enterprises,[1] but in essence advisory boards are small groups with three to five paid members chosen by family owners and the founder for their complementary business expertise. They meet periodically, perhaps on a quarterly basis, with family members active in the business. They review business operations, financial performance, and strategic objectives. More than that, they are tasked with providing frank, objective and non-threatening business advice to the new executive team, completely separately from ongoing family dynamics. Their charge is to advise the business, not the family. An advisory board respected by the departing founder can provide material reassurance that there is an independent group willing and able to hold management accountable for its performance. At the same time, an advisory board offers the successor management team comfort that there is an independent group, trusted by the founder, that can validate management's performance. An advisory board also provides a hedge that the founder will not feel compelled to play 'saviour' and seize back control of the business at the first sign of trouble.

Finally, there remains the all-important question about what the founder will become once he or she steps down from being a senior executive. Is there life after business? Of course there is, in multiple soul-rewarding ways; and they should all be explored. But one role that founders are uniquely positioned to fill is that of mentor to other family members active in management and to non-family executives. The trusted adviser can assist the founder in evolving an exciting new set of relationships with younger members of the family and the business's management team as a life coach. This grey-haired (or no-haired) mentor has earned permission to dispense confidential and valuable life advice to both those inside and outside the business. A mentor role is one that the reluctant founder is likely to find especially fulfilling, because it taps into his/her central view of himself/herself – that of a wise family elder unselfishly committed to the well-being of not just the business that the family controls, but to the family itself.

---

1 See generally several of the chapters in the companion volume to this publication, namely *Family Enterprises: How to Build Growth, Family Control and Family Harmony* (ed Richard L Narva), Globe Law and Business, 2015.

5. Conclusion

The business founder who is reluctant to step back and allow others to begin a new chapter for the business and to take it in new directions is a familiar character in a play that is visible in the daily media generally as well as every day in the lives of millions of family and non-family executives and employees active in family controlled enterprises. The process need not end in tragedy for the business or the family. It will, however, demand difficult conversations, expert outside intervention, and the creation of new challenges for the still-energetic ex-leader. The results can be amazing for all concerned.

Optimising the advent of non-family executive management in family firms

George P Bukuras
Milestone Business Advisors LLC

1. Introduction

I was introduced to the idea of the family business at an early age. Many of my relatives and our close family friends who immigrated into the United States during the early and middle part of the 20th century became entrepreneurs. Although there were various motivations, central to each of their life stories was the need to support a family. As a young man, I never thought as respectfully about these familial businesses as I later would. They were too familiar to me, and often these entrepreneurs highlighted the consuming nature of the course they had charted for themselves, encouraging me to seek higher education. Tacit in their message was that life for me as a professional would be more fulfilling, somehow nobler, and certainly provide a better quality of life.

After completing my higher education I was fortunate to earn a position at a major international accounting firm. There, I had imagined, I would be exposed to 'real' business. Little did I know that I was to embark on a path that would bring me back to my roots in an extended family of entrepreneurs and engender a true appreciation for the magic of entrepreneurship, as well as a deep respect for those committed to their family's businesses.

I began my career more than three decades ago at the public accounting firm of Price Waterhouse & Co, as a member of their audit staff. There, for the first time, I was introduced to the workings of large, sophisticated, publicly traded businesses. Without request, and much to my surprise, I was selected in the early 1980s to participate in a US firm-wide pilot study designed to train professionals to become general business advisers to some of the firm's smaller middle-market clients. It was explained to us that the motivation for the pilot study arose as the result of a strategic planning effort focused on the future growth of the firm. At the time, there were eight major international accounting firms (the so-called 'Big Eight'). The strategic study participants had theorised that, over the ensuing years, each of the Big Eight firms would lose approximately the same number of *Fortune 1000* clients as it would gain; and therefore, any meaningful long-term growth would have to come from what was described as 'smaller businesses'.

The strategic planners considered that one of the challenges in this environment was that these smaller businesses, typically run by founding entrepreneurs and/or their families, did not have the time or patience for dealing with several partners from various disciplines (such as tax, audit and management services). They concluded that, instead, these businesses would be better served by a single trusted business adviser as the point person and coordinator of all of the firm's services. Accordingly, our new group was denominated Comprehensive Professional Services (CPS).

When those of us in the study were first introduced to the concept, we were not sure our selection to the group had been fortuitous – the path to partnership through the firm's conventional disciplines was well paved. Conversely, the success of this new endeavour was uncertain, and we wondered what the career implications might be if this programme were to fail. To assuage this concern, we were provided with a tremendous amount of propaganda from the firm, which described the importance of small businesses to the US national economy. The firm's assertions were supported by statistical data and various metrics, from job creation to contribution to GDP. This was, perhaps, my first realisation that 'small business' was real business.

What first seemed like conscription into the tsar's army ultimately proved to be a valuable event – one that, together with my familial DNA, set me on a path as a career-long observer of, participant in and then adviser to, family controlled enterprises. When I left Price Waterhouse I joined one of those small businesses, a second-generation family firm. I eventually became the firm's non-family chief operating executive. Additional adventures with other family businesses followed. Throughout my career I have experienced family businesses from the perspectives of family member, public accountant, lawyer, consultant, non-family executive, family employer, executive board member and non-executive board member. I have worked in very small and very large business enterprises. I have evaluated such businesses, in many cases as a prospective acquirer. Interestingly, as I matured in my business career, I came to learn that many observations I made as a young man about workplace dynamics with entrepreneurs, who then happened to be my family, were the basis of reasonable predictions applicable to other family-owned enterprises, both large and small.

True to the theme of this book, I will base my observations upon real stories about real people, with non-essential details edited in consideration of privacy.

2. Why family firms need non-family executives

In order to have a meaningful discussion about optimising the advent of non-family executives in family firms, two questions must be considered: why family firms seek non-family executive management; and why non-family executives are attracted to family firms. The short answer is, typically, that each sees in the other what they do not possess themselves but desire.

A family member – whether first generation or later – who is running a family firm is likely to have spent the majority of his or her career in the family's particular industry. The family member at the helm may be the founder – or, if not, someone directly or indirectly influenced by the characteristics, beliefs and cultural nuances first modelled by the founder. Generally, the family firm has growth objectives and therefore will often seek non-family executive management hailing from larger, more mature and (typically) more institutional environments. Essentially, this arises from a need to import skills to supplement the family's home-grown talent and experience.

On the other side, the non-family executive may find a family firm alluring for both career and personal reasons. Professionally, a non-family executive may see the move as an opportunity to make use of his or her skills and experience in a leadership position, thus avoiding the political and timescale risks of staying on track in a larger institution, where such a position may never be achieved. Migration into a family firm may also give opportunities for team building that are absent in the executive's present environment, and which the executive may believe will positively contribute to corporate growth and personal fulfilment. The non-family executive may be motivated by one or all of these attractions, as well as the opportunity for building personal wealth, for working in a more humane and less institutional environment, and for maintaining geographical stability in service to the executive's own family interests.

Despite the mutually complementary objectives and motivating forces at work, the decision for family and non-family executives to work together is rarely an easy one, because fear and a lack of understanding are often intruding factors. Both parties are likely to have had strikingly different formative professional experiences. For each, entering the other's domain requires great cultural adaptation. Both a family and a non-family executive may concur that the family enterprise needs to learn the ideas and language of contemporary business from the non-family executive. However, at the outset neither party can really know the other and both sides might well naturally fear whether the other will be able to adapt to their vision of this new world. Will the new executive be successful at mastering the culture and dialect of the family controlling the enterprise? Will the family have the will to endure the necessary elements of cultural change to allow enterprise maturity?

Ultimately, the results – successful or not – will be disproportionately weighted to the sensitivities, emotional intelligence and skill of the incoming executive. Professional researchers and practising observers alike will attest that the primary reason that chief executives recruited from outside the family system fail to achieve success in their new roles is their failure to understand and integrate the culture of the family firm into their organisational efforts. Often, the ironic misfortune is that such failures have at their core the same institutional and cultural differences that had once been the source of attraction for the participants.

In a *Boston Globe* article,[1] Harvard physicist Lisa Randall, author of the book *Dark Matter and the Dinosaurs*, calls attention to the invisible yet profoundly influential forces of dark matter on our daily physical existence. Dr Randall asserts that this invisible matter, which neither emits nor absorbs light, is as real to our existence as are soil, air and water; yet evidence of its existence is hidden. In her article, Dr Randall draws the parallel of how invisible cultural forces affect interpersonal, racial, ethnic and political understandings. These hidden forces, Dr Randall explains, animate us and our communities in idiosyncratic ways often unknown and/or misunderstood by those outside our particular silo of cultural experience. These forces, the reader comes to understand, though unseen and therefore mostly

1 Lisa Randall, "Seeing dark matter as the key to the universe – and human empathy", *The Boston Globe*, 26 October 2015.

unappreciated, affect our relational experiences just as solar energy affects our weather patterns. So it is with family firms.

Such unseen cultural formative forces, I submit, are at the root of fear and conflict within the dynamics of integrating the non-family executive into the family firm. The formative experiences of those in the family firm and the non-family executive are often very different, misapprehended and therefore foreign to the other. Thus, in order to successfully mediate between the conflicting forces at work in family and non-family executive management, it is important to endeavour to understand the professional journey and cultural leanings of the other, and to recognise how these different forces influence, inform and animate the participants. For both parties, a successful result will require the difficult task of not only embracing but also surrendering aspects of these divergent energies in service to the enterprise.

Finally, as will be discussed below, for purposes of achieving optimal equilibrium in this regard, it is important that the family firm adopt a process of governance that is both sensitive and responsive to the potentially combustible energies at work in the family firm.

3. Overcoming fear of the other

Just as fear is at the root of prejudice in our communities, when the non-family executive appears, fear is the spark to be prevented in the new atmosphere of the family firm. In these circumstances the fear may be nuanced, depending on whether the family firm is first generation (so that it is the founder's first experience of allowing another at the helm) or later generation (where a family member might be burdened emotionally by the familial mandate to do no harm and pass onto ensuing generations at least what the present generation stewards had been gifted). Family fear is rooted in the unknown and runs deep, to the essence of notions of familial security.

Let us remember that, as with my immigrant relative entrepreneurs, it will have been the business that has always taken care of the family. With the advent of non-family executive management, things will change. The family, especially the founding entrepreneur, is called upon to trust a stranger with the family's most precious and unique assets: its cultural legacy, its personal fortune, its hard-won respect in the community and what is often its members' primary source of personal identity. The process is not anything like the relatively simple transition from one chief executive to another in a publicly traded company.

The non-family candidate will have grown in a very different environment. He or she will likely have been impressively educated, often including a relevant postgraduate degree from a competitive institution. Their résumé typically reveals a track record of progressively responsible experience and recites a myriad of accomplishments, complete with measurements and metrics. Although the candidate will have been exposed to a certain degree of organisational politics, notions of organisational governance, budgetary control, strategic planning, management by objective, and financial analysis are all second nature.

From the non-family executive's perspective, joining a family business always represents a risky experiment. Even though the executive may have experience in matters involving economic risk, it is very unlikely that the executive is comfortable abdicating total control over his or her career to some other family's patriarch or another controlling family member. Ironically, for the first-generation family firm, career risk was one of the hallmarks of the founding entrepreneur. For the non-family executive, being on the outside and having a career destiny vulnerable to the peculiarities of family members, whom the executive cannot possibly understand fully without the passage of substantial time and numerous interactions with many family members, can be unnerving.

I recall speaking with a marriage therapist friend years ago who explained to me his theory that one of the many utilities to the institution of marriage is that it creates a familial gravity force that requires more than a modicum of force to exit. My friend explained that when inevitable periods of marital turbulence present themselves and the 'fight or flight' reflex surfaces, such gravitational forces contribute to keeping the partners from flight and encourage mediation. Whether reciprocal gravitational forces actually exist from the family's point of view in the non-family executive or the family-firm dynamic, I can assure the reader that the non-family executive takes little comfort from this notion.

Mutually respectful insight and accommodation to the natural anxieties of each party is essential if the union is going to work. Both constituencies will experience change over time in the same manner that in-laws first encounter, and then accommodate, the differences in cultures and practices between two different families of origin. The family firm must adopt different disciplines while maintaining its basic character from which it derives its commercial advantage; and the non-family executive must endeavour to do no harm to that basic character while also serving as the catalyst for growth and maturation of the family firm, based upon the professional manager's larger world view.

In order to serve effectively as a catalyst, the non-family executive will need to subordinate – at least for a while – learned behaviour that does not fit and that may in some cases be toxic to the culture of the family firm. Additionally, it must be acknowledged that the owner/managers of the family firm may, at times, be uncomfortable when the non-family manager they recruited initiates change. Both parties should openly acknowledge at the start that the task will be difficult. With first-generation businesses, such a union may be the first time the founder begins to think of the business as an entity truly separate from self. By contrast, later generations may view such a move as an abrogation of familial custom and duty. Both the family and the executive should assume that the melding process will not be linear, and that investing significant effort in individual relationships will be required. The will for each constituency to tolerate the change required must come from a devotion to the reality that it is because of their critical differences in experience and perspective that each has sought the other.

With this foundation, we can explore (in sections 4 and 5 below) some of the cultural experiences and leanings that may be unique to the family firm on the one hand and the non-family executive on the other. Then we shall discuss in section 6 how the challenges of melding two distinctly different cultural forces may be mitigated.

4. We are products of our early experiences

Just as Aristotle's *Politics* begins with an examination of relationships within the family unit, the complex dynamics at work in family firms are often best understood by studying the most fundamental stage where esoteric energies first appear and are most easily observed. Accordingly, although the objective of this chapter is to discuss family firms that have attained some sizeable mass, in many respects some of the forces that will be described are best illustrated, in their most exaggerated form, from the perspective of the founding entrepreneur. This approach is based upon the observation that just as the young adult is a reflection of parental and other influences occurring during the individual's earliest years, so too do businesses reflect the legacy of their early years; and no legacy is so profound as the thumbprint of the founder. Accordingly, later-generation family-firm controlling parties may find most meaning in some of what follows by looking beyond the description of the first appearance of some of these forces and consider, by extension, the later and perhaps more muted effect of the tendencies described.

Successful entrepreneurs often exhibit unbridled initiative combined with a penchant for action. Among the most successful entrepreneurial founders, self-esteem and ego are generally subordinated to the importance of the task at hand, whatever that task may be – from maintenance of the washroom facilities, to preparing samples for a potential customer visit, to persuading a lender that the business is bankable, to calling the state governor to complain about recent anti-business legislation. Most successful entrepreneurs do not tolerate well those who allow formalities to stand in the way of action. Placing a focus on organisation at this early stage in a company's existence is a wasteful focus on form over substance to the entrepreneurial mind. In such an environment, there is little distinction made between the value of an individual's time as compared with that of another.

Compare such egoless devotion to the business mission with the yearning for the trappings of status that some strive for as evidence of movement up the corporate ladder in a large publicly traded firm. I remember how, in my own early professional life, at various stages a person's rank within the firm would be revealed by the style of briefcase with which he was issued. I can still recall my youthful pride when being issued with that flat, sleek leather satchel that was so easily distinguished from the bulky utilitarian audit bags carried by the junior staff whose responsibility it was to transport files to the client location. The sleek bag connoted that, because of the value of my time to the firm, I was now above such pedestrian tasks. How might that early moulding experience have translated later in my life when I was to report, as a non-family executive, to my new founding entrepreneur leader?

I was reminded of what might be termed my naive 'satchel pride' some years ago when accompanying a client – a very successful entrepreneur – to an important meeting at a bank. It was during the winter, it was cold and there had been a recent snowfall. When I picked up my client he was wearing boots, a hat and a heavy winter coat and he was carrying one of those inexpensive canvas carry bags sold in the check-out queue of most supermarkets. When we were ushered into the banker's conference room and my client removed his coat, I saw that the entrepreneur was wearing a short-sleeved Hawaiian shirt and discovered that he had grabbed the supermarket carry bag on his way out of his office to serve as his briefcase. Neither his choice of shirt nor his style of briefcase was intended as a statement; yet they both minimally but effectively served his purpose without any pretence whatsoever. It is highly doubtful that Messrs Price or Waterhouse would have either approved or dared to don similar business casual clothing.

Many entrepreneurs have a keen intuitive sense when it comes to economics at work in their business – not in the formal, conceptual Keynesian sense, but in the feral sense of a wolf on the hunt. They seem to just get it, and they expect those around them to just get it too. I remember working with one particular entrepreneur who owned a manufacturing company. It is relevant to the story that he knew that I had been trained as a certified public accountant early in my career and that, as a result, I was not intimidated by matters financial. Nonetheless, the entrepreneur's frustration with me would reveal itself in this particular meeting because I was unable, as quickly and intuitively as he, to understand why a particular fixed-price contract would be profitable and should be accepted. The experience caused me to question how, given that with my training and business maturity I had to defend my confusion to this impassioned and impatient entrepreneur, an employee with less formal training and self-confidence (and much to lose) would fare by questioning the master. I came to learn that the answer was that no one at this company questioned the founder's decisions. Perhaps this was a good thing at first, when no critical mass of business existed, speed was important and it fell to the entrepreneur to create something out of nothing. It was a quite different matter, however, when the entity had matured such that structure and process became important.

Contrast this with a more mature environment where analysis precedes virtually every decision. Moreover, the analysis in such an environment typically works its way up the chain of command to the relevant executive. The executive has to make the ultimate decision; and although some intuition may be involved, the organisation is not built upon one person exercising intuition as if by some divine power but, instead, on repeated analyses of data, and the conversion of that data to information on which to base a decision.

Hiring in a small and growing business is different from hiring in a mature business enterprise. Hiring in a small and growing business is like trying to hit a moving target. Often, the target is moving fast and the hiring has to follow suit. The wise entrepreneur recognises the issue of whether the skills he or she is seeking in a hire are those that are necessary for the present or those that she anticipates the business will need in the future. Almost always a compromise is necessary, which translates to hiring someone who is affordable and capable for today's need, leaving the worries of tomorrow for another time.

Often, the entrepreneur will not conduct an aggressive search but lean towards hiring someone the entrepreneur knows. To the more seasoned businessperson the folly here is clear. However, the early-stage business is often thought of by an entrepreneur as simply an extension of self – indeed, as family – and so there is comfort in bringing someone in that is known to and trusted by the founder. This is especially the case when there is little organisation and the entrepreneur is in need of loyal followers who will reliably execute tasks based upon the entrepreneur's instructions. As the organisation matures, however, such behaviour may result in loyal friends working in roles for which they are no longer sufficiently skilled or talented – a challenge with which the non-family executive reader will be familiar.

Compare such apparently cavalier hiring behaviour with the more defined, competitive searching and hiring processes at work in larger, more mature organisations. They have robust search processes, personality tests, professional reference and background checks, and collaboration among several interviewers.

Entrepreneurs are in the business of doing more with less. Professor Howard Stevenson, referred to by many as the godfather of entrepreneurship studies at Harvard Business School, famously described entrepreneurship as "the pursuit of opportunity beyond resources controlled". Compare such an approach with that of a business-school-trained executive climbing the ladder in a large, publicly traded company environment, where resources abound and cash is rarely an issue. The question is often whether to make or buy a new product, or whether to enter into a new geographic market organically or through acquisition. The task is one of how best to deploy plentiful resources, not how to stretch the meagre resources available in a relatively newly formed family business.

Having worked in both small and large businesses, I have experienced many cultural differences. Although the nature of these differences varies depending upon circumstance, there remains one difference common to every such comparison. In the large business the idea of, or concern for, cash was absent from almost all considerations. In a family firm, there is never a question about the importance of cash, and there is always a visceral understanding of whose cash fuels the enterprise.

5. Clash of culture

Let us accelerate forward on the business cycle timeline and study the possible aggregated effects of some of these formative tendencies to a point when a non-family executive is first being recruited by the family. What might the non-family executive come to find of the family controlled enterprise? Perhaps:

- a company that appears to have either no organisation, or more organisation than really exists;
- a company that is not practised in managing by objective or using shared information for decision-making;
- a company for which the annual budget exists principally to appease lenders;
- a company staffed with loyal associates of the founder, in positions where they may no longer belong and with titles unfulfilled; and/or
- a company with loyal long-term employees whose career progression has been subordinated to a style of paternal dictatorship – ie, being led by an army of one in the form of the founder, who knows something different is needed but lacks the experience to know what that is.

Now let us exaggerate, as well, the path of our fictional non-family executive – the one with a business school pedigree; the one who has participated in the management training programme of a major corporate conglomerate; the one who, at various points of time, served as general manager of different business subsidiaries of that conglomerate, in different parts of the world; the one who has others reporting to him with similar credentials, but junior experience and status. The non-family executive's experience has been in constant ascent. When called upon to describe his professional experience, he will do so by pointing to progressively more responsible experience and a resulting string of successes.[2]

With the foregoing in mind, think of the clash of cultures and experiences. Despite well-intentioned empathy, the non-family executive cannot truly understand the entrepreneur's journey. What the executive succeeds in understanding about the entrepreneurial experience is built on illusion; reading biographies and assumptions not based fully on fact. Similarly, the family founder, who has been in a business environment of his or her own creation, cannot truly understand the non-family executive's journey.

With such culturally diverse experiences, when introducing an executive from a large corporate setting into a family firm, even small and seemingly inconsequential transactions can portend consequential cultural conflict.

I was involved at one point in my career with a family firm in a capacity that afforded quite intimate insight into the firm's first attempt at retaining a non-family executive. The firm, which was engaged in the manufacture of specialist equipment, was in its second generation. The firm's chief executive officer (CEO) had returned to the US at the end of World War Two to a business that had been started by his father. Together with his three siblings, the returning veteran grew the family business significantly.

Even though the CEO had an impressive military record and held a command rank, the only business experience that this entrepreneur had ever had was within his own family business. Adding to the CEO's overly humble sense of self was the fact that his undergraduate education had been in agriculture before his war service as he had intended to pursue a career in farming. Despite his many talents and accomplishments, given his lack of business education and non-family business experience, this entrepreneur questioned his ability to lead the company through its next levels of growth. Desiring to see the business continue to grow, the entrepreneur and his siblings therefore decided it was time to bring in someone from outside the family as president.

Rather than conduct an exhaustive search, as some had advised, the entrepreneur settled on a man who was a neighbour of many years. The neighbour had an impressive background. He was well educated, had attended the right schools and had risen to an impressive post within a celebrated, well run, publicly traded company. Although it was never stated, I remember having the distinct sense that the entrepreneur was eager to select the neighbour rather than conduct a search out of a sense that, somehow, the neighbour would represent a safer choice than an unknown personality. He was a man whom the siblings could trust.

The seeds of discontent were planted early in the relationship. Since its inception,

---

2 The founding entrepreneur, on the other hand, when asked for a measure of his or her experience, will likely point to the number of times he or she 'got back up' after trying and failing, before true success was achieved.

the family firm had expressed its identity publicly by relying on a general corporate letterhead that was designed by the entrepreneur's founding father. Aside from address changes when necessary, the letterhead had remained the same for more than four decades. Used by everyone within the company, it was simple, understated and adequate. In his first month in office, the newly appointed president purchased a new personalised corporate letterhead, including his name and title, on the highest grade of paper available. Although the CEO never commented on this to me, I knew him well enough to sense his displeasure at the move.

Evidence of their differences began to accumulate like moths to a lantern. No one event carried a fatal sting, but the weight of seemingly constant petty insult eventually took its toll on the quality of life for the CEO, his siblings and some of the company's loyal and long-term employees. Eight months after his new letterhead arrived, the new president was negotiating his termination package. The CEO resumed the post of president and remained in that position until the family firm was sold, several years later, to a large publicly traded company. Between the time of the non-family executive's termination and the sale of the business, company revenues and profitability remained flat.

Even so, the terminated non-family executive went on to successfully grow another family-owned business quite dramatically. It was not ability which stood between the CEO and his new recruit, and it truly had little to do with the new president's choice of letterhead. The letterhead was merely the first small symptom of a much grander cultural clash in which the parties lacked the knowledge, will or tools to effectively mediate their way through. The newly hired president was fluent in the language of business; yet, overly eager at his task, he was not adequately inclined to learn the culture or dialect of the controlling family.

Whether it is the founding entrepreneur who is the first to solicit the assistance of non-family executive management, or a family successor to the founder years later, the environment into which the non-family executive will enter will have been influenced in some nuanced manner by the legacy of early factors unique to the particular family firm. The metaphor of the 'family tree' that is used in the study of genealogy is just as relevant in the study of generational family businesses.

6. The essential role of governance

Turning now to solutions, consider that, in the field of conflict resolution, disputing parties often seek the intervention of a respected, independent third-party neutral to serve as either arbitrator or mediator. Although the label 'disputing parties' does not fit the family firm or the non-family executive dynamic described above, reliance in a structural way on a respected independent third party is perhaps the only sensible way to mediate the natural conflicts inevitable when non-family executives are placed at the helm of the family firm. A fiduciary board of directors, or a non-fiduciary independent council of advisers, may serve as a reliable forum for the intervention of neutrals loyal to the enterprise yet independent of the parties in conflict. Such concurrent independence and loyalty are characteristics that are essential to the proper functioning of the business enterprise and the cultural melding called for in a family or non-family dynamic.

In my experience, a functioning fiduciary board composed of a sufficient number of non-executive independent directors (such that the board may be considered Sarbanes–Oxley compliant in this regard in the US) acting as an independent voting entity would be most effective for governance purposes. However, it is a rare first- or even second-generation family firm that will have the appetite for such a truly independent fiduciary board. A more common early attempt at governance will typically involve a non-fiduciary council of advisers (COA).

A COA can be almost as effective as a fiduciary board provided there is proper selection of COA members and that COA meetings, processes and procedure mimic the more mature liturgy of the fiduciary process. The parties – both family and non-family executives – essentially conduct themselves as if the non-fiduciary board is cloaked with fiduciary board authority. Of course, such action is only possible if the family commits to the principle of effective corporate governance with honesty and prudent fortitude. Adoption of such discipline has the added advantage, together with an equitable severance agreement, of helping to assuage the fear of the non-family executive of having their future determined by the whims of a family member. Without the safety of such constructs, attracting a suitable non-family executive is unlikely – more likely is that the family firm will find someone with an impressive résumé in need of a job.

Establishing an effective COA is similar to designing a complex floral arrangement. Colours and textures must simultaneously complement and challenge, without clashing. There is a synergy of sorts, where the differences add rather than detract. Moreover, both colour and texture must be in harmony with the overall space. However, when asked to explain the alchemy described in the context of forming a COA, most family firm founders will think two-dimensionally in terms of individuals with complementary, non-overlapping disciplines (such as marketing and finance, or manufacturing and human resource management). Few would focus on the temperament or personal qualities of the individuals – traits which in fact are of primary importance to the success of any governance body.

Although the process of bringing in non-family executive management often represents an organisational attempt at enterprise growth, in order to achieve the melding of cultures described earlier – essential to creating harmony and unity of purpose between family and non-family executives – personal growth among the participants is also required and the COA can be a catalyst for such growth. The suggestion is not that a COA should be made up of family therapists; rather, the COA should be established with individuals whose contributions will add perspective, will be forthright and independent, and (most importantly) will be heard even when these qualities are difficult to bring to the table. Furthermore, consultation with a professional with, at a minimum, soft science sensibilities might add to the effectiveness of the COA, just as an interior designer might bring a wise eye to the optimum construct of a floral arrangement for the space in which it will exist.

Bringing such emotional intelligence to the process is critical. For example, a forceful and controlling founding entrepreneur is likely to receive little benefit from having a Nobel Prize-winning economist as an adviser, if that adviser's personal manner was to be conflict-averse and compliant. Likewise, the same founding entrepreneur would benefit little by having a personal friend or business acquaintance whose experience and style mirrors that of the entrepreneur and whose personal friendship might trump independence, or provide the appearance of a lack of independence in the eyes of the non-family executive and other COA members.

As has been touched upon above, the non-family executive will typically present with impressive credentials and experience in more mature business environments. When establishing a COA, therefore, the family would do well to be sensitive to preventing a dynamic where a new non-family executive is (or, even worse, considers himself/herself to be), by training and experience, the most sophisticated individual in the room. Accordingly, both from the perspectives of oversight and accountability as well as for the support and growth of the executive, a properly formed COA should command the respect of the non-family executive based upon substance, not simply status.

Just as a fiduciary board will have its duties and authorities articulated in corporate governing documents, so too the COA should have a written charter. Advisers should know what is expected of them. The non-family executive also needs to understand the COA's role. Additionally, notwithstanding the non-fiduciary nature of the COA, the charter is the place where the family representative can formally set down in writing the intention (without imposing legal obligation), to the extent possible, to respect the authority of the COA as if it were a fiduciary board.

In addition to helping to facilitate the melding process referred to earlier, a proper functioning COA will assist in increasing the quality of decision-making on major issues, will enhance discipline in the conduct of the business and will instil a measure of accountability and responsibility from which both family and non-family executives will benefit.

In the case of later-generation family firms, it is equally important that the family adopt familial systems of governance that dovetail at appropriate 'touch points' with the family firm's corporate systems. Such familial systems will serve to mediate family issues, provide non-operating family members with a window into the affairs of the business, serve as a vehicle for the family to maintain its special imprint on the business, and provide the non-family executive with a sense of who the ultimate family head is.

The message here is not that having a well-functioning COA will cure all ills; growing a business is a continual challenge. What is being suggested is that just as a child requires different nurturing and exposure to various experiences at different developmental stages in order to thrive, so too do businesses and those who operate them. A board of directors or a COA can provide the parenting, so to speak, that is needed to nurture the business through impending stages of growth in light of competitive realities. Systems of corporate governance are necessary to provide the framework in which this individual and organisational growth may occur, and to mitigate the inevitable challenges that will surface.

7. Conclusion

Founding family members and later-generation controlling family members may have different issues when bringing non-family executives into the family firm.

However, such differences are simply variations on a theme. The business has always served the family. With the advent of the non-family executive, together with a fiduciary board or a non-family COA, the family is being asked to adopt a manner of existence that is different from what has succeeded for the family historically. It is a frightening moment in time.

The irony is that choosing not to go outside the family at the appropriate point in time should itself be cause for anxiety. Positioning the family firm to exist and thrive with non-family executive management at the helm provides the family with choices beyond simply selling the business when there are no longer family members interested in, or competent to assume, executive operating roles. Properly managed, the process of securing non-family executive management, possessed of skills and experiences that are different from those possessed within the family, can leverage the firm's commercial advantage and security across generations of family control.

I close with a quote from Charlie Munger, the nonagenarian vice-chairman of Berkshire Hathaway, which appeared in an article in *The Wall Street Journal* in 2014.[3] When asked to explain Berkshire's success, Mr Munger responded as follows:

> *Warren and I know better than most people what we know and what we don't know. That's even better than having a lot of extra IQ points. People chronically misappraise the limits of their knowledge; that's one of the most basic parts of human nature. Knowing the edge of your circle of competence is one of the most difficult things for a human being to do. Knowing what you don't know is much more useful in life and business than being brilliant.*

Having the courage and curiosity to search outside of the family as a means of expanding the family firm's 'circle of competence' is a worthy growth strategy, and one that will likely provide the family enterprise with greater long-term security than any alternative.

---

3 Jason Zweig, "The Secrets of Berkshire's Success: An Interview with Charlie Munger", *The Wall Street Journal*, 13 September 2014.

Transformation and tradition: transitioning to a non-family leader at the family firm

Roger Patkin
Next Generation Group

1. Introduction

We all have witnessed the transformative power of the right leader at the right time within an organisation, and this potential for transformation is particularly profound in a family controlled enterprise (FCE). Combining the richness of tradition, culture, values and relationships that define family enterprise with the fresh energy, thinking, skills and experience of a next-generation leader can be game changing and can provide an indispensable boost to the competitiveness of an FCE. At the same time, it is likely that as an FCE grows and passes from generation to generation, there will be a period of time when this new leader is not a family member. For this new non-family leader, the top job at the family firm can be the opportunity of a lifetime. However, it can also be the most challenging assignment any leader tackles throughout his or her career.

The purpose of this chapter is to set out a process for making a match between the FCE and a professional non-family leader, and then successfully transitioning leadership. This process has been developed in our family for our FCE over decades of navigating our company through multiple leadership transitions, including two successful transitions to remarkable non-family leaders.

This leadership transition process can be broken down into three major components:

- *Governance and guiding principles* – The first step in a successful leadership transition process is for the family to provide a clear understanding of the principles that guide both the enterprise and the family that controls it. Core values must be established prior to designing and implementing a leadership transition strategy. Next, governance structure and process must be built in order to create effective decision-making, and to align the family and company on the cornerstones of vision, values and guiding principles. With this in place, the family and board of directors are ready to define and prioritise the qualities and competencies they are looking for in their new leader.
- *Leadership search and selection* – The second component of this transition is a well-structured search-and-selection process that has the full support of the family and board. This initiative is essential to hiring the right leader and setting that person up for success. Working through this process with rigour instils confidence in the final decision and ensures alignment across family,

company and new leader on expectations and other important aspects of this new relationship.

- *Leadership and organisational development* – The last section focuses on embracing the new leader, and providing him or her with the support needed to be successful. This includes the right internal reporting structure, and access to an external trusted adviser. Finally, the family, board and new leader must align around a set of objectives for working together. This includes creating a common understanding about lines of communication and the day-to-day decisions of the leader that need to be communicated to members of the family and board.

I will describe in detail these three components in the context of my experience transitioning leadership of our 60-year-old auto parts distribution company (Autopart International, Inc (AI); formerly Foreign Autopart, Inc) from myself to our first non-family leader, Jim Durkin.

2. Background of Autopart International

My father, Stephen Patkin, founded our auto parts business out of the parts counter of my Lithuanian-born grandfather's Renault/Peugeot car dealership in Watertown, Massachusetts, in 1957. The parts distribution networks of both Renault and Peugeot were in their infancy and neither could supply my grandfather's dealership with parts in a predictable or timely manner.

At the time, my father had just graduated from college and was working in the family business for a summer prior to embarking on a career as an engineer. He was working in the accounts receivable department and heard from unhappy customers that it was taking more than a week for the dealership to service the cars it was selling. He identified the parts supply issue of the car manufacturers as the cause of the problem and aimed to solve it. He drove to New York City in the family station wagon with a couple of hundred dollars and a stack of note cards, each with original equipment (OE) part numbers written at the top, to explore the nascent industry specialising in non-OE parts for imported cars. He returned with a car full of parts in boxes with an array of unfamiliar logos and names. He stocked the shelves of the dealership's small parts room and the mechanics got to work. The parts were identical to corresponding OE items, but much less expensive. Happy customers were having their cars serviced in a day.

This vast increase in customer satisfaction drove car sales, which in turn drove increased demand for post-sales service. Soon word got out, and independent repair businesses began to call the dealership for parts for Renault/Peugeot and for other car brands as well. As a result, my father tested the business model of stocking parts for cars that the dealership did not sell and it worked. The family financed the start-up and Foreign Autopart, Inc was born. When the family divided ownership and leadership of the parts business from the automobile dealership business, my father owned the parts business equally with his youngest brother and they employed their eldest brother.

My younger brother joined Foreign Autopart in 1987 and transformed our 17-

store parts chain into a powerhouse. He brought great energy and talent to the strong, stable business that our father had built, and he became an expert in leading and expanding the parts stores. After practising law, I joined the parts business in 1990. My brother and I each led separate though intersecting halves of the business. He drove all customer-facing activity, while I built our brand and strengthened our manufacturing base and our corporate and supply-chain infrastructure. Our sister, Kimberly, ran our North American sales division for a time, and our mother Sally still greets everyone at the reception desk several mornings a week.

After a difficult ownership transition in 1994, when the company bought back my uncle's interest, my brother and I ran the business as co-presidents, while our father served as chairman of both our fiduciary corporate board and the very active advisory board. Shortly after this recapitalisation, my brother and I purchased in equal portions a majority of stock in the company from our father. Subsequently, in 1997 my brother began to pursue outside interests. I was appointed president and chief executive officer (CEO) in 1998 on the recommendation of our advisory board. My brother announced in 2002 that he would like to pursue a different path, and although there was no urgency, he asked that we begin working on an exit strategy for him. We had the opportunity to sell the business to Advance Auto Parts, Inc (AAP) in 2005, now the largest auto parts supplier in the United States. After a 10-month process, the sale was finalised.

I continued to run AI as a wholly owned subsidiary of AAP until 2010 when I hired Jim Durkin, the former executive vice president of the Global Business-to-Business Division of OfficeMax, as our first non-family president. I continued to serve as a member of the board of directors and assumed the role of senior adviser. Jim is a superb leader. He and I formed a strong relationship based on trust, respect and learning from one another, and this relationship remains strong today. In 2012 he was promoted to a senior leadership position at our parent company, and I was asked to return to the role of president with the express assignment of hiring our second non-family leader. After another long search-and-selection process, I hired Mike Creedon, the former leader of Tyco's Sensormatic Division, to lead AI. Mike and I have developed an equally strong relationship and he is doing an outstanding job leading our company.

To summarise, over a 30-year period our family business:

- split into two separate companies with separate ownership and leadership – an automobile dealership business and a new business selling auto parts for imported cars;
- leadership of the auto parts stores transitioned from my father to my brother Todd;
- ownership of the parts business transitioned from my father and uncle to my father through a leveraged recapitalisation;
- a second transition of ownership took place from our father to myself and my brother;
- leadership transitioned to a co-president model, with my brother and I leading the company and my father moving to the role of chairman;
- we then transitioned to a single family CEO;

- we sold the company to a public company buyer;
- the family CEO ran the company as a wholly owned subsidiary of AAP for five years;
- we transitioned leadership to a remarkable professional non-family president, and the former family CEO retained his board position and assumed the role of senior adviser; and then
- we transitioned to a second remarkable non-family president when the first was promoted to the parent company.

As I look back, this is a great deal of ownership and leadership change over a 30-year period of time.

Along with our successes we have had our share of family heartache, a description and analysis of which deserves its own space at another time. For the purposes of this chapter, it is important to note that unless the family issues that leadership transition almost always triggers are identified and addressed, heartache for the family is likely to ensue. This is heartache that could be greatly reduced, if not eliminated, by the ownership control group employing the same skill, insight, courage and guidance to address the impact on the family that it employs to address the leadership transition in the business.

The following sections set out the steps we have used to execute successful leadership transitions, including the transition of leadership to me and then from me to each of our non-family leaders. I will use examples from our experience with Jim and Mike to illustrate these concepts.

For the purposes of this chapter, the term 'family' refers to those family members or their representatives with power or standing to impact the enterprise. Each family, for a variety of reasons, may have all of the members of the family shareholder control group on the family council or they may not. There may be a family member with standing (founder's spouse or sibling) who is highly influential and not a formal member of the shareholder control group or the family council. Further, we will assume that the chairman of the family council and the chairman of the advisory board is the founder. Finally, we will assume that the advisory board consists of family members, independent directors and the new leader.

3. Governance and guiding principles

Governance consists of the structure and process for:

- delineating responsibility over foundational issues such as strategy, policy and key leadership roles;
- making decisions on these foundational issues; and
- creating alignment on these decisions at the family, shareholder and board levels.

Governance in a large privately held family firm typically consists of a family council, a corporate advisory board, and a fiduciary board of directors. Active governance in a small private company is often the work of just an advisory board, depending on the complexity of the family system. Good governance is necessary to ensure a well-run family business, and non-family candidates for the top leadership position in a FCE are likely to ask about the nature and effectiveness of governance. Much has been written on family business governance in Richard Narva's book, *Family Enterprises*.[1] Here, I will focus on what we accomplished with our advisory board and board of directors.

Prior to transitioning leadership to our first non-family leader, we codified the company's culture, values, vision and guiding principles. From there, we built alignment at the family and board levels around these four cornerstones. This enabled us to be clear and consistent on the essence of the company in the interview process. Both the family and the company's board of directors needed our new non-family leader to embrace these four cornerstones of the company's success. Alignment with these cornerstones was, and continues to be, essential to creating contiguity of culture and values from the family to the new leader, and this contiguity is essential to the success of the new leader and the company. Further, candidates for the leadership role need to know the culture and values of the company so they can begin to appreciate the uniqueness of the opportunity and help decide whether the job is a good fit for them. Research has shown that the primary reason that chief executives chosen from outside a company do not succeed as leaders is their failure to understand and embody the culture and values of the FCE.

We found that it is essential to establish consensus at the family and board levels when it is time for a non-family-member leader to be appointed, and a governance structure and process facilitates this agreement. To the extent that there are dissenters, they need to be heard and their concerns need to be addressed. If they do not agree with the decision, it is important that they nonetheless respect and support the decision. If this cannot be accomplished, they need to not act against the decision either in word or deed. If this is not possible, putting off the hiring process should be considered.

Next, the decision needs to be explained to the executives of the business. This explanation should include the reasons for the decision, and the fact that the decision is fully supported by the family and board. Authentic optimism for the future of the business and for all the company's employees is important. Again, dissenters should be listened to and their concerns addressed. The current leader and his or her executive team need to demonstrate unity and confidence around this decision. The decision should be presented by the executives to the management team in a similar fashion, and the management team should have the opportunity to ask questions. Once everyone is on board, the decision should be presented to all of the employees. Everyone should be able to communicate the reasons for the decision with confidence. When I hired Jim, I reiterated to the company my open-door policy and that they were welcome to stop by to discuss our decision at any time.

The family, board and business leadership need to approach the selection process with the intent of choosing the best leader for the business and then embracing that leader and doing everything possible to help him or her be successful.

---

1 Richard L Narva, *Family Enterprises: How to Build Growth, Family Control and Family Harmony*, Globe Law and Business, 2015.

With a new non-family member leader, governance needs to be flexible and efficient. If governance bodies meet quarterly, there should be a mechanism for making decisions on an interim basis. The governance process may need to be adjusted from time to time in order to keep up with the rapid pace of change that can result from the new leader's work, and to address the unsettling impact that might stem from these changes.

Importantly, vision, values, culture and guiding principles are enduring but not immutable. When changes to these fundamental tenets of the enterprise are considered, these changes should be subject to a structured decision-making process and be well communicated. For instance, a new president may want to add innovation as a value. The family and business may be very innovative, but innovation has not made the list of core values up to this point. Making such a core value explicit can be a driver for needed corporate change.

This was the case with our family business. In fact, most of the family stories about the business were about innovation although they were framed to show a tradition of grit, resilience and hard work. We reframed the narrative to accentuate the equally strong, though up-to-then less pronounced, thread of innovation in our family story. One example is our earliest story of my grandfather, at the age of 14, sweeping floors in a relative's small car rental business in Malden, Massachusetts, to earn money for the family, and to be around and learn to repair cars. He loved cars. After a few years, he had saved enough money to have his own rental car, which he rented and serviced. From there, with financial support from the family, he acquired a Ford dealership. Always wanting to stay a step ahead of the competition, he sold the Ford dealership and became the first Renault/Peugeot dealer in the greater Boston area. As set out above, the supply of parts from these car companies to their dealer network in the US was in its infancy, and their growing pains, and lack of parts at the dealership to service cars, were the catalyst for my father to innovate and start our parts business. We added the theme of innovation to these historical narratives, and added innovation to our core values.

Family support for a change in core values can be a powerful way of emphasising support for a new leader. It also dramatises the importance of this less prominent family business tradition, now brought to the forefront under the new president's leadership. Public displays of support such as this from the family and board for a new non-family leader are extremely important.

4. Leadership search and selection

Success in selecting and bringing on board the right non-family leader rests on defining a sound process and executing that process with rigour.

The first part of this section focuses on our search process, which we developed over time and refined over the course of hiring two outstanding non-family member presidents. The second part provides more detail on our application of this process and our experience.

4.1 The search process

(a) *Search personnel*

First, we selected an internal leader to champion the search process. Requirements included gravitas within the organisation, bandwidth, and experience leading a complex process in which maintaining alignment among several groups (including the family, the board, the executive team and the hiring committee) is essential.

The hiring leader appointed two people to the hiring committee. This committee was responsible for:

- outlining the search process;
- building a schedule with a timeline and deadlines;
- assigning responsibility amongst the hiring committee members for the various steps in the process;
- scheduling interviews and committee meetings; and
- ensuring proper execution.

Our hiring committee met weekly for two hours. We spent the first part of the meeting on a call with the search firm, and the second part reviewing our process and feedback on candidates.

(b) *Search process*

The following is a summary of the executive search process we developed. By using this process, the new leader will have been formally evaluated and selected.

This approach often raises important issues that should be addressed before an offer is made. Further, going through a well-structured evaluation and decision-making process that has the full support of the family and board is the best way of instilling confidence across all stakeholder groups in the final decision. Even with known candidates, there is value in going through the entire interview and hiring process.

Several of the following steps occur simultaneously:

- Unless there are known candidates, enter into a contract with a retained search firm.
- In three separate lists, prioritise the most important qualities, competencies and experience that the company is looking for in its new leader. Then ensure the family, board and executive team are content with these priorities.
- Draft a job description and include in the requirements section the qualities, competencies and experience noted above. Start and end the job description with the most compelling aspects of the job.
- Make a list of questions for the board to answer including:
  - To whom will the new leader report?
  - How will the new leader's performance be evaluated?
  - What is the high end of the pay range (salary, bonus)?
  - What are the components of the compensation package? In particular, is equity (phantom or real) an option?
  - What is the firm's policy on hiring family members?

  - Will board approval be required before the new leader can make a change to any of his or her direct reports?
  - How will the final candidate selection be made?
  - Are there any strategic imperatives (initiatives that must either be built into a strategic plan or excluded)?
- Decide who will interview the candidates, and work with them to prepare a list of interview questions. Typically, the same four-to-six people, including family, board and leadership team members, interview each candidate. Each should focus on the subject matter that plays to their area of expertise. Use Behavioural Event Interviewing (BEI)[2] to begin to develop a picture of each candidate's leadership style, values, and the culture they promote. (There are several good options for getting up to speed quickly on this useful interview practice, including online resources and human resource consulting firms that can train your team on BEI in a half a day.) This needs to take place prior to discussing the company's culture and values with the candidate.
- Build spreadsheets that can be shared and a process for collecting, standardising and reviewing interviewers' assessments and feedback. One option is to list qualities, competencies and experience down the left-hand side and candidates across the top. Also set up a text document for qualitative comments. Use a 1–10 point grading system for the top four-to-six attributes on each of the three lists noted above. Weight the attributes based on priority and generate an overall score. Material outliers should be footnoted next to the score.
- Determine how the committee will screen and choose candidates to interview from the search firm's documents. In our case, each person on the committee selected the candidates they thought should make it to the next round. Then together we reviewed each of these candidates and made a decision.
- Decide who will follow up on the top candidate's references. It is best if the same person follows up all of the references. The committee should make a standardised list of questions to ask each referee, and decide how the team will keep track of and share responses and team member comments.
- Select an external leadership assessment firm. Decide which assessments are most relevant, and negotiate a price. Be sure their availability lines up with your timing.
- Develop a process for keeping the family, board and executive team informed of the search committee's progress.
- Near the end of the process, develop a presentation for the family and board that highlights the process, including the top qualities, competencies and experience the company is looking for. In this (initial) presentation, make a recommendation.

---

2 Behavioural Event Interviewing (BEI) is a technique that asks the candidate to describe a situation or an experience they had in a previous job. Responses may not be as polished as the traditional type of question-and-answer approach because they cannot be rehearsed ahead of time. Nonetheless, the interviewer gathers valuable information from experiential responses because past performance predicts future performance.

4.2 The selection process

Ideally, at the end of the search process the committee will have two or three candidates who are well suited for the position and are highly interested in the job, and from among them the committee has a top choice to recommend to the family and board.

The next step is to call the top candidate's references. Assuming there are no red flags, have this candidate in for a final round of interviews. At that time, discuss compensation and next steps. Have a couple of people take this person to dinner and two others take him or her to breakfast or lunch. Have topics to discuss, and questions to ask. Often this includes going into more detail on specific leadership situations that were discussed during the interview process, in order to gain deeper insight into those qualities, competencies and experience that are most important to the company. Note relevant feedback. Once compensation and other key details have been agreed upon, proceed with an external leadership assessment. With a favourable assessment in hand (which includes a valuable list of areas for development), finalise the presentation to the family and board with the committee's recommendation.

The family and board will then proceed with their decision-making process. Once a candidate has been selected, call to congratulate him or her, and go over the major terms of employment. Then have legal counsel prepare either a letter of agreement or employment contract for the parties to sign. Do not end the process with the other candidates until an agreement is signed.

Work with your new leader to plan a warm welcome for their first day at the company. This should include a welcome from the family, showing unanimous support.

4.3 AI's approach and experience

The power of family is fundamental to family enterprise and was front and centre in our search process. We asked a family member to describe this power and its importance to the business to each candidate by telling stories. Stories are often the most effective way to portray family business history, culture and values – the sources of this power. In our experience, these stories, when delivered with warmth and enthusiasm, are met with sincere interest and understanding by the right candidates. These stories should then be followed by a clear description of the culture and values that underpin the success of the business.

Since inception, AI has had a strong, well-established culture and clearly articulated values. Our culture and values are those of our founder, and our top value is that we put people and relationships first. In particular, we put our employees first, and have a 'do what it takes', blue-collar culture. Our whole AI family takes great pride in the culture we have created and the values we live by. Continuity of culture and values from generation to generation, and from leader to leader, has been essential to the company's success.

After describing our culture and values to interviewees, we explain that our top priority is to make sure that our values align with theirs and that they are a good cultural fit. At the same time, we ask each candidate to tell us what is important to them professionally and personally. We let them know that if we feel we cannot meet their needs, we will be open and honest with them. We kept track of their answers, and for candidates asked back for second interviews we provided tangible ways that the company could fulfil their needs. This is one step in developing a relationship early on with the candidates where we are working together to determine fit. We view the interview portion as a process of coming together, and building trust and confidence.

When we hired our first non-family leader, we contracted with a leading retained search firm and conducted a 10-month national search. Reaching alignment among all our internal stakeholders on prioritised lists of qualities, competencies and experience was painstaking. The top of each list is presented here:

- *Qualities:* cultural fit, values fit, emotional maturity, and a 'growth mindset' (since capability, including intellectual capability, can be developed with effective effort).[3]
- *Competencies:* sales leadership, communication, performance management, and talent acquisition; and
- *Experience:* leading multiple departments within an organisation, profit and loss responsibility, and holding a senior level position in a public company.

Our new leader needed blue-collar values, the interpersonal warmth to connect with our people, and a strong presence in our parent company's boardroom.

4.4 AI's first non-family leader

We had reviewed more than 50 résumé files (each containing a CV and an executive summary) from our search firm and we had interviewed about a dozen candidates over six months, yet no candidate excited us. Late in the search process, I was reading résumé files that made it through the search firm's first pass and one file stood out. I liked his story of growing up with blue-collar values and working his way up to the position of executive vice president of the Global Business-to-Business Division of OfficeMax.

I liked him even more when I met him. He possessed a combination of warmth, authenticity and directness that our team would embrace and respect. I also felt that we would work well together and learn from one another. He made it clear in our second meeting that he wanted the job and that he could be trusted to lead our family's business to the best of his ability.

We discussed the knowledge and capability he would need to develop quickly. He needed to get up to speed on our company, industry and family as well as on running an entire company for the first time. He put together 90-day and 180-day plans that addressed this and more. We then worked together on a second pass of these plans. This gave us the opportunity to see what it was like working together prior to signing a contract.

This work included coming up with ways that the family and board could show the company and industry its unanimous support for Jim, and ways Jim could show his respect for the family and commitment to its values and culture. Jim suggested

3 See Carol Dweck, *Mindset: The New Psychology of Success*, Ballantine Books, 2006.

the idea of a founder's award that either my dad or I would present at our annual meeting. It would be presented to the person who personified the values of the company and our founder's entrepreneurial spirit. This was one way that Jim publicly acknowledged the importance of the family and the continuity of its values. I thought the idea was brilliant and said I would build in an introduction welcoming Jim to the company and family – another display of unanimous support. My dad accepted the idea graciously and with humility, and asked that I present the award. We also discussed communications to the company and industry, expressing our enthusiasm for Jim as our new leader.

With the support of the family and approval of the board, we hired Jim. He was a terrific fit from the outset. He and I formed a close relationship built on trust, respect and learning from one another. He asked me to attend his weekly leadership meetings with our twelve department heads so I could be more helpful to him. In addition, we met privately once a week, and I sat on his executive team and board.

5. Leadership and organisational development

This section focuses on embracing the new leader, and providing the leader with the support needed to be successful. This includes the right internal reporting structure, and an external trusted adviser, so that the new leader can continue to develop appropriate skills and be aware when improvements can be made in their performance. Finally, the family, board and new leader must align around a set of objectives for working together. This includes creating a common understanding around lines of communication and which day-to-day business issues the family and board may want to get involved in.

5.1 Embracing the new leader

The family and board must embrace the new leader in ways that are visible to both the company and industry.

A few days before Jim arrived for work, our executive team and I met with our management team to announce our decision to hire Jim to be our first non-family president. Here are the five objectives we had for the meeting in order of priority:

- to be clear that the entire family and board are thrilled to have Jim leading our company;
- to go over Jim's background and explain why he is our top pick among a very competitive field;
- to explain our new organisational structure;
- to let them know what I would be doing and how my role at the company would change; and
- to let them know that we are counting on their support.

I told them how happy I was to pass the leadership of our company on to Jim. I reiterated that I was looking forward to having the time to pursue other professional endeavours, such as teaching and advising leaders of social enterprises and other family businesses. I told them that I was committed to Jim's success, their success and the success of the company, and that I would continue to serve on the board and would now be a senior adviser to the president and his executive team. I was clear that my role would be to advise, not lead, and that my plan was to be at AI on Tuesdays because Jim asked me to sit in on his management and executive team meetings. I remember joking that he was already putting me to work.

We told the management team about Jim's background and how he had worked his way up to the position of executive vice president of the Global Business-to-Business Division for OfficeMax. We emphasised cultural fit and shared values, and that Jim was eager to learn from us. We told them that this presented an important opportunity for each of us to learn from him, and to take our games to the next level. We reviewed the exponential growth of all of our team members that came from working with our parent company. We now worked with state-of-the-art systems, and held ourselves to their high expectations around business planning, key performance indicators, and bringing multiple opinions and data points to bear in decision-making. Together, as AI's management team, we were committed to making the transition to our first non-family leader a catalyst for accelerated growth in all areas of our company, and for each of us personally and professionally.

Furthermore, we were specific as to what we needed from the management team members themselves. First, we needed them to use their management expertise and the strong relationships of trust they had formed to help their teams understand and become comfortable with the change in leadership. Next, we needed them to use their subject matter expertise to help Jim get up to speed. We talked about this being a historic time at AI, and the important opportunity it presented for the company and for each of us and the people on our teams.

I told our management team that they would be called upon to lead early in the next week when we sent out an announcement to our staff, customers, suppliers and the press regarding Jim. I asked them to meet with their teams and let them know how they saw this transition from their perspective. It is part of our culture to be open, authentic and supportive with all of our employees.

In addition to displays of support at company events such as our annual meeting, and the awards speech noted above, the family invited Jim and our other non-family executives to major family celebrations and other life events.

Finally, it is important that the family member leaving the top job be committed to a new chapter in life. They must limit their time at the company and let the new leader lead. Every few weeks, Jim and I would check in with each other to make sure the norms we were establishing around my advisory role at the company felt right to both of us.

5.2 Leadership development

A new non-family leader will bring a wealth of fresh ideas, perspectives and expertise to the company. At the same time, there is much for that person to learn. He or she needs to learn about the company and its employees, the industry, the family, the board and more. A detailed plan for this learning process needs to be part of the new leader's 90-day and 180-day plans. Start with a prioritised list of work (relationships to build, subject matter to learn, etc) and the most effective way to begin to accomplish each item.

Next, the new leader needs feedback weekly on his or her work. This can be challenging, assuming he or she reports to the board and the chairman is no longer in a day-to-day operating role at the company. There are several ways to obtain appropriate feedback:

- Even though the chairman is no longer in an operating role, meeting with him or her weekly provides an opportunity to learn about the business and the family, and to receive whatever feedback can be given. At the beginning, employees may feel more comfortable talking with the chairman and this is a valuable way to obtain feedback.
- The new leader should let his or her direct reports know that their feedback is valuable and welcome. The management team should be told the same, and anonymous feedback can be placed in the leader's inbox if preferred.
- Finally, after 180 days a '360' performance review is an effective way of obtaining useful feedback.

Guided self-appraisal is an important part of this process. The new leader should choose, and the company should retain, a trusted adviser, and together they should draft a list of questions for the new leader to answer periodically. They can review and discuss the answers together. This relationship is an important way for the company to show its commitment to the new leader's success. This external resource is responsible for building a relationship of trust with the new leader, and providing support, advice and mentorship. It is an opportunity for the new leader to hone his or her craft by working to strengthen areas of leadership that are noted in the leadership assessment portion of the interview process and through the various methods of feedback set out above. These areas and others should be part of a development plan that the new leader builds with the trusted adviser. It is with the trusted adviser that the new leader can discuss confidentially anything on the leader's mind, including matters relating to the family and board.

Finally, the new leader can take advantage of external opportunities for learning. This may include leadership workshops, industry seminars, and classes. In addition, some of the most important learning opportunities will come from meetings with customers and suppliers.

5.3 Aligning around a new work dynamic

(a) Norms of communication

To set the new leader up for success, the family, board and new leader must align themselves around a set of objectives for working together. This includes creating a common understanding about lines of communication, as well as the day-to-day business decisions the family and/or board would like to be involved in. Governance is the first step and provides a formal structure that delineates decision-making authority. Everyday norms provide an equally important informal structure and must be developed in an intentional way.

Typically, after the first year, norms develop around the issues that need to be communicated and discussed among certain family and board members. Until then, being deliberate is the best course of action. The new leader, working with his or her trusted adviser and the board chair, should set out a list of desired outcomes around communication and day-to-day decision-making with the family and board. In this way, intentions and objectives are clear and everyone can pitch in to get it right. An example of desired outcomes is set out below.

- Empower the new leader and the executive team to make decisions in an effective and efficient way. These decisions include business planning, operational policy and other decisions of major scope and importance.
- Avoid making certain decisions at the executive level around strategy and other sensitive matters that certain family and board members may want to be involved in.
- Create a culture where the new leader feels free to tap into the wisdom and experience of the family and board.
- Build confidence among the family and board that the new leader is capable of making important decisions on his or her own.

To some readers, especially to owners of family firms not engaged in management, this process may seem exceedingly formal. However, in my experience it is through being deliberate – and painstakingly so at times – that we can greatly increase the likelihood that the transition to a new non-family leader will go well. This includes the attainment of the following shared goals: continuity of family culture and values, increased competitive strength under a new non-family leader, and enhanced harmony and teamwork by and among the management team, the family and board.

(b) 'Leading up'

Creating clarity around vision, culture, values and family strategy as it relates to the business is the work of the family and the board. It starts by building alignment at the family level. This alignment then cascades to the board, and then to the new leader and the executive team.

The work of the new leader includes integrating these foundational principles into the strategy, business planning and day-to-day decision-making of the company. Through this process at the operating level, changes in the way these concepts are communicated and executed may require adjustments to them. To the extent that these adjustments are material, they need to be communicated upwards – first to the executives, and then to the board and the family – in order to maintain alignment throughout the organisation. Managing this interplay is important work for the new leader and is part of the process often termed 'leading up'.

6. Conclusion

Alignment is the single most important success factor for a new non-family leader in a family controlled enterprise, and much of this chapter has been devoted to achieving alignment. When the goals of the family, board and new leader, and the strategy for accomplishing those goals, are aligned, all effort is focused in the same direction and the new leader can chart a clear course to everyone's desired destination. Moreover, the family, board and new leader will have created common high ground to jump back onto if the seas get rough. Although the journey is not likely to be smooth or linear all the time, with alignment the family, the board and the new leader have greatly increased their chances of success.

Family governance: questions and answers

Daisy E Medici
GenSpring Family Offices

1. Introduction

A fascinating reality of families who control powerful family enterprises and/or great wealth is that success and wealth accumulation can and does happen for all types of families. Any attempt to understand how families govern their family dialogues about wealth and the enterprises that create it must begin with understanding that each family approaches communication and decision-making uniquely.

As advisers, it is critical never to assume that high levels of experience and sophistication will accompany the highly successful family members who come to talk about the future of their families and family enterprises. Additionally, it is important to understand that in some families there is a tremendous range of educational accomplishment, life experience and sophistication among members. It is the responsibility of the professionals who work with these families to bridge that divide. In order to be successful in our work around governance and family communication, we must level the playing field so that all participants fully understand and feel included in the process. Helping more astute family members understand the importance of this objective is critical to the successful outcome of advising these families.

2. Frequently asked questions on family governance, and some considered responses

Using the premise set out in the preceding paragraph as a starting point, this chapter poses a number of typical and frequently asked questions from family members who are interested in family governance.

2.1 What is family governance and how do I know if my family needs it?

Let's begin by demystifying this intimidating topic. Family governance, simply stated, is about shared decision-making. The field of family enterprise borrows the concept of family governance from the world of corporate governance, and both forms of governance stem from the overarching system of societal rule. Corporate governance is about joint decision-making for the continued growth and success of a corporation, whether public or private, while family governance is about joint decision-making as shareholders of family-held or family-controlled assets.

The reason that people need a government, companies need corporate governance and families need family governance is that without guidelines in place and someone to police those guidelines, humans cannot coexist harmoniously to make effective joint decisions. As people are forced to interact in business, especially about emotionally powerful issues, it can seem impossible without some basic rules to follow, whether formal or informal.

The next generation needs to understand and work through how they, as a generation of family members, will make collaborative decisions about the assets of which they share ownership – decisions once made for them by their parents and/or other close relatives. While theoretically it's simple, developing an effective system of family governance and facilitating the complex conversations that a family must have in order to put the proper structures in place is very complicated. Every family member is at a different age and a different stage of his or her life, has had different experiences, has different levels of information, has different (possibly competing) interests, values and priorities and, perhaps, has a different vision for the future.

The core developmental process in each individual family member's life journey is called 'differentiation'. Indeed, it is critical to the overall health and well-being of a family that family members naturally find their way to individuality by differentiating themselves from their parents and their siblings so as to form their own identities. Therefore, even in the healthiest of families, where family members have been allowed to find their own path it is the juxtaposition of those very differences with their shared family history that makes joint decision-making so challenging. Family dynamics cannot be ignored when preparing to sit with families and help them grapple with the challenges of inheriting and overseeing jointly owned assets, regardless of how healthy they seem.

In conclusion, if the senior generation of any family has designed an estate plan that has its next generation inheriting assets as shared owners, that family needs family governance and they need it urgently.

2.2 What if my family is not willing to participate in this type of discussion?

This question begs a two-part response. First of all, this work is not for the weak of heart, nor is it well suited to families with members who are not speaking and/or have gone their separate ways with no wish to reconcile. Those families need more than family governance can provide in order to reach consensus on issues or decisions regarding assets. However, any family who seeks advice on how best to move forward in a focused and collaborative fashion as shared owners will benefit greatly by working to improve family communication and to establish an effective system of family governance. This may appear to many families to be a high-risk voyage – as welcome an opportunity as a storm at sea. But the voyage is one of high reward if the family chooses an experienced and highly qualified adviser.

The answer for family leaders who question whether their family members are willing to meet is typically an easy one: "Let's ask them." Family leaders need to gather their adult family members and explain their wish to enlist the help of a qualified professional to provide some education on the benefits of family governance, and describe the process and time commitment on the part of the family, as well as the outcome they hope to experience. When presented in this manner, most family members will choose to engage in the process.

In traditional patriarchal families where there are significant assets and inheritance, the matriarch and her children usually have so many questions and concerns that they jump at the opportunity to participate in an organised forum for constructive and well-guided discussions to better understand their complicated futures. For example, think of this common scenario: the family's chief emotional officer, usually the matriarch, worries herself sick about how her children will maintain their familial relationships while working as shared owners in a family whose culture prohibits open discussion about money and power. Add to the mix normal sibling rivalries, the addition of in-laws who almost always originate from families with vastly different cultures, disparity of wealth, geographic dispersion and a litany of other issues, and the future may seem rather hopeless. However, working with qualified professionals in order to manage their lives as members of a family shareholders' control group and an extended family system can bring the family renewed hope that an organised process for moving forward is possible.

(a) A positive story of family governance

While the above scenario is a common one, a particular family story comes to mind. The patriarch of a large family enterprise (we'll call him Bill) was sharing some concerns with a friend (let's call him David) who also led a large family controlled enterprise. David shared in return that his family was engaged in a governance process that was allowing them to have structured and facilitated conversations on an ongoing basis, addressing the very concerns that Bill was sharing. David encouraged Bill to work with his wealth adviser and learn about the governance and education offering at the firm. Bill did as he was advised, but after a couple of hours of conversation with the governance and education adviser he said: "Well, this has all been very interesting, but I don't think my family needs any of this work." Perplexed, knowing there must have been an underlying reason why Bill originally talked to David, the adviser asked: "If your wife and adult children were here with us throughout this meeting, do you think their response would have been the same as yours?" Bill admitted he did not know and the adviser gave the aforementioned suggestion: "Well, let's ask them."

Arrangements were put in place and the adviser met with the whole family. Ninety minutes later all family members – led by the matriarch – said, "Sign us up!" In that moment, through effective joint decision-making, they had begun the governance process. Over time, the family did a tremendous amount of work. They worked hard to assess their current activity as a generational family of wealth, identified where they were strong and where they needed to build competencies, and drafted a code of conduct to guide their interactions as they moved forward working together. They committed themselves to taking time to meet for a whole day once a quarter. They endeavoured to talk respectfully about some of the past pain points that had seriously clogged the system; and they identified and articulated not only their shared values as a family, but also the values unique to each of them individually. They engaged in mission work to get a clear definition of their shared vision for the future, they established goals and they set a strategy for how to achieve those goals. They formalised their shareholder meetings and not only revisited their shareholder's agreement but redrafted it as well. They identified their strengths and weaknesses as a family and as individuals in an effort to make sure that everyone's developmental passions were met and that they were optimally harnessing their family talent. While their initial meetings only included lineal adults, they also put a family assembly in place, for a time to include spouses and next-generation family members.

While this example is only one family, this is a family whose very charming patriarch did not think his family needed to take on any of this work. Fortunately, he was a loving, smart and open man who wanted the best for his family and was willing to go the next step and ask for their input.

2.3 We never talk about the future in our family and there is so much secrecy around money that it is impossible to broach the subject. Is there any hope for us?

Learning a new way to interact as a family about an issue as emotionally powerful as money takes time, perseverance and commitment. There are many reasons why family leaders don't talk to the next generations about money. One of the simplest reasons is that families have cultural norms, traits and behaviours that function as patterns in family systems. In the culture of many families, talking about money is taboo. More traditional families and many 'baby boomers' (born in the 1950s and 1960s), for example, were raised on the doctrine that money is a private matter and that talking about money is socially unacceptable within the family as well as outside it. Meanwhile, the subsequent generations of Generation Xers and Millennials, who are accustomed to information at their fingertips, are seen to be chomping at the bit to open the conversation on this subject and know more.

While family culture and generational differences may prevent open conversations about money, there are also appropriate and significant motives for such reticence. Most parents with wealth are concerned about the impact of their wealth on their children. Quite frankly, they have reason to worry. Scores of stories surround us of family wealth gone wrong and fortunes lost, so one does not have to consider things for very long before feeling nervous. Fear that family wealth will disincentivise and demotivate the next generations, or preclude them from identifying their passions and pursuing fruitful and meaningful lives, tops the list of reasons why financially successful parents may choose not to disclose or discuss their family's wealth.

Fortunately or unfortunately, wealth acts as a magnifier. For instance, when a family has no real disposable income and children ask for something unaffordable, saying "no" is not only a natural response but a necessary reply for the parents and an understandable one to the offspring. However, when a family has great means and, to complicate matters, lives an opulent lifestyle, and children ask for something and the answer is "no" in order to impart a sense of discipline or to help engender the value of money, the answer takes on a whole other meaning. The child, regardless of age, knows the family has the means and is left to draw their own conclusions about the rejection. Those conclusions can range from thinking the parents are selfish to thinking they themselves are not loved, and so forth. This parent–child dialogue appears to be only about money, but it is rarely understood as such by the younger generation.

Conversely, a scenario might reveal well-intentioned parents keeping their wealth a secret from their children and purposely living below their means in the hope that it won't affect their children negatively. In this scenario, when the children discover the wealth, it can cause a whole set of other issues unrelated to money. Often, the children convince themselves it was because their parents didn't trust them or consider them mature enough to handle the truth. No matter what conclusion is drawn as to the 'why', the results are that the children are left unprepared to handle life with wealth, and the parent–child relationship is perceived inaccurately by the offspring, leading to other adverse consequences.

It must be emphasised how important it is for younger generations to gain an understanding of their family's wealth – the way the wealth was created, the values that have allowed the family to sustain the wealth thus far, the senior generation's expectations of their next generation with regard to the family wealth, and how the wealth will serve the family into the future. These are all topics of conversations that must be undertaken in order to raise responsible, motivated, productive and healthy next-generation inheritors. But even the best overt communication about wealth is by itself insufficient, as parenting in wealthy families has the most significant impact when viewed through the prism of parental modelling. The values and messages that parents are trying to impart must be modelled through their own behaviours.

In many ways, parenting with wealth is no different from parenting without it. Think of it this way: there are disadvantaged families with few means who raise successful offspring who assume leadership positions and contribute to a better world. Conversely, there are wealthy families of privilege who raise children who get sent to prison. It is not simply having money that enables children to be successful in life; it is the parenting or some combination of nature and nurture that leads to outcomes in each individual case.

Families need to communicate. Unfortunately, constructive communication in which everyone is valued – communication that would allow for open conversations about wealth – can seem unfathomable for many families. A family of next-generation members who were somewhat reluctant to have a meeting once said to me, "If this meeting turns out to be just another venue for our father to hold us captive while he pontificates about how great he is and how far we have to go, we guarantee that it will not only be the first meeting but the last." Many professionals in this field who are not trained therapists learn about family communication and family systems by continuing their professional education. Likewise, educating families in these topics helps them to better understand each of their family members, their family system and their own role within it. Helping a family learn why families behave the way they do is fascinating and engrossing, and these educational sessions elicit such positive feedback because family members are learning about themselves and gaining insight and perspective on their own behaviour, all the while learning to see themselves and their family members in a new light, which permits them to enhance their family relationships.

While it is difficult for parents to talk about net worth and it should not be rushed, educating the next-generation inheritors over time about what the family owns, how assets are held, the scale and nature of any business(es) the family controls and what the estate plan looks like is an essential and rewarding process that every wealthy family should employ. Governance is the overarching construct that allows for the most crucial communication and decision-making at critical moments. However, it is not a one-time event; it is a process that creates new ways for the family to move forward and that prepares future generations. It is the process through which our great fifth- and sixth-generation family businesses have succeeded.

2.4 As families begin to focus on governance, who should be involved and what is the best advice on including in-laws?

The answer to this question is unique to every family, and the process of discovery is crucial.

Understanding the family story by way of the family genogram is a great way to start. A family genogram is a graphical representation of a family tree that displays detailed data on relationships among individuals. In addition, the advisory team must be clear on the family's assets, how they are currently owned and how they will be owned in the estate plan. An in-depth review of these important pieces of information will begin to identify who should be included in a family governance structure. It is important to note, however, that family governance is most effective when it is inclusive. Typically, including all adult members of the family is a good way to think about who should be in the room. As the family progresses, plans for incorporating next-generation family members into the family governance plan can be designed and implemented. However, one cautionary statement is necessary here: culture and ethnicity play huge roles in families' recognition and acceptance of both improving communication and extending participation in the business affairs of the family.[1]

Families begin governance work at different stages. Many family leaders start to think about the future governance of family assets when they are 60–65 years old. From that age until sometimes well into their nineties, family leaders actively work with their families on succession planning. Where families are in their lifecycle drives when they become curious about the work and, often, concerned about the inclusion of in-laws. The question of how and when to include in-laws in family governance is an interesting and complex one.

Industry literature tells us that families who are successfully defying the odds (70% of wealth is lost at every transition) practise inclusion. Experience has shown that families with divorces are more likely to question the inclusion of in-laws than families where strong, lasting marriages prevail. Experience has also revealed that much of the reluctance we deal with regarding in-laws stems from concerns with privacy and confidentiality. One client articulated to his lineal offspring his trust in his next generation's loyalty regarding confidential information, but added that, likewise, his in-law children's first loyalties were to their families of origin. This patriarch's ability to articulate his fears and concerns was helpful for solving problems in his extended family because they were out in the open, allowing for a full discussion about exactly what scared him. That admission allowed for a robust conversation that included the many positive reasons in-laws should be included.

1 See the chapter entitled "Culture and ethnicity in family enterprises" by Everett Moitoza in Part I of this publication.

Family governance is a forum that allows for the education, preparation and development of next-generation leaders and/or inheritors. Why miss the opportunity to further educate and mentor in-laws in the values and mission of the family? Further, if it is the wish of the family leaders and lineal descendants to include young next-generation family members as age permits, a family governance plan that excludes in-law spouses puts young next-generation family members in an awkward position when one of their parents has been intentionally left out. It is also important to understand that next generations inherit their core values from both parents, so including in-laws in family values conversations is recommended for that reason as well. One thought to consider is this: when family members are not included in important planning conversations within the family, they are left to operate from assumptions.

In the case of the family mentioned above, it boiled down to actual numbers. The patriarch was uncomfortable with in-laws and young third-generation family members participating in financial reviews and/or discussions. It took a long time for him to be able to share his real angst; but once he did, everyone understood. In fact, his children-in-law made it perfectly clear, in unison, that they did not want to be included in any part of the financial discussions and such exclusion gave them a sense of relief.

In this same case, lineal family members expounded on the intellectual capital of the in-laws and the value they could bring to other important family conversations. So the family governance structures they put in place were:

- a family council that included all first- and second-generation family members;
- an executive committee of first- and second-generation lineal descendants where all financials would be discussed; and
- a family assembly that included all first-, second- and third-generation family members, where the young members of the third generation could begin to learn about the purpose and mission of the family and be educated in financial literacy and other topics relevant to living with wealth responsibly.

The family also identified the purpose of each of their three family governance entities, decision-making policies where appropriate and the responsibilities of engagement for each entity. They fully participated in developing a litany of family policies to guide their interactions, the most important to this family being a family confidentiality policy. Finally, all of these decisions were clearly documented in their family constitution, a morally binding document intended to serve as a guide for family decision-making going forward.

2.5 How can parents and grandparents, who worry about the impact of wealth on their families, prepare their children for living with wealth?

(a) Achieving financial literacy

There are many facets to preparing children for living with wealth, but everything begins by teaching them the basics of financial literacy. No matter how or when children are in line to inherit assets, if they are guided to develop solid money management skills when they are young, they are likely to carry those skills throughout their lives and apply those same skills when they inherit.

Think about where children start these days in regard to how we pay for purchases. They rarely see cash change hands. They see plastic cards that, magically, produce purchased items and machines that swallow plastic cards, eject money, and even return the card! But, do they see the bills their parents are paying for all the goods they are consuming? How many children are exposed to that part of the process? The key to mentoring children in personal money management is to begin early and be disciplined about the process implemented.

Learning to manage personal finances is essential, and young adulthood provides a further excellent opportunity for mentoring. This is a critical turning point in the lives of young family members, who might be managing their personal budgets for the first time, made even more difficult for young adults who have never had restrictions on their spending. Think of Allison, for example, a young adult starting to struggle with her expenses, which were often beyond her income and forcing her to withdraw more than recommended from her family trust. Working together to closely examine her expenses, it was determined that Allison had very few areas where she could realistically cut back her spending. Our conversation moved to how she might increase her income in order to balance her budget, which inevitably led to a focus on her career. We worked for several months, brainstorming the next step in her career, revising her résumé and coaching her to create a network of people who could help her reach this next step. Through this work, a new career opportunity surfaced, enabling Allison to increase her income enough to completely eliminate her dependency on her family trust.

There are many more areas of financial education in which younger family members should have a basic understanding, and these fundamental skills are rarely taught in school. Yet a basic knowledge of economics, taxes, credit, interest, debt and investing are essential for successful personal money management, and this requires a helpful learning environment in which to pick up these skills.

(b) A helpful learning environment

To help one's heirs obtain appropriate financial knowledge, it is best if families have something to gather around. For instance, families who are philanthropic gather around family foundations and/or donor-advised funds, which can be superb solutions for crystallising and transmitting a family's cultural and spiritual legacies. Philanthropic venues constitute the perfect forums for youngsters of all ages to learn family values about giving back, about how the family has organised itself around its giving values and why it's so important to the family members. Additionally, foundations are business enterprises – non-profit business enterprises but businesses just the same. Thus, they offer excellent opportunities for teaching business skills using the legal, operating and reporting documents of the family foundations. For tax reasons, foundations – whether held in trust or formed as corporations – also require sound governance, allowing the next generation of young people to also learn the basics of governance by participating in the foundation. Given that the size of grants that a family can make in the name of the foundation is as a result of investment performance, younger family members are also well-positioned to learn the basics of investing through tracking the performance of the investments that fund their family giving.

When working with a family to bring their next generation into the family foundation, one young family member, with a sigh of frustration, said to me, "I have no idea where the foundation gets its money to give away." There are three lessons here: there are no bad questions; never assume what your offspring know or don't know; and make sure you create a safe environment for the family to learn together so the younger generation feels comfortable being vulnerable. Whether you move towards a family foundation or donor-advised fund, or utilise a more informal method of charitable giving, including your children in your giving plans remains an excellent forum for mentoring children of all ages and passing important family values downstream.

Families with operating companies seem to more naturally indoctrinate their children into the inner workings of the family business early, simply through dinner table conversations and regular childhood visits to the business(s). These children are raised from the outset with much more awareness of the families' holdings and values than children born into families who manage liquidated wealth and/or inheritance. Therefore, families with operating companies have a somewhat natural venue for teaching children, especially if the company offers family members summer job opportunities, internships and/or employment opportunities. Family governance is also important to business-owning families because mentoring, succession and leadership development is critical to the success of families who envisage their family business leading their family controlled enterprise for many generations.

For other families, the ideal vehicle could be a family bank. In one example known to the author, first- and second-generation family members began by learning about the concept of a family bank and worked together – spouses included – to design an entire process for operating such a bank. The bank was intended to fund entrepreneurial opportunities for second-generation family members who were enterprising enough to identify an opportunity, conduct proper due diligence, draft a solid business plan and present it to the family, who then served as the governing board. Replete with governing documents, operating documents and financials, a family bank is a business in itself and can develop good business skills in those who don't have them, sharpen business skills where they are rusty and benefit greatly from the business skills of those who are endowed with them. There are a number of different ways in which families design family banks. Formalising them with very well thought-out and agreed-upon guidelines is the most important takeaway here. Like most good family work, family banks require an organised process. That said, it is a wonderful way for families to allow their financial capital to serve the continued development of the human and intellectual capital of the family.

The general theme is that it is important for families who control substantial assets to find something to gather around. These best practices require time, patience and discipline, both on the part of the children and the parents. As in most situations, follow-through and accountability are crucial to successful outcomes.

2.6 In order to put an effective system of governance in place, if we were to commit to meeting regularly as a family, how long would it take and what would it involve?

The first response to this question is always the same: it depends how often the family is able to take time away from their day-to-day responsibilities to hunker down in a conference room for a full day at a time; additionally, it depends on the complexity of the family and the family enterprises.

Quarterly meetings is a fairly workable frequency for most families with shared assets. After two years of quarterly meetings, the vast majority of families can really measure their growth. At that point, they know they are having conversations and making progress they never thought possible. However, family governance is an evolutionary process requiring constant affirmation of goals, continual revisiting of policies and procedures, ongoing implementation of agreed procedures, and expert facilitation. If there are no operating companies or shared assets, and everyone owns their wealth outright but gathers around a family foundation, meeting once or twice a year is usually sufficient.

For the purposes of answering the question more fully, let's assume the former scenario rather than the latter: let's assume we're talking about a family that has a large global operating company, some real-estate assets, a shared family farm and both beach and mountain homes. This family has agreed to meet quarterly. The founder and those of his/her generation are elderly, the second generation consists of four siblings, all married, and members of the third generation range in age from 21 to 41. Some family members in both the second and third generations work in the business, but most do not. Some wealth has been passed downstream already, including shares in a large operating company and some real estate, along with a significant family foundation.

The process for achieving a workable structure for family governance would be as follows:

- First, an advisory team would need to be appointed, with the aim of understanding the family genogram, the family story, its culture and ethnicity, what the family owns in its entirety, how all the assets are held and what the family is trying to achieve.
- Then the advisory team would have to help the family identify their collective goals, their shared values, their shared vision and their mission as a family and how, over time, they are going to achieve their vision.
- All family members must be clear, at least at a high level, on what the family owns and how the assets are held. They must also understand how each entity is currently governed and why. Many legal entities have governance requirements, but many family members have no understanding of the legal aspects of these entities and must be educated in these areas in order to be thoughtful and engaged participants in the process. It is important to note that family governance protocols must align with the governance requirements of legal entities.
- Once all family participants are clear on their values, vision, mission and ownership, they should align themselves around their family mission and

begin to put family governance structures and policies in place to guide their joint decision-making. How will they work together to achieve their mission? What decisions will need to be made and who will make them? Will they keep decision-making as a function of the lineal descendants, or will in-laws be included? Should committees be formed or should they all participate in every project? How will they keep themselves informed on a regular basis about the performance of the operating companies and other assets, and who will have that role? What should the family governance structures be and does the family need all of those structures to efficiently serve the greater family? Who will be the main liaison officer between the corporate board and the family council or assembly or executive committee? What about the education and preparation of the next generation of young people? At what age will they be included in decision-making? How will next generation leaders be cultivated and developed?

- Once families determine what their governance structures should be, it is time to focus on what kind of policies they need to craft in order to guide their interactions. Once introduced to this practice, families always know what they need. What they typically don't know is that successful families attribute much of their success in working together to creating family policies that were adopted by all family members and codified in family constitutions. While industry literature has espoused this best practice for decades, advisers to these families must not assume each family is aware of the significant role that a family constitution can play in constructing effective family governance.
- Leadership is critical for the family governance system to be successful. There are scores of books and articles about leadership and it still remains one of the greatest challenges for these family enterprises. One of the most thought-provoking questions that family members must ask themselves when identifying next-generation leaders is, "Would I hire this person for this job if he/she were not a family member?" That said, young family members who wish to develop into family leadership positions should be hard at work during their school years and in their career efforts after college, building their experiences, résumés and successes so that their family members see their value and encourage and support their interest in leading family enterprises. Finally, it is important to note that leadership of families requires even more emotional intelligence than corporate leadership. Education for family leadership should take cognisance of this important reality.[2]

3. Conclusion

I have been fortunate to be invited by dozens of families to lead them through the experience of creating their family governance process. Facilitating hundreds of family governance meetings has been, and continues to be, a rich and rewarding learning experience. In closing, a few thoughts come to mind.

---

2 See the chapter entitled "Vertical Leadership" by Greg McCann in this publication.

It is love, connection, courage and wishes for healthy, happy, productive, responsible and successful family members that brings to the table these multi-generational families who control powerful family enterprises. It is their willingness to learn how governance works, how it can be helpful to their families and the enterprises they control, and their trust in the process that allows them to participate patiently. It is their patient participation that allows them to develop hope and experience success.

These families come in all types and styles. They can be small families with simple enterprises, small families with complex enterprises, large families with simple situations and large families with very complex situations. Just as every family is different, every scenario is different. But each one benefits from thoughtful, well-planned and guided conversations – from establishing their shared goals to embracing their shared values and aligning themselves with their mission, to designing governance structures to allow for joint decision-making designed to fit their unique complexity. Of great importance are the policies and guidelines they put in place to guide their interactions as they work together to develop strategies for sustaining wealth into the future, while allowing that wealth to have a positive effect on their greatest assets, the human capital of the family: their precious family members.

Awareness and action: transforming a family business via family enterprise and vertical leadership

Greg McCann
McCann & Associates

1. Introduction

Family enterprise, by its very nature, is among the most complex and integrated of systems in contemporary society. Now, more than ever, families who work together need agile leaders who can navigate this complexity within the context of exponential change and diverse stakeholder interests.

As the culture, society and technology in which business operates evolve, the nature of family enterprises also must evolve. I believe that as this process unfolds, two new perspectives can be employed to fundamentally reshape family business and ensure long-term viability: vertical leadership development and the family enterprise model.

Vertical leadership development is a process of leadership development that, rather than focusing on the knowledge necessary to manage a changing business, improves the leader's skills in making use of that knowledge by addressing how the leader thinks and acts. The resulting increase in emotional intelligence and self-awareness endows the leader with the increased agility necessary for navigating family and business dynamics within the context of rapid global change.

At the same time, evolving toward the family enterprise concept shifts the pre-eminent identity away from business activity and toward family. This evolution redefines the notion of stakeholder value, broadens the scope of influence, and implicitly requires the family to take a proactive role in defining both its purpose and how that purpose translates into sustained competitive strength, continued family control and enhanced harmony in the family shareholder control group.

In this chapter I will discuss how some family businesses are adapting to today's changing world through vertical leadership development, and demonstrate how the resulting agility of leaders trained in and effectively using vertical leadership development creates the values-based emotional capital that is a hallmark of sustainable family controlled enterprises. I hope that business consultants and advisers will see the merit in integrating these concepts into their practice as well as bringing it to their clients, thus greatly increasing their positive impact on the family businesses they serve.

2. A case study

Haws Corporation, based in Nevada in the United States, is a family business that is transitioning its leadership from the third to the fourth generation, and it epitomises many of the trends and challenges facing family businesses globally. Its adoption of both vertical leadership development and the family enterprise model offers a compelling study of how these two concepts can enhance family businesses outcomes.

Stephanie Kilroy and Tom White are agile leaders in this family enterprise. Each views the family's involvement as both a cultural and strategic advantage to the enterprise; simultaneously, each sees the enterprise as beneficial to the family in ways that are financially and non-financially rewarding.

Stephanie is a fourth-generation family member, daughter of the retiring patriarch, sister of the other majority fourth-generation owner, head of the family council, and a newly elected member of the board of directors. She plays multiple concurrent roles and represents a variety of stakeholder interests and perspectives. Stephanie recently transitioned from the firm's director of human resources to the newly created position of family governance director. The job description for this new position includes the task of ensuring that the family's involvement becomes, and remains, of greater strategic advantage for the enterprise.

Tom is Stephanie's brother-in-law. Married to the other major fourth-generation owner and chief executive officer, he also serves on both the board of directors and the family council. Tom has been leading the effort to help diversify the family enterprise holdings. In the process, he has added more independent directors with experience in acquisitions and start-ups to the board, encouraged additional education for family members, and made innovation a main focus of all groups of stakeholders.

Tom and Stephanie – with the family council, management team and board of directors – have struggled in the last decade with the challenges of buying out another branch of the family, preparing for an eight-member upcoming generation, diversifying the company's holdings and professionalising their corporate governance. They face a tough, highly complex task: to confront these challenges while honouring their heritage, building on the family's purpose, navigating global trends and creating an effective group of leaders.

Their leadership has reframed Haws Corporation into part of Traynor Family Enterprise (TFE). This was not just a legal change nor a branding initiative; it was a complete shift in their identity and thinking. The TFE identity statement reads:

Traynor Family Enterprise is a family-owned business that dates back to 1906 and our founder, Luther Haws. Now in our fourth generation of family ownership, our focus is on the future rather than short-term financial results. We are a family enterprise – not simply a business – that fully leverages the competitive advantage of our family ownership. We are driven foremost by our values, which serve as a compass for our enterprise. And while values remain constant, how we create value changes over time and will continue to do so. We give equal emphasis to education and governance, business development and vision, employee growth and achievement, and financial performance. We value family, so our legacy is important to us. We conduct ourselves with honesty and integrity. We value leadership, education, innovation, and fairness and we understand the importance of investing in relationships. We have fun. We accept responsibility for our actions. We recognise that much of our success comes from attracting and retaining the best available talent and then supporting their efforts to build and deepen our desired core competencies. We provide a safe, open, and collaborative environment that fosters candid, respectful dialog and a willingness to challenge the status quo.

Given the complexity of this leadership challenge, it is clear that increasing leadership agility is absolutely imperative for that leader's own development, for their family, and for their enterprise.

3. Overview of vertical leadership within a family enterprise

The fates lead those that will follow; those who won't, they drag. (Seneca)

The more complex, interdependent, and rapidly changing an organisation, the more agility is required from its leadership. This is especially true for firms adopting the family enterprise model. Family enterprise is a mindset that requires more agile leaders who don't just know more, but who also cultivate the higher levels of awareness that lead to more informed action. In other words, it's not just what they do that matters, but also how they do it. Given the world of today, it is clear that integrating vertical leadership into the family enterprise model may be less of an option for cutting-edge family enterprises and more a requirement for success.

The term 'VUCA', frequently used in the US military, is an acronym for 'volatile, uncertain, complex and ambivalent'. It is used to frame strategy within contexts such as World War Two, the sixties, and other periods of sustained instability and change throughout history. While each of these periods left a significant impact, they were generally followed by a return to greater stability and predictability, along with more conventional approaches to strategic decision-making.

Today, we can no longer predict a return to stability. Furthermore, we have not completely grasped the full implications of exponential change and interdependency as they currently exist. As indicated in Figure 1 below, we are at the so-called "knee" of the change curve, which measures the combined rate and complexity of change over a period of time. The overriding message here is that there is no return to normal. Change and complexity will continue to increase exponentially.

Given the current rate of change, 'normal' and 'conventional' thinking are obsolete concepts. To rely on them for a family business is dangerous. We need new, innovative approaches to leadership that incorporate and integrate five major trends that affect family business:

- exponential change;
- globalisation and interdependency;
- entrepreneurship;
- family and generational differences; and
- technology.

All these trends interrelate and create an alchemy of change in the world we

Figure 1: Exponential change through technological capability

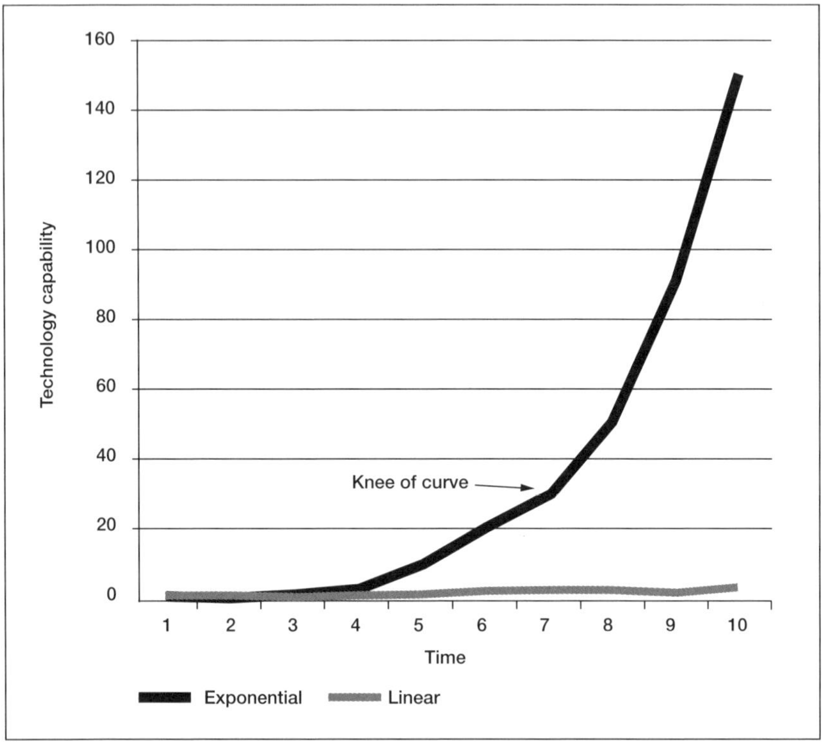

inhabit, and thus will require leaders to adapt and think differently. Agile leaders will need to become ever-increasingly aware of when and how to use the innovation that technology offers in order to improve effectiveness and profitability without eroding the necessary intimacy of key relationships.

3.1 Exponential change

As the rate of change itself increases, this momentum builds on itself. In his book entitled *The Singularity is Near*, futurist Ray Kurzweil posits two profound ideas:

- In this century alone, we will experience 20,000 years of change as measured at today's rate of acceleration. This is incredibly hard to grasp. Though not mathematically precise, I use this metaphor with families to convey the general idea: "What would you do if you knew that your industry was going to change as much in the next three to five years as it did in the last century?"
- Kurzweil also contends that humans tend to think in terms of a constant rate of change rather than in exponential terms. This may be at least in part why there is so much resistance, denial and avoidance of the reality and magnitude of this systemic change. One may liken it to trying to make a family's Blockbuster video store more efficient as opposed to creating a more effective and technologically relevant system such as Netflix.

Today's leaders have to deal with change at a much faster rate than their forebears. While a software update that previously took 180 days now takes a few hours, for instance, breakthrough and disruptive innovations occur at similarly increasing rates.

Consider knowing with certainty that a family's industry would be obsolete in five years. Agile leaders must realise that exponential change is happening at an ever-increasing rate and their industry, family and individual perspectives will undergo systemic shifts with greater frequency.

3.2 Globalisation and interdependency

Any business that has a website – which is virtually all businesses – is global in its visibility and vulnerability. Couple exponential change with global interdependency and it is clear that not only mobile phones and computers change at mind-boggling speeds, but business cycles are shorter, valuation models are less reliable, regulations can't keep up, and we all are at risk of mistaking a frantic pace of activity for productivity. A flight out of London can be impacted by a terrorist attack in Mumbai; a supply chain in Ohio can be interrupted by a tsunami in Malaysia; and a bitcoin crisis can affect contracts in South Africa.

Awareness of this interdependency is critically important. A leader cannot merely continue doing things the same way. However, at the same time, keeping too narrow a focus is dangerous. Since everything that happens in business affects everything else, the complexity and rapid change means leaders must be constantly and continually developing themselves. Leaders must focus as much beyond their business as they do on their business.

3.3 Entrepreneurship

With shortening business cycles, ever-accelerating change and global competition, there is pressure for every organisation and every business leader to be more entrepreneurial. In family enterprises, that entrepreneurial energy often comes from within the family.[1] Additionally, from the family perspective, entrepreneurship may be one of the best ways to counteract a sense of entitlement or low credibility in the rising generation within wealthy families.

For leaders, this may require a shift in mindset from 'being the hero' to cultivating talent in each member of the organisation. For both enterprise and family reasons, everyone must be entrepreneurial, especially the next generation.

3.4 Family and generational differences

The very concept of 'family' is being redefined legally and socially, and this is also relevant in how it relates to enterprise. Although a full discussion of this topic lies outside the scope of this chapter, I will assert that the trend toward having four generations working together in a family enterprise is more common than ever.

The millennial generation (known as Generation Y) may have the audacity

1 See Babson College's STEP (Successful Transgenerational Entrepreneurial Program) website at www.babson.edu/Academics/centers/blank-center/global-research/step/Pages/home.aspx.

required to bring about the needed change, perhaps tempered by the hard-earned wisdom of senior generations. Meanwhile, retirement for the senior generations may be less likely than in the past. To have senior family members move into roles that value their experience and wisdom while acknowledging their different life stages is a challenge for many families.

In my firm, we encourage families to see these generational differences with the open-minded curiosity one would bring to visiting a new country. One client led his family business through transitions into three different industries in just over a decade. He said it was indeed hard work and the family dynamics were like "playing three dimensional chess".

Leaders must see that managing family dynamics, even more than managing the business, requires increasing agility and emotional intelligence. Family cohesiveness, especially across the generations that follow the founder of a family firm, cannot be taken for granted. Families must be intentional, take the initiative, and be explicitly committed to the enterprises they undertake.

3.5 Technology

Technology is the arena in which we are most likely to notice and appreciate exponential change. As the cost of accessing information becomes exponentially cheaper, businesses face unforeseen consequences. Among those consequences I predict that future generations may have a greater ability to innovate, but also a concurrent decrease in social skills and intimacy. Research on emotional intelligence indicates that Generation Y is superior at adapting to change but inferior in self-awareness and empathy than previous generations at the same age.[2]

4. Vertical leadership

The #1 reason people leave a job is due to a bad boss. (Gallup Poll findings)

[M]ature business families understand the value of embracing multiple perspectives of thought and balance the contradictions while seeking synergistic insights. (John Ward)

In previous generations, leadership development was horizontal: it focused on increasing a leader's bank of knowledge. Vertical leadership development, however, involves changing how thinking is structured, not simply how much is known. Reading a book or taking a course on accounting is an example of horizontal leadership development, whereas developing the insight necessary to understand how brainstorming creates chaos when used at the wrong time is vertical leadership development. That is to say, through vertical leadership development, one becomes more self-aware about when introducing a new skill is relevant and useful, and thus tailors one's actions accordingly. Vertical leadership development focuses on cultivating more innovative and multifaceted leaders.

---

2 See Travis Bradberry and Jean Greaves, *Emotional Intelligence 2.0*, San Diego, CA: TalentSmart, 2009, pp236–240; and Greg McCann and Leah Sullivan, "Gen Y: Engaging or enraging?", *Family Business* magazine, Autumn 2010.

Leadership agility can be thought of in comparison with gears in a manual-transmission car. One might be expert at driving in second gear. However, if the car has five gears plus reverse, an agile driver is mindfully aware of how and when to switch gears to make the best decisions and progress. This will happen based on changing terrain and the actions of other drivers. In a business, an agile leader will 'switch gears' based on greater interdependency and faster rates of change.

The idea behind leadership agility grew out of research that Bill Joiner and Stephen Josephs did with approximately 800 leaders.[3] They found, as have other noted researchers, that we evolve through stages of leadership. This is similar to the stages identified by childhood development theorist Jean Piaget and ethicist Lawrence Kohlberg. In a nutshell, as we live, learn and adapt to the challenges of life, our level of awareness naturally evolves.

Horizontal leadership development is essential as well as interdependent with vertical development. My experience as a teacher, consultant and practitioner also shows that vertical leadership can be accelerated. For example, providing someone with a roadmap for their leadership development will increase their rate of development.

My colleague, Rich Morris says, "It may have been true in the past that one good business idea might last three generations; now, each generation may need three good business ideas."[4] Without vertical leadership, effectively responsive innovation is simply impossible in today's environment. It is essential, then, that advisers and consultants offer clients this roadmap to vertical leadership development. This roadmap essentially consists of the four agilities and stages outlined later in this chapter.

5. Why the family enterprise model is emerging

The family is keeper of its values and culture. If the goal is to succeed across generations, the family must take responsibility for deciding the future of the family and the business.[5]

Family business may be older than civilisation itself, but as a field of study and professional practice it is incredibly young. Although scholars could debate the exact dates and events, the field began emerging over the last 30–40 years (since the 1970s and 1980s) as family business-focused practitioners, scholars and university programmes began to emerge.

Many people see the idea of a family enterprise as a stage in the evolution of a family business.[6] However, family enterprise can also be described as more of a mindset than an evolutionary stage.

---

3 See Bill Joiner and Stephen Josephs, *Leadership Agility: Five Levels of Mastery for Anticipating and Initiating Change*, Jossey-Bass, 2007.

4 See my article with Rich Morris, "Economy Next", *Family Business* magazine, Summer 2011.

5 See my article with Andrew Keyt, "Managing the family/business overlap", *Family Business* magazine, July/August 2013, p13.

6 See my article with Andrew Keyt, "Managing the family/business overlap", *Family Business* magazine, July/August 2013. See also Sara Hamilton (founder and CEO of the Family Office Exchange), White Paper entitled "Taking the Long Term View of the Family Enterprise", Southeastern Family Office Forum, September 2014.

Since its early days, the field of family business has relied extensively on an iconic study of succession to frame family business theory and practice, namely John Ward's study of one industry (manufacturing) in one state (Illinois), which focused on how family-owned businesses survived.[7] Even though an innovative and groundbreaking study, it framed success in terms of whether the business continued with family ownership – it was a business-centric approach. Indeed, many of the field's practitioners and scholars, and even university-based family business centres, defined 'success' with great, if not sole, emphasis on the perpetuation of the business by the family. Ward's study is perhaps the most often cited in the field of family business but may warrant reconsideration.

Only those core businesses continuing under family ownership contributed to the overall measure of success in Ward's study. Families who sold the core business and reinvested their wealth in new ventures, for example, were not seen as successful. Under that model, the purpose of the family was to serve the business; no aspect of the family's well-being was directly addressed – hence my use of the term 'business-centric' above. As my colleague Dennis Jaffe says, "'Family' was merely an adjective that described the business." 'Family' then becomes just a modifier like 'agri-' or 'retail', not a co-equal subsystem with the corporate endeavour.

In 2011, the Family Firm Institute (FFI) and accountant Joe Goodman commissioned research to reframe the notion of successful family business outcomes. The study examined family-owned businesses in their second generation and older across the US and across multiple industries, and made some astonishing discoveries:

- Approximately 90% of the respondents own more than one business.
- Approximately 20% of the respondents own five or more businesses.
- The average respondent had changed its core business more than twice.

The FFI/Goodman study targeted only for-profit businesses that had actual sales. It did not count family foundations, family offices or social entrepreneurship activities. The study also reinforced the notion that family business leadership can be cultivated not just within the ranks of management, but also in the family council, board functions, the family office and the family's philanthropic activities. See Figure 2 for two ways of thinking about a family enterprise. One notable additional piece of validation for placing greater emphasis on family outcomes as well as business outcomes is worth mentioning here. The STEP research project started at Babson College and focuses on the entrepreneurial activity of the family in multigenerational enterprises.

Two key conclusions have emerged from these recent studies on family business: the family should be seen as the primary vehicle for wealth transfer; and families will own a number of enterprises. Reflecting this change in emphasis, a family enterprise should be considered as having shifted its focus to the family as the anchor, and the values and purpose of the family then define value. Building on concepts outlined

---

7 See John Ward, *Keeping the Family Business Healthy*, Jossey-Bass, 1987. It should be noted here that John Ward has done as much to influence, define and lead the field of family business as anyone, and my critique of the field's use of his study is merely that.

Figure 2: Two constructs of family enterprise

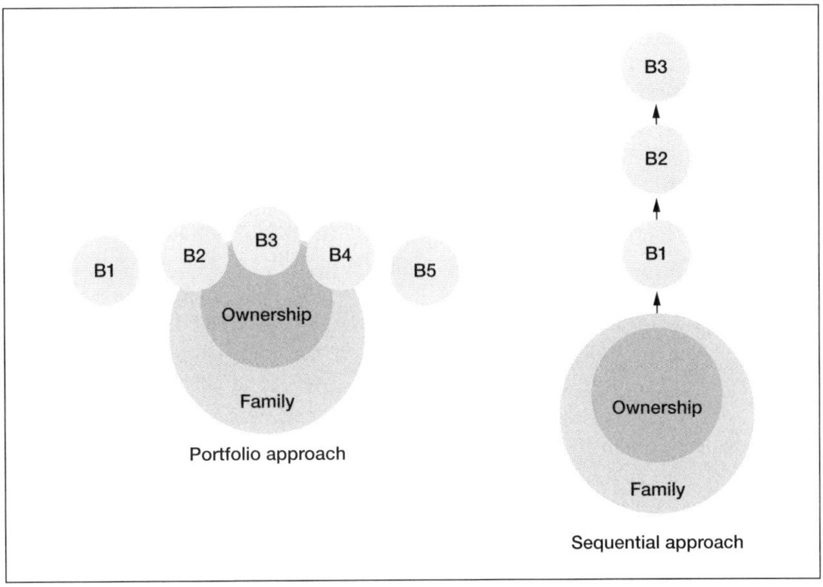

by James Hughes in his seminal book,[8] it is clear that that the notion of 'value' in family enterprises is being defined more holistically than in the pioneering days of family business research, incorporating broader terms for stakeholder value that include human (talent), financial (assets), and social (relationships) capital.

For example, one family business that I profiled in an article in Catalyst magazine worked this way. The article describes the family values – "We care about people" – influencing business values, specifically towards its employees, suppliers and customers. The family leadership set up measurable metrics, such as what it called 'regrettable turnover', as a way of operationalising stakeholder values and making the family's values and culture a business advantage. As a result, Mark Johnson, the non-family president and chief executive officer (CEO) at Bird Technologies, said that the biggest advantage of this process was to enable him to create a culture of trust where he and the managers could clearly see the goal and where 'out of bounds' lay.

Connecting this back to Traynor Family Enterprise (TFE; see section 2 above), that company's identity statement says that the purpose of TFE is as a values-based family enterprise. In essence, the firm communicates the idea that how it does things is as important as what it does. It has clearly defined its purpose and is defining stakeholder value in broader terms that include, but are not inclusively focused on, financial value. TFE brings the family's values to all its enterprises, be it the family council or a for-profit business – see the 'portfolio' approach in Figure 2. TFE's values

8 See James E Hughes Jr, *Family Wealth: Keeping It in the Family – How Family Members and Their Advisers Preserve Human, Intellectual, and Financial Assets for Generations*, 2nd edn, Wiley, 2004.

as listed in their identity statement are: family, honesty, integrity, leadership, education, innovation, fairness, fun, accountability and empowerment.

This evolution reflects the values that so many family enterprises nowadays embrace, and it resonates with the famous Peter Drucker quote:

Profit for a company is like oxygen for a person. If you don't have enough of it, you're out of the game. But if you think your life is about breathing, you're really missing something.

In this case, the family has to be more proactive – not just about its core business, but about aligning all its enterprises with its values and purpose. To accomplish this, the family needs to develop a proactive practice so that the talent – the human capital – is developed towards becoming agile enough to handle the exponential change, complex interdependency and diverse stakeholders.

As a starting point, each adult family member has to develop a practice that encourages thinking like an owner as well as a leader, both personally and professionally. This approach broadens the notions of management succession and ownership transition as well. The former once-per-generation leadership transition is now seen as too narrow and too late – analogous to changing captains on Titanic after it's hit the iceberg. To effectively manage an entrepreneurial family enterprise requires leadership agility, and thus a programme of vertical leadership development.

6. Vertical leadership development and leadership agility

We cannot solve our problems with the same level of thinking that created them. (Albert Einstein)

As discussed above, vertical leadership development involves changing the leader's level of thinking or overall awareness. It is less about knowledge and more about deepening awareness of thoughts and feelings (of one's self and others). At its core is the ability to step outside a system ('jutzing' is a term that I coined, and I have used it in my writing, teaching and consulting for more than 20 years), whether that system is family, organisation, culture or even one's own ego. From this place of great awareness, a leader is able to take action that is far more informed and therefore more effective. Cultivating this ability is the backbone of vertical leadership development. This greater awareness is crucial to more effectively lead complex and interdependent systems – ie, every family enterprise – through exponential change.

The world's premier leadership organisations, including the Center for Creative Leadership, Harvard University and Cambridge University, all state that vertical leadership development is the number-one leadership development trend today. Leadership agility is the specific model of vertical leadership that I have used with clients, executives in our EMBA program and with my own leadership practice. In this model there are four key agilities, and I have paraphrased them here for simplicity. All involve greater awareness coupled with action. According to the research conducted by Joiner and Josephs, the top 5% of leaders are likely to have three relevant things in their life: a daily reflective practice; a workout regime; and a creative practice outside work. We will discuss this finding further in section 7.1 below.

6.1 The four agilities

Figure 3 shows the four agilities – self-awareness, empathy, framing and innovation – and they are described further below. All four revolve around an axle of cultivating awareness by stepping back and looking at the system from outside (ie, jutzing).

Figure 3: The four agilities needed in vertical leadership

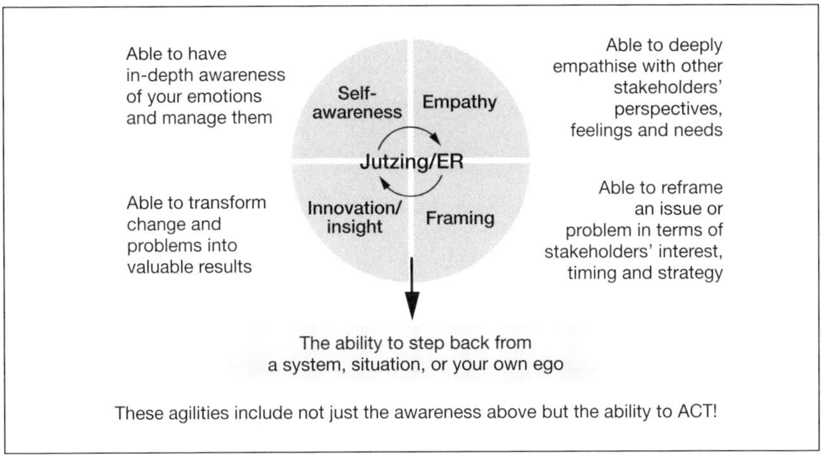

(a) Self-awareness

In my interpretation of this model, self-awareness ('self-leadership agility' in the leadership agility model) is the first and most important agility to cultivate. Awareness changes everything, and a leader who does not cultivate self-awareness will not evolve vertically regardless of the credentials he or she earns. Self-awareness is the ability to see oneself, including not only one's strengths but also one's weaknesses and blind spots. It includes the willingness to appropriately reveal more of one's self. A meditation teacher I practised with years ago referred to meditation as "solvent for the ego" and I think that is an apt description of self-awareness.

Leading a family enterprise requires an awareness of one's multiple roles, the roles of others, how one is perceived, and how one presents one's self. Tom White, for example, is a former naval officer, family member, business leader and board member. He is aware of who he is, how he presents himself and how the stakeholders perceive him.

(b) Empathy

Empathy (or 'stakeholder agility', as the leadership agility model terms it) is the second agility and can be seen as the other side of self-awareness. In my coaching, I see a very strong correlation between self-awareness and empathy. Does a leader see other people as merely resources, or can they place themselves in another's shoes and imagine what that person might think and feel? I worked with one leader who could viscerally experience what others felt as they came into his office. That is pretty evolved.

In a family enterprise, the importance of process often trumps the utility of a particular solution. If the relationship is important, empathy is crucial. When people feel heard, understood and validated they are more open to compromise, especially when the family is involved, since family ties are so profound. Expert advisers often have a blind spot when it comes to this reality, but it is critically important to recognise. This is precisely what makes advising family enterprises fundamentally different from advising other kinds of enterprise. Stephanie and Tom of TFE (see section 2 above) both invest a great deal of energy in not only cultivating their own self-awareness but also reflecting on what the other stakeholders think and feel, given their unique roles and perspectives. Thus, members of the family, the management team, and the board of TFE not only respect them but also feel heard and understood by them.

(c) ***Framing***

The third agility, framing (or stakeholder awareness), describes the ability of a leader to take on an issue, challenge or circumstance and see beyond a narrow foreground, such as one's own department within a company. Incorporating self-awareness and empathy for the relevant stakeholder concerns broadens one's view in a family and culture-encompassing context.

(d) ***Innovation***

The fourth agility is innovation (or, in terms of the leadership agility model, 'creative agility'). This requires the individual leader to spearhead and support innovation throughout the company, such as the management team and family council. In TFE, the way in which Tom and Stephanie led the effort to reframe the initiative to make the family a cultural and strategic advantage for all its enterprises led to the creation of Stephanie's position as family governance officer, as well as the innovative reframing of the entire organisation as TFE.

(e) ***All four agilities together***

At higher levels of leadership agility (see section 6.2 below) – ie, the post-heroic stages, where the leader isn't attached to being the person who comes up with the solution – the four agilities are particularly relevant and can be wielded together by a leader in the same way that a champion athlete uses a combination of strength, flexibility, endurance and speed to develop his/her overall performance. When all four agilities are accessible simultaneously and in the moment, an alchemy can arise that drives truly great leadership.

6.2 The stages of leadership agility

There are six stages of leadership agility. However, since most leaders fall into one of only three stages, we will mainly discuss those: experts, achievers and catalysts (see Figure 4).

(a) ***Experts***

Experts comprise approximately 45% of leaders. At this stage, leaders feel pressure to

Figure 4: The three levels of leadership

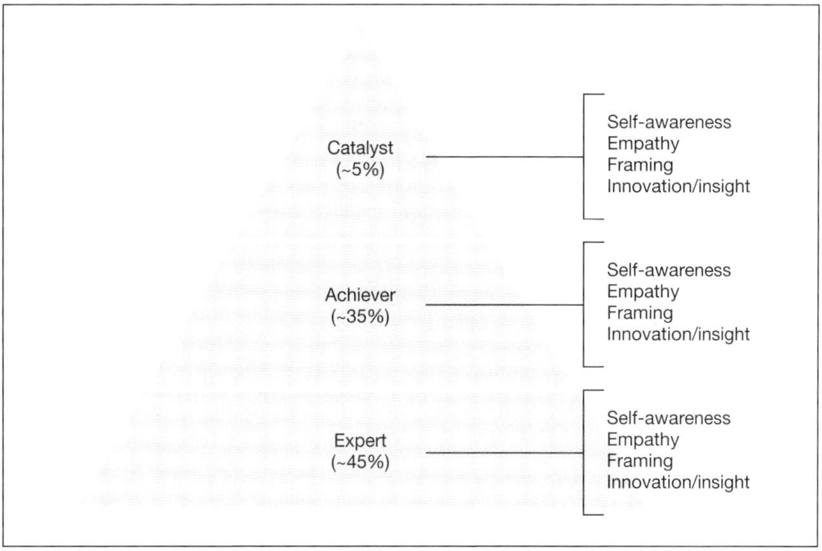

Adapted from Leadership Agility *by Bill Joiner and Stephen Josephs.*
Note: There are three levels of leaders above or below these levels that are ~15% of leaders. For simplicity, the above three levels will be discussed.

be the smartest person in the room. They often see problems, and thus tend to see people relative to their utility in addressing these problems. This need to 'be the hero' can be draining; it can also create a resistance to feedback and blind spots when it comes to mistaking perception for facts. Without deeper self-awareness and empathy for others, the expert can feel heavily burdened by pressure to solve all problems personally.

In terms of the four agilities, the expert begins to develop all four. However, he or she might resist the tools available for cultivating self-awareness, because the suggestion may seem like criticism or a threat to their identity, which is anchored to the need to be right from the outset.

Framing a problem and its solution typically focuses more on the problem than the stakeholders, and empathy tends to take a back seat to intellect. As a result, innovation is likely to be incremental, more focused on the organisation and more likely to arise from their own efforts. The expert's vision tends to focus narrowly, from his/her personal perspective of the organisation.

(b) Achievers

Achievers account for approximately 35% of leaders. This type of leader begins to see things from a systems perspective and to develop all four agilities. With this shift in awareness, the leader can shift focus from the problem at hand to view the broader system and develop a strategy, as opposed to merely solving the presenting problem. He or she might still be the hero, but is more defined by a penchant for strategy than problem solving – they realise they need to get buy-in from everyone involved in the situation and that others may have some experience or expertise that could inform their strategy.

The achiever is in the midst of developing all four agilities, though more often after the fact rather than in the moment. He or she might reflect on a meeting during the weekend while jogging, or realise that Mary, a single mother in the accounting department, is very worried about job security and will likely view most ideas through that lens. This leader uses empathy as a tool to help get buy-in and tweak a plan. Framing a solution to a problem is derivative of strategy, so innovation occurs within that broader vision. Such innovation is therefore more likely to be linked to industry developments or best practices.

(c) ***Catalysts***

Only about 5% of leaders are at the catalyst level, the first of the post-heroic stages. (Note that there are two stages above the catalyst stage, which comprise another roughly 5% of leaders.) The catalyst leader is no longer concerned with being right all of the time, or with being the hero – although he or she can step into that role when needed. Catalysts mainly focus on developing the people whom they are leading.

At this stage, the four agilities interact, often in the moment. The catalyst can jutz in a discussion and realise that he or she is feeling defensive, identify it, and ask the participants in the discussion to help him work through it. Catalysts empathise with the people they lead so that when they are emotionally stuck, they sense it and can address the issue of their being stuck rather than failing to progress.

For example, Mary, the single mother described above who fears risks, may argue about a new investment based less on her accounting concerns than on the emotional issues arising from her personal situation that may be absorbing much of her psychic energy. While the expert may try to get her buy-in based on the merits of the investment – which largely ignores her true, personal concerns – the catalyst is more likely to see her resistance to the merits of an investment in light of the bigger picture and see not just the organisation or the industry, but the social issues. So at this stage social responsibility begins to play a role in the leader's choices, and she or he might try to target their personal concerns as a way of enhancing the effectiveness of a potentially important contributor to the enterprise.

7. Why family enterprises need vertical leadership

Success is not counted by how high you have climbed but by how many people you brought with you. (Dr Wil Rose, late CEO of the American Indian Heritage Foundation)

For a family shareholder control group endeavouring to turn a family firm into a family enterprise, developing agile leaders is the most important initiative it can undertake. Any enterprise that involves a family becomes more complex than any non-family controlled competitor. Merging two business systems or business cultures in the context of an acquisition is complex, and the reason why such a high proportion of corporate mergers fail. Managing and leading a family shareholder control group and the enterprise it controls is vastly more complex than merging two corporate enterprises because family enterprises merge two different types of cultures: the family culture and the corporate culture.

Families have permanent, unconditional relationships – a leader is less likely to fire a family member because of a slow quarter – and positions are determined by relationship. Harmony is often a core value. In most enterprises, however, relationships are temporary and conditional: a CEO does not usually retain a poorly performing sales manager just because he or she loves him. Positions are defined by function, and performance is the core value that drives the outcome of whether an employee retains a job, gets promoted or is terminated.

Consequently, leading any family enterprise is a more complex undertaking than leading a non-family controlled competitor, all other variables being equal. There is greater interdependency between the family and business system and thus a greater need for the leaders to be fluent not only in the language of business but also in the dialect of the controlling family – and at the same time they must switch easily from one tongue to the other and back again.

7.1 How to cultivate leadership development: it has to be a practice

In some ways, leadership development is analogous to athletic training. Although some people are born with great natural talent, even those individuals have to develop that talent if they want to excel at the highest and most competitive levels in their field of endeavour. And just like an athletic training regime, leadership is a practice. If company leaders merely read best-selling books on relevant subjects and attend seminars to cultivate their leadership, and do not implement real change in their daily practice at the organisation, they will not have success.

In my experience, too few managers and owners have a well-defined vision of what leadership is or can be. However, we know a roadmap for leadership development will accelerate skill improvement. And while horizontal leadership development is important, it is all the more valuable if it is supported by vertical leadership development.

Vertical leadership development should begin with reflection and jutzing. The top 5% of leaders are likely to have a daily reflective or meditative practice. One thought leader in this field interviewed a group of these top leaders and found that all of them write in a journal, another reflective practice. Therapy and coaching are other modalities to help leaders explore their purpose, their presentation and their blind spots.

Many leaders are exploring the field of emotional intelligence, which is where a leader can identify emotions as they arise, label them and regulate how they want to act on them, causing them to be far more effective leaders.[9] In an exercise we do in our EMBA course, executives are required to get three words from ten people on how they present themselves on a good day and on a bad day. Almost everyone is very surprised to hear that most stakeholders very accurately perceive how they are perceived on a bad day. As one colleague put it, "We are all professional boss

9 See Daniel Goleman, *Emotional Intelligence*, Bantam, 1995.

watchers." As to the good-day feedback, people generally find it validating and occasionally discover a strength that others see in them that they may have overlooked.

This leads to another essential tool that all leadership models highly recommend: seeking feedback. The Center for Creative Leadership posits that as one moves upwards in any organisation, the lack of objective feedback is the number-one factor than can derail effectiveness as a leader, and even a whole career. If this is true for a police officer, professor or politician, then it is even truer in a family business where that core value of harmony will often constrain the truth from coming out.

Given the dual dynamics of resentment and fear, a family member may be justified in being cautious with feedback: Does the sender resent me? Is it because of who I am in the family, or are they sucking up to me? Feedback is also essential to the work of aligning a person's self-perception with how others in a company perceive that person's leadership – which is an ongoing, and profoundly meaningful, endeavour.

Finally, and more specific to vertical leadership development, tools for growth include a basic personal commitment on the part of a leader to development. This involves taking time to have new and complex experiences, such as immersing oneself in other cultures and connecting with people who are also engaged in business practice, as well as remaining endlessly curious.

7.2 A peek at the potential

In my experience, vertical leadership development, especially within the intimate, complex, inspiring and occasionally humbling world of family enterprise, can dramatically transform people and the family enterprises they lead. At the top levels where leadership abilities combine, some truly amazing things occur. We see leaders helping to change estate laws in their states, as Jim Ethier has done in his role as former chair of Bush Brothers and board member of the Beacon Center (a think tank that has led the effort to eliminate inheritance tax in Tennessee). We see the reframing of business into so-called 'conscious capitalism', as John Mackey, co-founder of Whole Foods, has done. And we see social entrepreneurial programmes that require no government funds and become models for the future, as Mark Peters, CEO of Butterball Farms, has done.

Enterprises need inspiring leadership if, as Rich Morris said, businesses must "go from having one good business idea that lasts three generations to each generation needing three good ideas". I believe it is crucial that today's leaders develop the agilities suited to the values-based, patient, emotional capital inherent in the family enterprise mindset.

The author would like to thank Audra Jolliffe, Project Consultant at McCann & Associates, Kathleen Hoye, Director at the Family Business Center of the University of Louisville, Joshua Nacht of Family Enterprise Systems, and Tom Epperson, Senior Director of Human Resources for the Luck companies.

Leading from the self

Robert Goodman
RGoodman Associates LLC

1. Introduction

Everyone thinks about changing the world, but no one thinks of changing himself. (Leo Tolstoy)

Based on my years of coaching executives, training leaders and preparing advanced doctoral students to lead systems-wide transformational change, I have come to believe in the value of a personal leadership approach to leadership development. I believe it is the path to great leadership.

'Personal leadership' in this context is leadership rooted in one's personality and personhood – of being an individual having human attributes and feelings. It is leadership anchored in the self. When a person leads from this stance, that person is tapping into his or her unique set of personal abilities and strengths, life experiences, motivations and values, as well as understanding and ameliorating limitations, 'triggers' and blind spots. Authentic leadership evolves from that. Most great leaders eventually learn that there is much to be gained from knowing deeply who they are, rather than leaving behind their personal selves at work's threshold in order to assume a 'leaderly' persona in the office. When someone practises personal leadership, that person leads from the inside out.

In order to lead in this way, a person must firmly commit to developing self-awareness, answering questions such as:

- What are my true strengths and limitations?
- How do others see me?
- Why do I do what I do?
- What has shaped my assumptions about how I lead?

That person must be willing to explore deeply and assume ownership of his or her actions, resisting the tendency to blame others when something doesn't work out as planned. The leader who assumes ownership of self takes full responsibility for his actions. He looks inwards first, to understand his 'triggers' – ie, what or who in the environment sets him or her off and poses a threat, causing knee-jerk unconscious reactions. The personal leader works towards minimising the strength of these triggers through awareness and by managing emotions internally.

Increasing self-awareness and the assumption of ownership of self are life-long developmental processes. I operate from the critical assumption that adults can change and evolve in their thinking, self-awareness and emotional and interpersonal maturity if the environment has the right mix of challenge and support. An interested manager, a coach, a partner and a trusted colleague – each can play a role in facilitating the development of these critical capabilities.

The field and practice of personal leadership development is growing and, with it, the tools and methodologies that support it. The power of this field of thought for all individual stakeholders in family controlled enterprises who seek leadership roles is clear: notwithstanding the power of the culture of a family shareholder control group, each individual immersed in that culture and in the affairs of the enterprise has the opportunity to seek the pathway of personal leadership development. In this chapter I will describe selected cutting-edge tools and methodologies that are helping leaders to develop in these areas.

2. The tried and true

Self-awareness has been an aim of the practitioners of leadership development thinking for many years. The typical approach begins with the leader considering any of a number of psychological and personality measures in order to create a leader profile. For example, it is possible to engage in a 360-degree feedback process. Or one can take the Myers–Briggs Type Inventory, or the DISC or the Thomas Killmann Conflict Management Style Measure. But new measures are being developed every year; in fact there is a glut of measurement tools, which can be very confusing to leaders.

While the information culled from these measures is absolutely helpful in building self-awareness of preferences, strengths and blind spots, they often do not automatically lead to deeper levels of self-awareness. This is because of superficial analysis or lack of integration of the results into the leader's past experiences, motivations and beliefs. Let me illustrate through an example how a personal leadership approach moves beyond such superficial analysis.

2.1 An illustrative example

Jason is the marketing team leader in a digital advertising agency. He is aware that he is avoiding the conflict that periodically erupts in his team. The recurring conflict has got to the point that it is now affecting the team's productivity and efficiency. He decides to participate in a workshop on managing conflict so that he can identify his typical conflict management style and learn techniques that allow him to be more comfortable addressing conflict as it arises. Some of these techniques resonate with him; some do not. He has some success applying this new knowledge, though it is limited and somewhat short-lived. A few weeks later, he experiences what many who take these workshops often do: he cannot even remember the techniques that felt so resonant, much less use them in the moment. Before too long Jason is back to burying his head in the sand. This is a familiar story, one that I hear often in my work as an executive coach and organisational consultant: "The workshop was useful at the time, but I can't get these ideas to stick!"

If Jason were to take a personal leadership route, he might seek the guidance of a coach who would help him to make sense of the results relative to his work context and personality – in essence, a more customised and personal approach. Jason might be asked questions that would allow him to gain insight into why he is conflict avoidant. Some of these questions may bring to the surface some experiences that were not entirely conscious to him. Jason might write a biography about his conflict avoidance and discover that he has been operating under an assumption that if he confronts conflict, he will lose his temper because that's what has typically happened for him for as long as he can remember. He has little patience and empathy for adults who can't "figure it out and get along".

Jason might then be asked first to observe his assumption in action. When does he see his assumption operating? Is it true in all contexts or in particular ones? What does he feel and think about when he witnesses conflict? Whereas this assumption was operating fully in his past, is it still true for him now? What can he do to put himself more in the driver's seat so that he can exert more control? How can he become less at the mercy of this assumption and the fear it generates?

Jason might run an experiment – ie, try out some new ways to address conflict in a calculated and low-risk way, so he can have the experience of remaining in control. And he could gradually run more tests of his assumption that are increasingly riskier. He is examining and challenging the truth of his (buried) assumption and way of operating, which has become an entrenched, unconscious belief. The process of identifying, working with and overturning personal assumptions that work against development and change is the central work of Lisa Lahey's and Robert Kegan's Immunity to Change process,[1] which we will discuss later in more detail.

You might be saying to yourself at this point that the personal leadership route, while interesting, is a lot of work! It is a lot of work to unearth root causes. Yet the chances of Jason making a more long-lasting change to his leadership, resulting in an increased capacity to effectively address conflict, are far greater than has occurred through his experience in the workshop. In the end, the return on his investment in time and emotional energy is well worth it, since it leads to change that is more durable.

3. The growth mindset

One day while in prison, I nearly attacked a prison guard – I had to work hard at controlling my anger … [I]f I had not gone to prison, I would have not been able to do that which is most difficult – to change yourself … I see myself as a work in progress … never forget that a saint is a sinner who keeps trying. (Nelson Mandela)

There are two *a priori* states of mind that sit above the leader's goal of self-awareness and ownership of self, and that must be embraced for development to occur. The first is the idea of the growth versus the fixed mindset, an approach developed by Carol Dweck;[2] the second is the notion of vulnerability as a critical leadership attribute, developed by Brené Brown, a Canadian sociologist and researcher.[3] I highly recommend reading both Dweck and Brown, in addition to viewing them on *Ted Talks*. (Brown's Ted talk is among the most viewed in the world.)

---

1 See Robert Kegan and Lisa Laskow Lahey, *Immunity to Change*, Harvard Business School Publishing Corporation, 2009.

2 Carol S Dweck, *Mindset, The New Psychology of Success*, Ballantine Books, 2006.

3 Brené Brown, *Daring Greatly: How the Courage to be Vulnerable Transforms the Way We Live, Love, Parent and Lead*, Random House, 2012.

3.1 A growth mindset, not a fixed mindset

Dweck and her research associates have identified two distinct habits of mind or belief that have profound implications for leadership and, more broadly, life. The fixed mindset is the belief that your qualities are carved in stone. Many of us are trained in this at a very early age, thinking that it is one way or the other; you are either smart or you're not. Your IQ tells the whole story of who you are. Avoid looking dumb at all costs and get that A! If you can't, then keep striving for it until you do. Life is very much about proving oneself, and the nagging questions of a fixed mindset are: Will I succeed or fail? Will I be accepted or rejected? Am I a winner or a loser? Notice where the focus is in this mindset: in the future and on performance. Not in the present and on the process of learning.

In contrast, the growth mindset posits the idea that your basic qualities can be cultivated through effort. The hand you were dealt at birth is merely the starting point in development and life. Everyone can change and grow. No one kind of person has a corner on that market! We all know of people who are born with certain towering talents. The growth mindset people develop them and become highly successful in their fields. The highly talented fixed mindset people become fixated on winning and getting the A or the first chair in the orchestra and avoid failure at all costs. Yet without failure we cannot learn.

Take a moment and try to see the connection between failure and learning. If you can't do that, consider an experience in which you 'failed' – a mistake that you felt at the time was HUGE, and one from which you felt you might never recover. Or if you did recover, it would have caused irreversible serious negative consequences. Did you recover? And now the most important question is: did you learn something from the experience? If you were fortunate enough to have the resilience to bounce back, you probably did learn, and for some readers it may have been among their most important lessons ever.

The growth mindset does not suggest that anyone can learn anything or that anyone can be anything. Instead, the growth mindset assumes that a person's true potential is unknown and that it is impossible to know what can be accomplished by that person through hard work and a learning stance. Development unfolds over time. I recently heard a presentation on autism in which the boy's father refused to believe that his son would never be able to talk. He spoke normally prior to two years old and then reverted to one word, "juice", for many years. But, in his repetitive rewinding of countless Disney videos, the child was learning the character's dialogue. All his parents needed to do were to join with him in the dialogue by playing the parts of the characters. Before long he was speaking again and expressing a range of emotions, just like the Disney characters.

So what does this have to do with leadership? In order to develop a deep level of self-awareness and self-ownership, you need to believe that you can learn, that you can always learn more and that, finally, you can learn until you die. Leaders need to believe that the level of self-awareness they currently possess is a snapshot, a moment in time. Leaders who believe that the level of self-awareness they currently have is fixed will need to overturn that belief. Self-awareness does not have a cap. The same can be said for ownership of self – there is always more to learn about the myriad of ways that we hide, often unintentionally, from taking responsibitity for our actions.

Let me introduce a young leader to illustrate the idea of growth in comparison with fixed mindsets. Her name is Samantha. She thinks quickly on her feet and is analytical, strategically focused and very personable. She had been focused on her next big promotion for the last 18 months. Four months ago, she heard from her boss that she got the promotion to Senior Manager for Finance. She's 120 days into her new job, making the transition from doing the work to ensuring she gets the work done through others. This means she must leave her area of competence as a rock star-like numbers analyst and enter into the arena of managing others while influencing her cross-functional colleagues, over whom she has no formal authority. She is no longer getting an A grade; in fact, she is performing at a C-level. She is losing sleep and focus. Here is her mind chatter: "I feel like a reject. I'm a total failure. Why can't I get this!" She sees her struggles as a direct measure of her competence and worth. She tells no one about her fears and anxiety. "Are you kidding? That would be like committing suicide. I'll just keep my head down." This is the fixed mindset.

You can see where her focus is: on processing – one might say obsessing on – her shortcomings. This focus takes enormous energy away from other more positive things she could do. She is allowing herself to be consumed by her feelings of inadequacy and appears too afraid to let anyone know, typical of the fixed mindset.

What if Samantha were to view her challenge from a growth mindset? What might she be telling herself? She may be saying to herself: "I will look around and see how others get work done through their direct reports. I'll talk with Jason. Maybe I'll experiment with a new way of coaching. I wonder if others in my situation go through this too? I know I have to go about things differently. I'm on a new planet." The growth mindset views struggles associated with a new challenge as normal and something to figure out. The leader who adopts the growth mindset takes the risk to reach out and admit the challenges inherent in a new situation. An inability to function in this new world is not experienced as an indictment of one's abilities or value. The growth mindset is oriented toward learning.

Adopting the growth mindset is not the whole story, though. There is another stance that Samantha must adopt in order to become a successful leader. She must make herself vulnerable. For most people this means admitting mistakes and asking for help. Many people would prefer death to confessing vulnerability. Yet, ironically, if those same people don't embrace a vulnerable stance, they die as leader–learners.

3.2 The courage to be vulnerable

Vulnerability sounds like truth and feels like courage. Truth and courage aren't always comfortable, but they're never weakness. (Brené Brown, in *Daring Greatly*)

A fundamental dilemma is that leadership roles constantly generate feelings of vulnerability, but we typically condition leaders to hide their vulnerabilities at all costs. (Ed Batista)[4]

---

4 Ed Batista of Executive Coaching Change Management, in "Coaching Your Employees", *Harvard Business Review*, HBR Publishing, 2014.

Brené Brown, a renowned Canadian sociologist, has researched and championed the notion of vulnerability and its connection to leadership. Her work has a growing international reach. She defines 'vulnerability' as "uncertainty, risk, and emotional exposure". Since we all experience vulnerability daily, some days more than others, it is essential to learn when it is present, how we respond to it and use it, and how we manage the feelings associated with it. It's uncomfortable – and humans have a desire to lessen uncomfortable (and often anxious) feelings. And the desire to avoid feelings of discomfort can be especially strong for leaders who are on the line day in and day out. The stakes are high. And when emerging leaders are engaged in leading an enterprise founded by their families and led by generations of their forebears, the stakes are even higher.

According to Brown:

The perception that vulnerability is weakness is the most widely accepted myth about vulnerability and the most dangerous. When we spend our lives pushing away and protecting ourselves from feeling vulnerable or from being perceived as too emotional, we feel contempt when others are less capable or willing to mask feelings, "suck it up", and soldier on. We've come to the point where, rather than respecting and appreciating the courage and daring behind vulnerability, we let our fear and discomfort become judgment and criticism.

To put our leadership and ideas out into the world with no assurance of acceptance or appreciation – that's also vulnerability. To risk failure is to be vulnerable. To admit to mistakes is to be vulnerable. Leaders who aren't comfortable with vulnerability often get angry, directing blame and responsibility on others. Anger serves as a socially acceptable mask for many of the more difficult underlying emotions we feel when we sit with our vulnerability like shame, fear, insecurity and incompetence.

Does this sound familiar to you? Do you run from your feelings of vulnerability? Do you know any leaders who do this? In order for Samantha to become the leader she aspires to be, she must embrace not only the growth mindset, but also her own vulnerability. She must allow herself to accept her vulnerabilities, to accept them as a normal part of assuming a new role while resisting the temptation to cover them over. Once she has acknowledged her vulnerable feelings, she can do something about them. She can end her isolation and silent suffering. She may even find it acceptable to ask for help.

A leader's ability to do this for herself has a very positive effect for those being led. The followers see someone who is comfortable in her feelings of not knowing and who then takes action to improve her situation. We know from decades of research that human beings connect around that which makes us human, namely our struggles. It is far more difficult to connect with the leader who presents himself as perfect and all knowing. Such leaders are usually put on pedestals and consigned to the world of the unattainable. "He is not like me! I have flaws. I struggle. I'll never get to where he is."

Why is embracing vulnerability important to leadership? Leaders must engage others in order to advance the work of the organisation. Which kind of leader is most likely to engage his/her followers and peers? The one who demonstrates that he's got it all together, or the one who can show that he is imperfect and striving? The chances of learning are far greater for the leader who accepts his vulnerability as a condition of growth.

4. The Immunity to Change process

Identifying some of the deepest, "below the surface" thoughts, feelings, assumptions, and beliefs is usually a precondition of behavioral change – one too often shirked in development programs. Promoting the virtues of delegation and empowerment, for example, is fine in theory, but successful adoption is unlikely if the program participants have a clear "controlling" mindset. ... It's true that some personality traits (such as extroversion or introversion) are difficult to shift, but people can change the way they see the world.[5]

The leader who embraces a growth mindset and works to increase his comfort level with his vulnerability is in a position to make optimal use of some of the tools of personal leadership. In section 2.1 of this chapter I spoke about Jason, the marketing team leader whose very human difficulty confronting conflict is affecting his team's productivity and ability to innovate. I contrasted two ways to approach his leadership development: the workshop; and the uncovering of limiting and very real assumptions driving his behaviour. I'd like to discuss further the latter personal leadership approach that I introduced earlier, called 'Immunity to Change' (ITC).

This groundbreaking work, co-developed by Robert Kegan and Lisa Laskow Lahey, is centred on the idea that, despite our best efforts, we are hampered in our ability to change by the (often unconscious) existence of powerful competing commitments. Although these competing commitments make a good deal of sense, they also work against realising our goals. Personal leadership goals almost always involve personal change.

Related to these competing commitments are powerful assumptions about what we believe, how we relate to others and how we move through the world as individuals. In many ways these assumptions have run our lives and held us captive. ITC work is aimed at uncovering well-worn beliefs so that ultimately we can be released from their grip. It invites the leader to enter into a discovery process of if and how these assumptions are operating now. It invites the leader to evaluate the potential gap between an internal reality and the external world.

Let's return to Jason. He has decided to explore his ITC process so that he can improve at addressing the conflict that is hampering him and his team's work. The four-column mapping process shown in Table 1, a personal leadership tool, is at the core of the Immunity to Change process.

---

5 Pierre Gurdjian, Thomas Halbeisen and Kevin Lane, "Why Leadership Programs Fail", *McKinsey Quarterly*, January 2014.

Table 1: Mapping goals in the personal leadership approach

Goal	What am I doing behaviourally that works against goal?	Competing commitment	Big assumption
I commit to addressing conflict on my team as it arises.	I don't say anything when I see it. I minimise it by calling it a miscommunication. I change the subject in team meetings.	I am committed to protecting myself from undue exposure and risk, and from losing control.	If I were to address conflict, I would get uncontrollably angry, because I truly believe people should be able to figure it out for themselves. If I get angry I will jeopardise my relationships and leadership, and there will be a stain on my performance.

Identifying and understanding a more personal reason for Jason's conflict avoidance is the beginning of this process. With the help of a coach, Jason will begin to test his big assumption in safe, low-risk ways to see whether what he believes to be true really is true. Will he get uncontrollably angry? Will he jeopardise or even lose his relationships? By Jason taking on this process he is clearly working in a growth mindset. He may not be 100% convinced that he can learn to do this, but he is willing to give it a chance. He is exposing his vulnerability in this area as opposed to covering it up. He is willing to risk failure.

Jason has also elected to work with a coach and a trusted colleague, who can observe him as he tests his assumptions. He is resisting his desire to cover up his fears and acknowledge this so-called imperfection. With a growth mindset and a growing ability to be vulnerable, he is using the ITC process optimally. He is practising personal leadership.

5. The Ladder of Inference

In our Practising Leadership Inside and Out class for doctoral students at the Harvard Graduate School of Education, my colleagues and I teach an important personal leadership tool, known as the Ladder of Inference (LOI). Chris Argyris, one of the founding fathers of the field of organisational development, created and developed this tool. It has become a staple in the field of communication, because at its core it is about deep self-awareness and ownership of self.

The LOI describes what happens internally as we move from direct observation of behaviour to the making of attributions and inferences about what we see and hear. The particular attributions we make are a function of our experiences, values and culture, and our history with those with whom we interact. We climb the ladder, making inferences about what a person's behaviour means, drawing conclusions and arriving at 'truths' on the basis of which we take action. Of course they are our truths. This process of attribution-making, often laced with critical and negative judgements, is something all people do, and it happens in an astonishing few seconds. Figure 1 should help to make the process of metaphorically 'climbing up the ladder' clear.

Figure 1: Jill is going 'up the ladder' on Paul

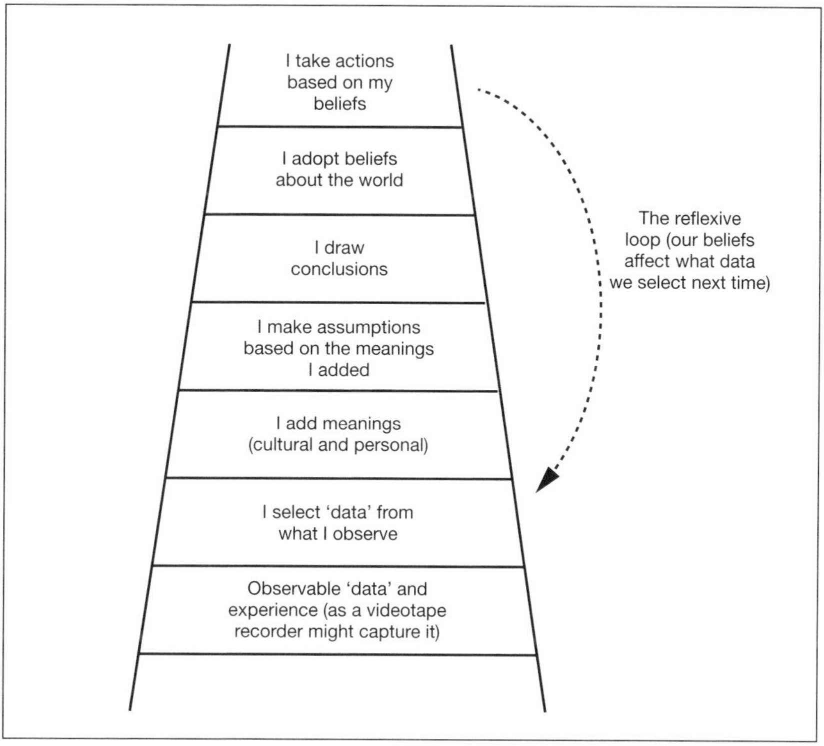

In the example we are using, Jill is a cross-functional colleague of Paul's and they are working on a project together. Looking at Figure 1, let's follow Jill 'up the ladder' as she tries to make sense of Paul's behaviour in a particular situation:

- **Observable data:** Paul has generally (though not always) delivered on aspects of the current project on time.
- **The data selected:** Paul has just swooped in with some last-minute changes to the current project – again!
- **The meaning added:** He doesn't seem to care about the impact on us.

- **The assumption made:** If he were more organised, this wouldn't be happening.
- **The conclusion drawn:** He seems totally incapable of sticking with a plan.
- **The belief adopted:** He is disrespectful of others.
- **The action taken:** I need to sit down with him tomorrow to have a talk.

Despite the fact that Paul has delivered on many aspects of the project on time, Jill is focusing on his last-minute changes – in other words, among all the data known to her this is the data to which she has decided to pay attention. (Historically, last-minute changes get under her skin.) She ascribes to Paul the behaviour that he doesn't care about the impact on others and that he lacks organisation. Jill is now up and running, so she considers that Paul is not capable of sticking to a plan and, further, is disrespectful. He needs a sit-down talk.

How can using the LOI increase Jill's self-awareness and thereby improve the relationship with Paul? First, Jill may not have been aware that she was doing this at all! Jill can slow down her 'laddering' of Paul and see that she is judging him and doing so in a way that is particular to her own belief systems. She can learn that what she observes may not mean what she thinks it does. Then, with this self-knowledge she can bring into question her assumptions and interpretation of his behaviour. Furthermore, she can begin to acknowledge that this is her interpretation. So she can refrain from blaming Paul and begin to ask questions about why Paul "swooped in" with the changes in the first place. She and Paul can begin a mutual learning conversation that could result in their evolving a shared understanding about how to move forward more collaboratively.

As Jill learns to use this tool in relation to Paul, she can begin to see in what ways she is also doing this to others. She can intervene in her own process of attribution and engage Paul in conversation aimed at collaboration and problem solving.

The general inference is this: once leaders become aware of the LOI, they can interrupt the way in which they react to situations and begin to question the very assumptions that are propelling them to the top of the ladder. I challenge such leaders to climb down the ladder and speak from the level of what they saw and heard while respectfully enquiring into its meaning for the person with whom the leader is interacting. This work is not for the faint-hearted. Why do I say that? Because we do not want to challenge our truths – they make perfect sense to us! They are comfortable and comforting, and in many cases they have been with us for a long time.

And to state the obvious: undertaking the process of climbing down the ladder in a family controlled enterprise can appear or feel like the most daunting task imaginable. Not only must one unbundle one's personal assumptions to do so, but one must also challenge many of the core cultural premises of one's family of origin, one's culture or ethnicity of origin, and one's superiors in the management and ownership hierarchies to which one has devoted one's career. These simultaneous challenges, when articulated, can seem insurmountable. And in reality they often are. To optimise one's endeavour to become an effective leader in a family firm requires, in my view, a well-vetted tool such as the LOI in order to manage the concurrent risks of simultaneously challenging some of the basic cultural assumptions of one's own nuclear family, extended family, ethnicity and corporate culture.

The Ladder of Inference is an excellent way to reflect on the self, deepening self-awareness and learning about oneself.

6. Threats and triggers

This [Pinch Analysis] is, I think, one of the most important elements of these personal learning tools: they help us gain real ownership over our experiences. I think one of the biggest transformations I've had over the term is gaining the sensation that negative interactions rarely just 'happen' to me. I've started to gain the capacity to turn them around as they are happening, rather than feeling helpless and then fuming afterwards. I see it as a step towards self-authorship to be able to take ownership for my interpretations of a situation or of others' reactions and behaviors. (Janet, a leader trained in the tools of self-awareness and ownership of self)

We can all imagine what a trigger means. It's the thing that catches us, and causes us to react rather than respond. It's the feeling a person gets when a certain someone walks into the room and by his/her presence generates strong emotions. Triggers provoke us and cause us to be reactive. In order to engage others in work, we need to understand our particular threats, what they feel like, what happens to our brains and emotions, and how to effectively manage our feelings when we are triggered. We need to do this so that we can lead well.

Leaders must know their triggers as they navigate their day's activities, encountering endless situations where they can get tripped up and react in unproductive ways. Who doesn't know a leader who has 'lost it' and then had to clean up the resulting mess. I know a leader who, when he became frustrated, would toss his head back and begin rolling his eyes when a team member disagreed with him. If he felt particularly triggered, he would then raise his voice, and then in some instances slam his hand on the table. Eventually his boss caught wind of his behaviour and it stalled his promotion. It was a while before he took the time to understand what he was experiencing and what he could do about it. Leaders are doomed to repeat ineffectual behaviour if they do not understand what is going on internally that generates strong feelings.

Parenthetically, his manager never asked this leader why he was behaving this way. Instead, he himself went 'up the ladder' and proclaimed him to be emotionally immature. This leader did not have the opportunity to identify his threat. He was stuck in the blame game: "My team repeatedly misses the point!" There are numerous versions of reacting to a trigger; some are much less visible, like the leader who withdraws from the slightest hint of conflict.

Why do people get triggered? In most cases it is because deep down they feel threatened. Originally as humans, our threats were from predators, in the form of competition for food or for a mate. The threats we experience today – experiences that are just as powerful as primordial threats – are social and interpersonal in nature: betrayals; one-upmanship; breaks in trust. If a peer who is in line for a promotion to the same job for which you have been preparing comes to a high-visibility meeting with an incredible idea, it is likely you will feel threatened. What might you do? You might try in subtle or not so subtle ways to diminish the power of the idea, or you might place another different and better idea alongside it. Or you might even withdraw and say nothing because you feel like you've already lost.

What happens when we feel threatened? Our brains are activated, and in particular the limbic system and, within that system, the amygdala or 'primitive' brain. When we feel threatened, we typically have a flight-or-fight response – ie, movement towards the threat or movement away from it. When we move towards the threat, it can look like anger, confrontation or competition; when we move away, it can look like disengagement, withdrawal and even denying that anything threatening has happened.

Here is the core idea: the person who said or did something that threatened you did not cause your feelings. What they did was to trigger and prompt your feelings. The feelings that you experienced are your unique feelings in response to a threatening stimulus. This may or may not sound logical to you. I know that some readers are saying right now, "No, that person was awful towards me, humiliated me, and was out to get me. In fact, they deserved every bit of my wrath!" While it is easy to admit to the notion of threat and trigger, it is very difficult for us to admit that the other person wasn't the cause of our reaction and therefore was not to blame. It's this difficulty that makes us point the finger. The true cause of our feelings and behaviour lies beneath the surface of our own lives, not in others.

The exercise of identifying threats and learning how to respond to them increases self-awareness. The exercise of taking responsibility for one's feelings in response to a threat increases ownership of the self. The language of self-ownership sounds like this: "I allow myself to get angry when I feel like my competency is being questioned;" or, "I allow myself to withdraw when I witness conflict on the team." When a leader takes responsibility for his actions, he is putting himself – not the other person – at the centre of control. The blame language of the leader who was fired from his job is what we hear when leaders fail to take ownership of their feelings – it is the other person's incompetence! Notice the link to Brown's concept of vulnerability: leaders who blame and get angry or withdraw are often covering over their feelings of vulnerability.

6.1 The SCARF model

David Rock, in his book *Your Brain at Work*, has proposed the SCARF model to help explain some of the types of threats that can trigger unproductive reactions. He has identified five domains of social experience that our brains treat as survival issues: status, certainty, autonomy, relatedness and fairness, expressed as follows:

- Status is defined as relative importance to others;
- Certainty is about attempting to predict the future;
- Autonomy provides a sense of control over events;
- Relatedness is a sense of safety with others, of friend versus foe; and
- Fairness is a perception of fair exchanges between individuals.

Returning to our eye-rolling leader, what threat do you imagine he was experiencing? As teammates brought up new ideas that challenged the leader's, it is likely that the leader's status as the person with the right/best/smartest answers was threatened. Might he have been able to modify his reactions if he had a deeper understanding of the underlying threats? It might take some work, but I can imagine that this leader might even have been able to make room for other people's ideas, and not just cover up his eye rolling, by learning how to self-observe his non-verbal messaging.

We can feel threat in these domains. But what happens if we experience reward – when our status is recognised and uplifted, or when we are given autonomy to design our work? The leader who understands his triggers and threats is the leader who is more likely to understand the value of rewarding his followers in these crucial domains. The personal leader takes his/her insights into the self and uses them to help develop the talents and achievements of others.

6.2 The Pinch Sort

LaL (Leadership as Learning)[6] has created a tool, named the Pinch Sort, which helps leaders to analyse what happened in a situation where there was a triggered response. It is a very useful tool for increasing a leader's self-awareness and ability to assume self-ownership of responses rather than reacting unproductively to the threat.

I'd like to draw from a personal example of an interaction between my adult son and myself that I analysed via Pinch Sort to better understand my reactions. The context for this example is as follows. Jen, a friend of mine and my 28-year-old son's, is in town. I think to myself, "Let's surprise Nick!" so after Jen and I have had dinner in town we head to Nick's apartment and ring the doorbell. I hide and Jen stands in front of the door. I am very excited about this fun plan! How my great plan played out is shown in tabular form in the Pinch Sort analysis of Table 2.

Here is my reflection on my use of Pinch Sort in these circumstances. I learned many things, the most important being that I had strong feelings of insecurity, rejection and shame. These are difficult feelings for me to deal with because, in this particular case, I didn't want to be seen as a bad parent or as having made a mistake. I believe that these feelings would have got covered over by secondary feelings emanating from my mind chatter. For example, I would have instead characterised Nick as rigid and lacking spontaneity or too hung-up on boundaries. In short, I might have deflected away from my feelings and made him the problem. I might have blamed him for my flop.

My familiar threats on the SCARF model are relatedness and certainty: relatedness because my relationship with Nick in those moments felt threatened as he felt like the foe not the friend; certainty because the incident made me feel out of control and unable to predict what would happen. I had come up with this plan and was thwarted when I tried to enact it; the outcome was out of my control. For me, who considers himself a strong planner, it was a very uncomfortable feeling.

One of my most impactful learning moments occurred after I left Nick's

6 See the learnaslead.com website.

Table 2: Pinch Sort analysis of a tense interaction

Interaction element	Commentary
A. What happened	His roommate answers the door and looks befuddled. We go upstairs, where Nick is watching TV, and yell "Surprise!!" I eventually sit down next to him on the couch and he is not looking at me, with no laughter and not much happiness about the surprise.
B. My mind chatter	Uh, oh! Maybe not a good idea! Why can't he just go with the flow? He's so sensitive! He's got so many boundaries! What's the big deal! He's making Jen feel uncomfortable.
C. My feelings	He's not looking at me. I feel cut off, rejected, disconnected, shut out, unable to reach him, frustrated and surprised by his reaction.
D. What I did in response	Nothing! Given that there were other people there, I maintained 'normality' because of the situation, pretending that everything was fine. I made small talk with his roommate, and I tried to establish some connection with Nick by talking about what he was watching. But he remained monosyllabic. I was aware of how uncomfortable I felt.
E. Benefits to me of acting that way	There was no 'scene' as I didn't respond in the moment – that's a good thing. And I didn't expose Jen to an uncomfortable situation. I didn't have to talk about my true feelings.
F. Costs and ripple effects	I was acting unlike my usual self, with very little conversation, low energy, feeling constrained, internal agitation, and a feeling of being less close to the people I love. The others in the room could also feel the tension.

continued on next page

Analysis element	Commentary
1. What is the (familiar) threat?	My status as the 'good father' is threatened by his response. On the SCARF model, my relatedness was threatened, and I was no longer safe, feeling my son was foe not friend.
2. Back to the present: reframe	What I had hoped for was to have a good time with all of us and for Nick to enjoy the surprise visit from Jen.
3. New course of action	Boundaries are important to respect. Refrain from making assumptions about what will be fun and what won't. Put a check on my thoughts and needs. Make sure to ask myself: is this for me or the other person?

apartment and went home. I attempted to compose a text in which I was intending to apologise. Lucky for me that I had two people with me who let me know that what I was actually saying was an attempt to right myself. My first text attempt was, "I didn't think you would respond the way you did. I meant it as a fun time." I went through two more iterations until I finally simply said, "I am sorry for what happened last night." What I learned was that there was still a part of me that was defending my actions because I didn't want to be the person who made a bad judgement, especially as a dad and because nothing had gone as I thought it would. I didn't want to be wrong. I didn't want to be perceived as insensitive. So it was hard to apologise because I equated an apology with admitting that I had made a big mistake.

7. Conclusion

All leaders want to be good at leading and most want to be great. Great leaders are aware that they live in a tension which they have to manage daily. On the one hand they want to be seen as highly competent, smart, incisive, thoughtful and great developers of people. But wanting to be seen that way can hinder the expression of failure, of not knowing the answer – in short, of being human. Great leaders know that they will lead best when they bring all of themselves to the table. This means their shortcomings too.

The question for the present or future leader in a family controlled enterprise – someone whose life choices clearly indicate that he or she is wholly committed to working in a family system, albeit one focused on sustained growth – is how to manage the recovery of the inevitable error in judgement that implicates not only parent and child, as illustrated by the example in section 6.2 above, but also extended family, ethnic group and enterprise stakeholders.

If it is true that leaders believe in the value of leading from the self, then it is essential that leaders understand themselves as deeply as possible so they can bring this understanding fully to their work and in the service of those they lead. The approaches and tools that I have discussed – namely the growth mindset, vulnerability, Immunity to Change, the Ladder of Inference, triggers, the SCARF model and the Pinch Sort analysis – are pathways to accomplish this.

To deepen self-awareness and self-ownership in the evolving context of one's own development is a lifelong endeavour. Learning to develop these critical capabilities are goals that should be on every leader's development plan at all times.

Creating a strong leadership team

Ann Lindsey
Lindsey Leadership Consulting

1. Introduction

Creating a genuine leadership team takes time, effort, skill and sometimes an outsider – a consultant. The consultant, not bound by the past, has the capability to envision possibilities, and provide both the structure and the environment to make a hoped-for vision into a reality.

In creating a genuine team, the first factor that must be developed is trust. Trust occurs (for adults) through open communication. Oddly enough, many organisations have unwittingly fostered a closed system of communication. Fear of losing control and the repercussions that might occur with that loss lead to a lessened openness; yet people long to say what is on their minds, to call things as they see them, and to help make changes that will make their own and others' working lives better. Thus, when setting the stage for genuine teamwork, the first step is to create an environment in which people can talk openly to one another. This includes the participants being willing to take some risks in terms of self-disclosure, as well as having some fun in the process. This first step is often the most difficult.

The process of becoming an effective and genuine team often has an unexpected and unanticipated effect: hope is created or, in some cases, recreated. New and powerful energy is released, and people find themselves reaching to attain goals that they had earlier never believed they could reach; collectively and individually they find a sense of creativity and yearning to go beyond the limits they have previously achieved. Often these limits have become feelings that have been buried under the weight of the demands of daily work and life, and the return to the uninhibited openness that was experienced early on in life is a joyful occurrence.

2. The leadership team, and creating a new organisational structure

One of the most effective tools for making positive change in any organisation is the creation of a strong leadership team, whether in a family-owned business or in a corporate-led enterprise. The difference between working with a leadership team in a corporation and one in a family-owned business is the potential added encumbrance of family dynamics. Family dynamics are, of course, very powerful; they are also deep-seated.

While the dynamics in a family-owned organisation may be complex and, indeed, daunting, the same kinds of interpersonal dynamics tend to occur in a corporate-led organisation. These dynamics often include the perception that others are stuck in their ways and not capable of change. Passive/aggressive behaviour, as well as dependency, control and competitive issues, are often at play. Family dynamics issues are often entrenched and so are played out at work as well as in personal lives. Within corporate structures, such dynamics are often quickly created because people bring their personal needs and wishes into their working lives. Work itself often comprises three-quarters of individuals' waking lives and, accordingly, any individual's needs and hopes may be easily played out within the business enterprise.

In building a strong leadership team in the midst of these dynamics, a consultant who is engaged to assist would seek to help the leadership team to:

- build trust among the members of the team;
- create team goals that support the mission of the organisation;
- use team members' voices and perspectives to understand the reality of what faces the organisation;
- develop effective means of resolving conflicts;
- create effective communication processes within the team and with the organisation;
- be innovative and thoughtful in all problem-solving processes;
- create an environment that will promote intrinsic motivation among the team members; and
- become adept at anticipating changes in the larger environment and responding successfully to these changes.

In the best of situations, the consultant would also work with multiple groups and teams in the organisation, using a similar process, until the entire organisation is embedded in a newly created organisational future. Once that is established, the company is more likely to use teamwork appropriately to sense the environment, plan, create and implement strategy, and ensure its future.

3. An instructive case study

3.1 Overview

In working with a family-owned manufacturing facility, we found that the leadership team members were set in their ways as well as in their belief that nothing could change. However, competition in the industry was forcing the company's leaders to consider ways of becoming more effective in their leadership. Clearly, a pivotal factor in their success or lack thereof would be to change their beliefs in their ability to work together and to be able to act on this understanding.

The senior leadership team was composed of seven men and included the company's chief executive officer (CEO) (who was also the founder of the company), one son who headed the finance function, and a younger son who headed up manufacturing. The company produced spectacle frames and sold to various distributors that carried brands from the lower end of the market to the designer end. The founder owned 50% of the company while the two sons each owned 25%. The company itself was located in the mid-west of the United States, had been in existence for 32 years and employed approximately 500 people in manufacturing and sales, many of whom were long-term employees due, in part, to the fact that getting another job was very difficult in that area of the US.

Historically, there had been a consistent pattern of difficulty in the relationships of all three family members in their roles within the company. There was little trust between them, and they were often suspicious of one another. They could not provide a sense of safety, either for one another or for the entire team. Modelling the behaviour of the controlling family owner/managers, the company executives acted towards one another in ways that reflected their suspicions of each other – they felt little safety in the team and lived with a concern that things might become chaotic at any moment.

The beliefs and behaviour of the leadership team were reflected throughout the organisation. Unknowingly, the team members were demonstrating the concept of isomorphism – that is to say, those below the leadership team members replicated the tone and behaviour of the leadership without a conscious knowledge of why they were doing so – and the consequences were damaging. This phenomenon of isomorphism is seen in many companies, and the majority of leaders of those companies do not know that it is occurring.

This particular leadership team could not resolve conflicts between its members. The sons were afraid of displeasing their father, who was perceived by everyone else in the organisation as very powerful. The sons themselves did not see eye to eye about a number of organisational issues. For instance, the head of manufacturing wanted some additional plant machinery and associated training to accompany the new machinery, while the head of finance strongly believed that with sales falling because of growing competition, no extra expenditures should be approved. Both positions were reasonable under the circumstances, and even appropriate for the executives advocating conflicting positions, given the explicit responsibilities of these two owner/managers.

The conflicts between the owners were easily seen by other members of the team, who had over the years grown fearful about expressing their personal views. Of course, since conflict avoidance was itself an implicit core value of the business enterprise, it is hardly surprising that the entire team was generally uncommunicative.

The team firmly believed that the controlling family shareholder's personal traits were unchangeable and that other team members were also incapable of change. In social psychology, this belief is identified as a 'fundamental attribution error'. By definition, this error is the tendency for people to place an undue emphasis on personality characteristics to explain someone else's behaviour in a given situation, rather than considering the situation's external factors. In an enterprise where fundamental attribution error had become a way of life, all the team members assumed that others could not change.

The leadership team members' reactions to one another were consistently negative. In reality, they were somewhat depressed and angry, and either did not know or could not acknowledge the depths of their despair. This reality was their past and unfortunately their present, so change did not seem a possibility.

At the same time, the outside factors affecting the company were having an increasing impact; in particular, new competition in the industry was growing. Company sales continued to decline, and the company was not innovative, consistently failing to think of new products or of efficiencies for its current product lines. From the human perspective, the reality that their employees' lives and abilities to provide for their families were at stake affected all the leadership team members. They were, however, too stuck in their ways to be able to effect changes that could ease their concerns.

It was at this point that we were asked by the manufacturing head – who had gained the tacit agreement of his father – to step in as consultants and begin working with the leadership team to "make things better". The specific remit was to work with the leadership team and the organisation to change the situation for the better.

We based our consultation work on the following principles:

- Successful teams coordinate individual efforts so that their results are greater than the sum of these individual efforts. Attaining such results requires attention to the team process and its growth; such attention requires time and effort.
- It is all too easy to approach team development as though the managing of relationships within the team will create success. Many team-building efforts are devoted to building stronger bonds among the team members. While this effort is valuable, it is important to understand other factors that are critical to the development of a successful team. An overriding critical component is that team members accept that that they must all pull in the same direction, and do so consistently. This analogy suggests that the fulfilment of the mission or vision of the team and its organisation is the ultimate goal around which all members are united. In order to attain the mission or vision, the team members must be united in their own goals and the performance needed to achieve these goals. Team members must also understand who needs to do what to ensure that the team will achieve its goals, and they must agree on what procedures will be needed for the team to do its work.
- It is imperative to recognise that when things go wrong in some way, the difficulties are often not due to individual members' characteristics or to difficult interpersonal relationships. If all team members agree on the organisation's mission or vision, the leadership team goals, the team members' roles and responsibilities, and the required changes of procedure and approach, then differences among team member personalities are less consequential.

3.2 Initial assessment

We started with an assessment of the situation we found. Each leadership team member talked confidentially with a consultant about being a member of the team. These interviews provided room to express frustrations. Some members talked quite openly and others were more guarded. Based on what the consultants were hearing from the leadership, we then delved deeper into the problems by talking with a cross section of the organisation's members. The interviews included open-ended questions about what the employees or management were experiencing in their work, and the responses allowed us to develop the significant themes that were impacting the organisation.

3.3 Guiding leadership team development

We presented the organisational diagnosis to the leadership team candidly without reference to any individual. Rather, we identified the themes that were expressed, such as "It is very difficult to trust/communicate/make decisions around here" or "I believe (or don't believe) that the leadership team cares about the organisation and its workers." The team was then asked to explore what these themes and comments meant for the organisation and its ability to thrive. The leadership team members expressed some surprise at how the consequences of their own behaviour were perceived throughout the organisation.

In order for the leadership team members to gain perspective about their situation, the consultants guided the team members in analysing the factors that were affecting their teamwork, the organisation and their industry. These factors included individuals, groups and organisations both inside and outside their own organisation (see Figure 1). Soon, they began to understand how these factors affected their team's ability to be a strong and resilient leadership team.

Figure 1: Factors that influence teamwork

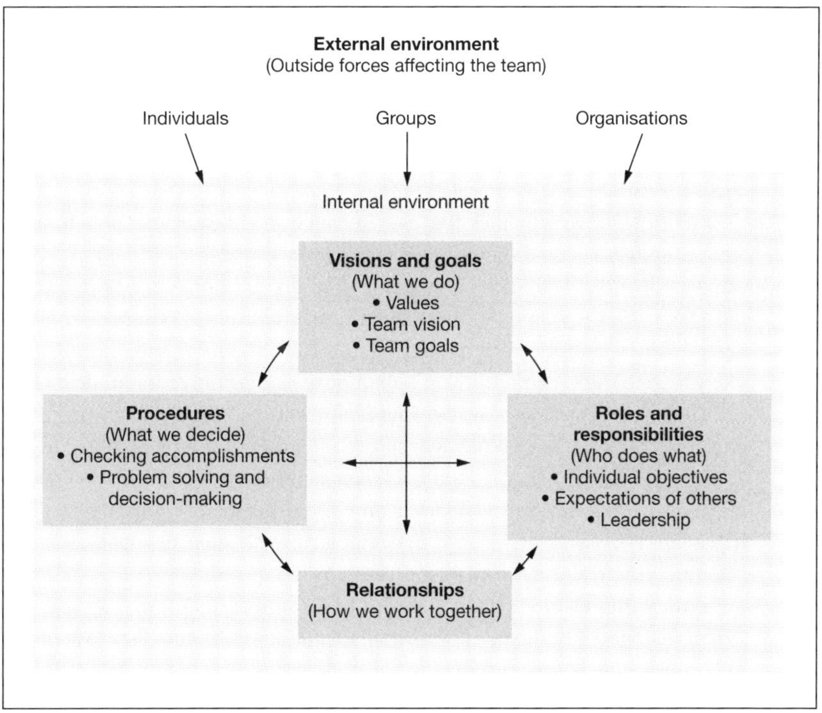

Next, we explored with the team the characteristics of ideal leaders and, by comparison, ineffective leadership teams, and we also discussed the consequences of each kind of leader for the team and for the company. We examined how ineffective leadership teams affect an entire organisation, and how their shortcomings can dramatically impact the members of the organisation as well as the organisation's own survival.

The next step was to effectively bring the leadership team back to its core mission as leaders of this company. The team members were asked to explore more concretely what their mission was (in other words, what their job was, what they were there to do, and what they could do to be more successful than they had been in the past).

We were then ready to have the leadership team create their operating philosophy or principles about how they would agree to treat one another going forward. We asked the team members to identify the values and characteristics that were important in creating a work environment in which people would feel intrinsically motivated to do their best work. These would form the basis for their operating principles.

An operating philosophy for any team includes a set of guiding principles that say:

- how team members will treat one another;
- what motivates the team;
- what quality of life the team members want; and
- how team members will treat others with whom they interact in their work, both inside and outside the organisation.

3.4 Commitment to change

After the operating principles were created, we asked each member to sign them as a pledge to abide by them in their work with one another, with company members and with those (such as suppliers) with whom they interacted on the outside.

The operating principles that were created read beautifully, but no one on the leadership team was convinced that it would be possible for them to follow through on their words, even with their pledges to do so. However, the leadership team recognised that it would be important to own the new philosophy. They also knew that if they used their former techniques of intimidation and control, they would likely negate their own efforts on behalf of their new operating philosophy.

They were also clear that they had a most difficult time confronting one another constructively. Having acknowledged the difficulty of their situation, the leadership team developed a simple approach of reminding one other of their (many) regressions in behaviour. Whenever any team member saw another team member behaving in a way that was not in accordance with their new operating principles, the observing team member would take a printed card from his pocket and hold it up to the other team member. The card had a simple question: "Are you Y'ing me?" Whatever the "Y" meant it was theirs to keep to themselves. We never knew, although we had our surmises.

In any event, the result was a good many instances of cards being pulled from pockets and held up in the eyes of the often unsuspecting yet offending team member. No words were ever spoken, no criticism was given, and no relationship was undone in the process. However, over time, this method led to a remarkable change in the actions and behaviour of the leadership team members. In fact, the head of manufacturing decided to take on a change management role. He began to read books about leadership and over time became very active in implementing important steps for positive change in the company.

In their actions, then, the leadership team had begun to create an environment in which they felt some sense of safety. An important outcome of the development of the operating principles for any team is the containment that begins to be established. People start to feel that they can disagree with one another without things coming apart. Tensions can be expressed and resolved and people believe that they can move through difficulties and come out with solutions. They begin to have a foundation for hope about the future.[1]

3.5 Development of team goals and roles

At this point the leadership team was ready to undertake the development of their team goals, with performance measures and time lines to accompany those goals. They then moved to developing their roles with regard to their work as a leadership team. Doing so meant that team members had to explore how each could contribute to the team and its goals. Additionally, each team member had to take full responsibility regarding his role in meeting the team goals.

The team members had to look specifically at how the leadership team got things done. They had to decide on and agree to procedures for various things such as making their leadership team decisions, resolving their conflicts, holding their meetings, negotiating (where necessary) with one another, including new team members when they came on board, and checking on leadership team accomplishments.

When the mission, operating principles, goals, roles, and procedures were developed fully, it became clear that even members of the team who didn't necessarily like each other could indeed work together. Their personality differences became far less important when it was possible to agree on how and what they were going to do.

3.6 Skills development

During and following these team development sessions, we also worked on skills development. There were many skills to understand and develop. Some of the important ones included the ability to listen to others, to give feedback, to resolve conflict, to understand the impact of the system that people are in with regard to their actions, to understand oneself and others, to understand change and using resistance to change to further the change process, and to learn to build an environment in which individuals' intrinsic motivation can be brought to the forefront of their work lives.

Since collaboration is a necessary and valued characteristic among a leadership team, we consultants introduced the following collaboration-building skills:

---

1 See Ronald Heifetz, *Leadership Without Easy Answers*, Harvard University Press, 1994.

- practising 'appreciative inquiry' – ie, asking questions without implied criticism, and listening very carefully to the response;
- maintaining caution concerning any assumptions made, by testing those assumptions by getting more information;
- assuming that others are making sense to themselves – and figure out how, usually by asking;
- sharing your own requirements, needs and hopes;
- not assuming that people and groups act as they do because of their stable characteristics – looking instead at the impact of the system on them;
- explaining your thinking fully to others – they don't necessarily know or understand your thoughts. Be willing to share the thinking process, including the uncertainty that may be involved; and
- focusing on others' strengths and accomplishments, and criticising rarely.

During all of the team development, it was important to shore up the leadership team members' resilience, courage and heart when they or other team members were having difficulty. Their developing capability to remain consistent and contained in their actions and reactions to others was paramount to continuing the foundation that was being built.

4. Extending the work into the organisation

Over time, our work as consultants extended to all levels of the organisation. We began with off-site sessions comprising the leadership team, managers and cross sections of employees. These off-site sessions helped the leadership team and others learn the importance of listening to and involving others in the creation of a new work environment.

In an off-site meeting devoted to working on a new organisational design, not only was a larger organisational philosophy created, but work plans were looked at for line workers. One worker, whom I remember vividly (as he was a tall, younger and red-headed man), said, "No one knows more about my work than I do." This statement became a model for looking at and exploring individual work, and for growing teamwork among the line workers.

4.1 The learning group process

One of the most important interventions that we implemented was the creation of learning groups, so that all members of the organisation could do their own mini-diagnosis concerning what had occurred in their company over the years. They could then, in their learning groups, begin to absorb new skills into their behaviour and understand what makes a real team.

The initial learning group discussions were some of the most important and more difficult parts of the work. But for me they comprised some of the most memorable times in my working life. People – managers at all levels and plant floor workers – had so much frustration, and were so very hopeless in the beginning, that I would finish a day of listening to and facilitating a given learning group completely spent. I remember one man who cried as he blamed himself for his wife's suicide because of the way he had acted at home as a consequence of the despair and anger that he felt at work. His learning group cried with him.

From these long days of honest discussion and education about how to have a new working life, hope began to emerge for the workforce in general. In my judgement, there would have been no way to move forward without this painful process of addressing emotionally powerful issues that impacted work performance. During this change process, of course, it became clear that as the work progressed, resistance to future change was being reduced and new forces for positive change were being planted.

4.2 The change to a 'new' organisation

During this time of development and change, several events occurred. The founder decided to retire. The manufacturing manager then moved into his place to become the new company CEO. The two brothers became equal co-owners of the company.

We continued to work at all levels of the organisation. This work included selecting and teaching several pairs of individuals (one man and one woman in each pair) to function as internal consultants to various areas of the organisation so that workers and their managers would have a source of help for problems. The efforts of one pair of these internal consultants, Marge and Josh, form a vivid memory for me of two individuals who took on their roles with tremendous initiative and a desire to make a difference for those whom they served. In time, Marge and Josh became the informal leaders of the small internal consultants' group.

Formal structures were also put in place that were advisory in nature. These comprised cross-sectional teams at various levels of the organisation, which served to keep necessary information flowing and to ensue that communication was occurring at all levels. In addition, the teams advised (where appropriate) in critical decision-making for the organisation. One such advisory team even had members ranging from the CEO to plant floor workers.

Plant floor workers were trained cross-functionally, became active members of their teams, and received performance-based pay both for their individual work and for their team's work. This new reward system supported and furthered the change to a collaborative, participatory and highly productive organisation.

When the leadership team became a highly functioning collaborative team and all related processes were successfully in place, our work was over.

5. Conclusion

Working with leadership teams is a process that is often initiated and furthered by an organisational consultant until the goals and goal results are embedded in that organisation. The work is not always straightforward; the process can be long and worrisome, and it is organic at its core. The leadership team itself must create the stepping stones for what it wants to accomplish on its own, as well as with the organisation.

The role of the organisational consultant is to build the containing environment – the safety net – in which the organisation's leadership team and the organisation itself can create the effective enterprise that all desire.

Mediating family business disputes: a primer for clients, family business advisers and other professionals

David A Hoffman
Boston Law Collaborative LLC

1. Introduction

Although the practice of mediation has an ancient lineage – dating back to Bible times and even longer ago in China – our modern era did not see a resurgence in the use of mediation until about thirty years ago. In law schools in the United States, for example, the first textbook[1] on mediation appeared in 1985, and many similar texts – aimed primarily at the legal market – have been published more recently. However, the public's knowledge of what mediation is, and isn't, is surprisingly limited. Because of that lack of awareness, the need for mediation far exceeds the demand.[2]

Accordingly, this chapter will begin with a basic introduction to the subject of mediation and then move on to more sophisticated aspects of the subject in later sections.

2. Overview of mediation

There are five different aspects that need to be considered when trying to understand the basics of mediation, as set out below.

2.1 What is mediation?

The simplest, two-word, definition of mediation is 'facilitated negotiation'. Mediators manage negotiations in such a way as to create a safe place for a sometimes difficult conversation. Unlike arbitrators, who are legally empowered to act as judges and make binding decisions regarding a conflict, mediators have no power to impose a solution. All of the power remains with the parties, while the mediator, using a variety of techniques discussed below, tries to help the participants find fair and reasonable solutions.

2.2 Who can serve as a mediator?

The short answer is, literally, anyone. Most professional mediators come to the field

---

1 Stephen Goldberg, Eric Green and Frank Sander, *Dispute Resolution: Negotiation, Mediation and Other Processes* (1985).

2 Bill Ury, co-author of *Getting to Yes* (see note 5 below) and author of many other books on dispute resolution, is the source of this observation.

from some other profession, such as law or psychology, but many distinguished mediators pursue mediation careers directly out of college or graduate school. Mediation is not yet a licensed profession in any state in the US, but a few states have certification programmes for mediators who receive referrals from the courts. In addition, there are professional organisations, such as the International Academy of Mediators, whose membership is selective and based on success in the field.

2.3 What do mediators do?

The mediator's toolbox is broad and deep – we use a variety of techniques, adapted to the specific needs of the situation. For example, if a family business is in crisis because of personality conflicts, the mediator's techniques might focus on fostering greater understanding among family members and improving communication. Or if the family conflict has arisen because of financial issues – such as some members wanting to withdraw, others wanting to continue, and the business lacking sufficient liquidity to pay those who wish to withdraw – the mediator's techniques might focus more on financial analysis and problem solving.

Mediators use active listening and reframing so that participants feel heard. They serve as referees and managers in a negotiation, sometimes coaching the parties on how to be more effective in communicating their positions and perspectives.

The mediation process begins with 'contracting' – discussions between the parties and the mediator (or someone on the mediator's staff) to determine the scope of the mediation, the logistics (such as location and cost) and the signing of an agreement to mediate (containing provisions about confidentiality).

Then the next stages are story, interests, options and alternatives:

- *Story:* Mediators often begin by creating an opportunity for each participant to tell their story in their own way. This might be in a one-on-one meeting with the mediator, or in a room with all participants present. People in conflict need to feel heard, and the best mediators are good listeners.[3] It is not uncommon – in family business disputes or any other type of dispute – for the collection of narratives that mediators hear to have a *Rashomon*-like quality. The stories are often one-sided, self-serving and drenched in blame and accusation. The participants often use their narratives to try to recruit the mediator to their version of the facts. From the mediator's standpoint, the stories are worth hearing regardless of how partisan or distorted they might be, because the manner of telling is highly diagnostic for the mediator and at least as important as the content of the story.[4] Each narrative reveals the emotional impact of the conflict, and the extent to which the teller can see the conflict from a balanced perspective, or not.
- *Interests:* As the mediator listens to each party's narrative, s/he is trying to discern what each side wants (ie, their positions or demands) and their underlying interests. 'Positions' are what we want; 'interests' are why we

---

3 For an excellent resource on attentive listening, see Rebecca Sharif, *The Zen of Listening: Mindful Communication in the Age of Distraction* (2003).

4 See David Hoffman and Richard Wolman, "The Psychology of Mediation," 14 *Cardozo L Rev* 759, 764 (2013).

want them. The value of shifting our focus from positions to interests was one of the central insights in *Getting to Yes: Negotiating Agreement Without Giving In*,[5] which revolutionised negotiation theory and practice. Before *Getting to Yes* was published, much of the literature about negotiation focused on how to manipulate a negotiating partner through a combination of threats, ultimatums, cajolery and even deception. The authors of *Getting to Yes* advised depersonalising the conflict (separating the people from the problem), looking for objective benchmarks of fairness, and communicating about underlying interests. They illustrated the latter point with a story of two children fighting over an orange, which has become a classic of negotiation literature. In this story, the children's parent settles the conflict by slicing the orange in half, without asking either child why they wanted the orange. The story's moral – based on the fact that one child wanted the orange to make juice while the other wanted only the rind for baking – was that disclosing interests could lead to win–win 'expand-the-pie' solutions.

- *Options/alternatives:* Once the parties in a negotiation know more about each other's interests, they can begin to explore more productively a range of possible options. Brainstorming solutions plays a major role in mediation, and the mediator may choose to meet privately with each party to discuss options, or generate options in a plenary session with all participants present, or do some of each. In any case, the ground rules are the same: everyone is permitted to float ideas and propose solutions without being committed to them, or even necessarily supporting them. I often tell people in mediations that generating a very broad, creative range of options – including even some bad or outlandish options – is useful because in our reactions to unattractive options, we might learn more about our underlying interests, concerns and goals.

In mediation, we use the term 'options' to mean settlement terms that the participants can agree on at the bargaining table – as distinct from 'alternatives', which are the solutions available away from the bargaining table. For example, if family members are joint owners of real estate and one family member wants to convert his/her stake in the property to cash, one option would be a buy-out of that family member by the other members of the family. Another option might be looking for a third-party investor to purchase the withdrawing person's share. If the family members are unable to agree on any of the available options, the withdrawing family member might consider the alternative of filing a lawsuit, seeking a judicially ordered sale of the property.

Fisher, Ury and Patton, in *Getting to Yes*, introduced the idea that effective bargainers need to compare the available options to their "best alternative to a negotiated agreement" (their 'BATNA'), and mediators can help the participants, individually and collectively, to make this comparison.

Although my mantra as a mediator – story, interests, options/alternatives – seems

5 Roger Fisher, Bill Ury and Bruce Patton, *Getting to Yes: Negotiating Agreement Without Giving In* (1981).

to be sequential, there is no required order. As mediator Brad Honoroff once noted, "Mediations have a beginning, a middle, and an end, but not necessarily in that order."

One of the important features of the mediation process is that, in most cases, the ground rules – established by an agreement to mediate signed by all participants – permit the mediator to speak with everyone together, or one-on-one, or in subgroups. The mediator, in consultation with the parties, decides which of these formats (joint sessions, private caucus sessions, or various hybrids) will be most useful at each point along the way in the mediation. In my own work, I usually meet with everyone together initially to describe the mediation process and the scope of the mediation (ie, the issues to be addressed), meet with the participants individually at least once and then, from there, use a combination of joint and separate sessions depending on the topic to be discussed and each participant's level of comfort discussing that topic with others present. In striking the balance between separate and joint sessions, the mediator is trying to promote both candour (which is sometimes easier in separate sessions) and communication (which usually requires joint sessions).

2.4 What are the ground rules?

Each mediator has his/her own form of an agreement to mediate, but the most common features are the following:

- Participation is voluntary. Any participant can choose to withdraw from the mediation at any time.
- The process is confidential. The participants and the mediator agree not to disclose the substance of their discussions with anyone other than a specified list of need-to-know people (such as lawyers, accountants, spouses, etc).
- The process is essentially forward-looking. Discussions about the past are welcome, and often necessary, but the main focus of discussion is what lies ahead. (This, I point out, is why car windscreens are bigger than rear-view mirrors.)
- There is a division of responsibility in which the parties are ultimately responsible for the substantive decisions about settlement, and the mediator is responsible for managing the decisions about the mediation process, such as making sure that everyone gets 'airtime' in the discussions.
- Occasionally, mediators will help the parties develop a set of communications guidelines that foster mutual respect.

2.5 How does mediation differ from other processes?

When members of a family business sense that third-party involvement and expertise are needed, they have a range of options to choose from: facilitators, mediators and family business consultants.

Facilitators help run meetings. They do not need in-depth substantive knowledge of the business, and they may be hired for one or more meetings. Their role is to help participants have a productive discussion and enforce guidelines about participation. Facilitators are hired for their process skill. And, while some facilitators become long-term participants in periodic family business meetings, sometimes they are hired just once to help with a particularly challenging meeting.

At the other end of the spectrum, family business consultants and advisers are often hired for in-depth, long-term involvement with the family business. They typically have expertise in both the psychological and business-management aspects of the family business enterprises that hire them. One of the distinguishing characteristics of the best consultants is their expertise in family systems analysis.

Mediators occupy a middle ground between these two poles. Mediators are usually brought into family business discussions to help the participants address a specific conflict, challenge or opportunity. Unlike facilitators, who generally meet with everyone together, mediators use a variety of meeting structures – sometimes meeting with participants separately on a confidential basis to learn about their individual interests and perspectives, and sometimes meeting with everyone together or with subgroups – with the goal of trying to identify some common ground. Mediators also get more involved than facilitators in substantive problem solving and in developing options.

Unlike family business consultants, mediators do not ordinarily give advice or make recommendations. Ethical rules governing mediation vary from one jurisdiction to another, but most prohibit mediators from providing professional services, such as law or therapy, in a mediation even if they are licensed in those professions. Also, unlike consultants, mediators usually do not take on long-term roles in a family enterprise.

One of the valuable services that mediators (along with consultants, facilitators and other family business professionals) can provide is triage – ie, serving as process experts who advise the family business on what services are most needed and most appropriate. For example, if one of the issues that the enterprise is struggling with is business valuation, a mediator can facilitate the negotiation of an appraisal process. Or there may be a legal issue, and the mediator can facilitate the process of getting unbiased legal advice for the enterprise.

Many mediators are generalists, working with many kinds of conflict. Even those who focus on family business conflicts may work with a wide variety of industries and work with both large and small enterprises.

3. How to select a mediator

The three most important characteristics are competence, chemistry and tenacity:

- *Competence*, of course, has multiple components. Does the candidate have experience with family business conflicts, and if so, how much experience? Are there lawyers or mediation participants who can vouch for the mediator's skill in the family business arena? Participants in a family business dispute often assume that the mediator must have industry-specific knowledge. For example, in one family business dispute involving the ownership of a hotel, the participants wanted to know how much experience I had in the hospitality industry; but the success of the mediation depended far more on my process skills than my industry expertise.
- *Chemistry* is hard to quantify, but (to paraphrase US Supreme Court Justice

Potter Stewart) "you know it when you see it" – or, to be more accurate, feel it. Hiring a mediator for a family business dispute is a bit like hiring a therapist or business adviser. Qualifications are usually not the deciding factor if the interpersonal connection does not feel right. With multiple family members trying to select a mediator, this can be complicated: Some family members might be looking for sensitivity to nuance, and others might be looking for a blunt, brass-tacks approach. (Of course, these two traits are not always mutually exclusive.) A mediator might not match everyone's preference perfectly, but the selection is not irrevocable. Some families try one mediator, and then move on to work with another. That said, choosing the wrong mediator can be costly, because the new mediator will have to be educated about the family, the business and the conflict.

- *Tenacity* is, like chemistry – ie, hard to measure. However, in interviewing potential mediators one can ask about their experience in their most difficult cases. Often, the best guidance for mediator selection comes from the people who have used the mediator's services. Although mediators are not usually at liberty to provide potential clients with the names of past clients, mediators can provide the names of lawyers who have been involved in their cases. From the lawyers' standpoint, tenacity is important because many lawyers tend to equate success in mediation with the mediator's settlement rate (as opposed to whether the parties reached a new level of mutual understanding but no settlement).

One option to consider in choosing a mediator for a family business conflict is whether the situation warrants the use of co-mediators. In commercial mediation, the parties to the conflict and their counsel usually opt for a single mediator. However, in family business conflicts, where communication and relationship issues introduce psychological elements to the conflict, it is not uncommon for two mediators to be used – often, the combination is one psychologist–mediator and one lawyer–mediator. The mediators work side by side, helping to manage the negotiation together but bringing somewhat different perspectives and skills to the table. If the participants prefer to hire just one mediator, and that mediator does not have psychological training, s/he should at least be someone with a high level of emotional intelligence.

4. The role of lawyers

In high-stakes family business disputes, it is not uncommon for lawyers to be involved. There may be one or more lawyers who work for the enterprise, and sometimes individual family members have their own lawyers. Access to legal advice is critical in some cases in order for the parties to be able to give informed consent to whatever deal is on the table for discussion. The risk, of course, is that the lawyers could go overboard and become needlessly adversarial. Thus, care in the selection of lawyers is important.[6]

In most family businesses, there is already a lawyer in place who has been

6 See John Talvachia, "Effective Legal Representation of Family Firm Clients" in Richard L Narva (ed), *Family Enterprise: How to Build Growth, Family Control and Family Harmony*, Globe Law and Publishing, 2015.

advising the enterprise for years. When conflicts arise, family dissidents may view this lawyer as partisan – ie, supporting the non-dissident family members. Accordingly, there are some situations where that lawyer can best serve the enterprise by recusing herself or himself from the conflict, even though the lawyer could add value by virtue of his/her familiarity with the enterprise and its history.

Another problem that frequently arises when several lawyers have been hired by various parties is that some lawyers may see their main job as adversarial advocacy while others see their job as interest-based problem solving. Adversarial lawyers usually evoke an adversarial response, and this can escalate the conflict. Mediators can sometimes get the lawyers onto the same page, and foster moderation among the more adversarial of the lawyers – but not always.

One technique that participants in a family business conflict can use is to hire the lawyers jointly. This could be done by having the family members interview all of the candidates who are interested in serving as counsel to one or more of the parties, and then the family members decide together which lawyers to hire and whom they will represent. By interviewing and hiring lawyers in this unconventional way, family members can feel more confident that the tenor of the negotiations will not sink to the lowest common denominator of adversarial activity, and that all of the lawyers support the family's goal of an amicable settlement. Mediators can also be a good resource for lawyer referrals, because they have seen numerous lawyers in action and can recommend those who have good track records at resolving conflicts constructively.

When lawyers are involved in family business mediation, the clients need to decide how involved they want their lawyers to be – in other words, will the lawyers attend every mediation session, or only a few that might involve legal issues; or will the lawyers be involved solely as consultants coaching from the sidelines and not attending the mediation sessions?

In some cases, one family member may feel that he/she wants to have his/her lawyer present, while other family members prefer not to have their lawyers present. This difference may be related to cost considerations or concern about levelling the playing field if one party feels less skilful as a negotiator. While there is no rule in mediation requiring all parties to have lawyers with them, if some do, it is essential that all participants in the mediation feel that they have the advice and support that they need in order to participate.

5. Advantages and disadvantages of mediation

From the standpoint of family business conflict, mediation offers a number of advantages. In cases where miscommunication contributes to conflict, mediators can provide coaching and serve as referees to enforce ground rules for discussion. In my experience, people generally behave (and negotiate) more reasonably when a disinterested third party is observing. (This is akin to the 'Hawthorne effect' that sociologists have established.[7]) After helping the participants better understand each

7 See Daniel Bowling and David Hoffman, "Bringing Peace into the Room", 16 *Negotiation Journal* 5, 10 (2000).

participant's underlying interests, mediators can help the family generate options, and focus on those options that best match the identified interests.

Mediators can also serve as deal brokers, speaking confidentially to individual participants, or to small groups of them, testing the waters with hypothetical proposals and thus determining whether there is a zone of possible agreement. For example, in one family business dispute involving two brothers who co-owned a mail-order business, it was clear from their history of conflict and their inability to leave past grievances behind that one of the brothers needed to assume full control of the business and begin a buy-out of the other brother's interests in the company. As their mediator, I was able to find out – confidentially, in separate meetings with each brother – how much money each would insist on as the price for withdrawal, and an agreement was reached.

Mediation holds four principal advantages over resolving disputes in court – although in many cases the choice is not mediation as opposed to litigation, but mediation as opposed to trying to manage conflict without the help of a third party. The principal advantages are:

- privacy – the parties' communications are protected by a legal privilege (similar to attorney–client privilege) in most jurisdictions;
- choice of mediator – as opposed to the random assignment to a judge or even greater uncertainties associated with a jury trial;
- speed – litigation can take years; and
- cost – mediation is almost always less costly than proceeding in court.

Among the disadvantages of hiring a mediator is the investment of time and effort. Time spent in mediation could be more profitably spent tending to the business. The mediator needs to become educated about the conflict, and, although lawyers can help, the need for direct involvement of the principals is unavoidable. In addition, there can be an emotional cost in addressing the emotional and psychological dimensions of the conflict. Even though the mediation process may be covered by legal privilege, many families find it uncomfortable airing all of their 'dirty linen' in front of an outsider. Some families may wonder whether mediation could actually worsen their situation by bringing painfully to the surface certain complaints and resentments that have been festering for years. Just as surgery may involve grave risk for the patient, so too with mediation, which might open wounds that will take a long time to heal and could complicate the task of focusing on a business's day-to-day operations.

In weighing the costs and benefits of using mediation, it is worth considering that the interests of the family as a whole may differ from those of individual family members. For example, in a recent family business mediation, it was clear that the family had suffered such a severe breakdown in communication that mediation was needed in order to keep the family's extensive investments in real estate from imploding. Even so, two of the 30 family members were so mistrustful of other family members (based on past conflicts) that they needed to be persuaded that mediation was worth the effort in the interests of all.

Because mediation is a voluntary process and not an irrevocable commitment, one option is to try mediation and then evaluate the experience. For most family businesses, mediation is an unfamiliar process; and a certain 'negativity bias' often colours our reactions to anything unfamiliar.[8] Most mediators are willing to participate in one meeting or mediation session without any obligation on the part of the clients to continuing the mediation, or continuing to use that mediator.

6. Myths about mediation

There are three particular myths about mediation that are worthy of note here:

- *Myth Number One: "If I agree to mediate, that would be viewed as a sign of weakness."* Conflicts often generate a phenomenon that psychologists call 'competitive arousal'. The phenomenon is illustrated in a *New Yorker* cartoon, in which two dogs, dressed in suits and drinking martinis, are standing at a downtown bar. "It's not enough that dogs succeed," says one. "Cats must also fail."[9] Especially in the US, the so-called 'argument culture' described by sociologist Deborah Tannen causes compromise to have a bad name.[10]

  However, mediation has become a ubiquitous feature of the business world in recent years. More than 4,000 large corporations have pledged that they will consider mediation before going to court.[11] Mediation statutes exist in every state in the US and most other countries. In other words, mediation is becoming a normal part of 'business as usual' when conflicts arise. Moreover, the proponent of mediation may, paradoxically, be perceived as coming from a position of strength if s/he genuinely wants to hear other perspectives before making a decision.
- *Myth Number Two: "Mediators just split the baby – we don't need to hire someone to do that."*

  Because mediators lack the decision-making authority of arbitrators, there is no baby for them to split.[12] If this myth is about mediators simply trying to herd people toward the middle, that may be true of inexperienced or inept mediators. The better sort are looking for opportunities to match differing needs and preferences so as to expand the pie (as in the conflict, described in section 2.3 above, over the division of an orange).
- *Myth Number Three: "If mediation isn't binding, what's the point?"*

  The fact that mediators cannot compel a resolution (and the parties retain 100% of the power over such decisions) is, as the computer geeks say, not a bug – it's a feature! The purpose of mediation is to identify options that work better for the participants than the *status quo* or alternatives available away from the bargaining table. If such mutually agreeable options cannot be identified, the wise choice for the participants is not to settle. The underlying concern that gives rise to this myth is the fear that one or more participants

---

8 See David Hoffman and Richard Wolman, "The Psychology of Mediation", 14 *Cardozo L Rev* 759, 789 (2013).

9 *New Yorker*, 13 January 1997.

10 See generally Deborah Tannen, *Argument Culture: Stopping America's War of Words* (1999).

11 See the website for the International Institute for Conflict Prevention and Resolution: www.cpradr.org/PracticeAreas/ADRPledges/CorporatePledgeSigners.aspx.

12 This is a biblical reference to King Solomon of Israel. See I Kings chapter 3 verses 16–28.

will not participate in good faith – ie, they might use the mediation simply to stall or stonewall – and that is a legitimate concern. Mediation participants should discuss with each other, and the mediator, their willingness to settle before investing in extensive mediated negotiations.

7. Beyond the basics (1): the emotional dimensions of mediation

In some cases, mediators are primarily deal brokers – for example, in disputes where there is no past relationship and no likelihood of an ongoing relationship, such as an accident involving a vehicle. In those cases, the issues are mostly monetary (how much compensation will be paid, on what schedule, etc). The negotiation is essentially a distributive zero-sum problem, where the only common interest is the reduction of the transaction costs associated with litigation. Mediators can add value in such settings by helping the parties assess their options and alternatives in a realistic way. The parties may have highly emotional reactions to each other's settlement proposals, and part of the mediator's job is to help the parties manage their emotions. Even so, at the end of the day the main issue boils down to money.

At the other end of the spectrum, mediators handle some cases that are primarily about managing relationships, such as when divorced parents are in conflict over how to raise their children or how to allocate parenting responsibilities. The parents have a common interest in reducing the transaction costs, but more importantly they share an interest in their children's well-being. Mediators can add value by improving the parties' communications with each other. The success of the mediation will be measured by the degree of improvement in the parents' future working relationship.

Family business conflicts occupy a middle ground between these two poles: relationships matter a great deal, as do financial concerns. In deciding, for example, whether the next chief executive officer (CEO) of a family enterprise will be a family member or someone else, feelings matter as do bottom-line results. In this setting, mediators face the dauntingly complex job of managing both the emotional dimensions of the conflict and the business dimensions, and the degree of success will be measured both in the bottom line and in the quality of family relationships.

Mediators use many techniques for helping participants manage emotions in the mediation process. Providing the participants with private-caucus venting opportunities can help, although the scientific literature suggests that too much venting simply reinforces the anger that the mediator is hoping to dissipate. These separate meetings also create opportunities for mediators to develop more personal connections with the participants, because they tell the mediator in less guarded ways what is at stake for them in the conflict. These private-caucus sessions are useful from the standpoint of brokered deal-making by the mediator, and they can serve the goal of preparing the way for more effective communication among the participants.

The importance of emotion in family business mediation cannot be overstated. It lies at the core of what drives most conflicts in that setting. During the years after the publication of *Getting to Yes*, mediators tried to use the principles of interest-based bargaining as a way of managing the intense emotions that arise in conflicts. The premise of the *Getting to Yes* model is that people will act in their own rational self-interest if we can help them discern it. However, there is abundant evidence that even ordinary day-to-day decision-making is largely driven by emotion rather than rationality.[13] And when people are in conflict, their thinking becomes even more prone to cognitive biases and the distorting influence of emotion.

A good example of this phenomenon can be seen in what is known as the 'Ultimatum Game', a game-theory experiment that shows that people in every known culture of the world will turn down free money if, in a proposed deal, the other player receives substantially more.[14] The ground rules of the game are simple. One person (called the proposer) is given $100, but only on the following conditions: the proposer has to offer a portion of it to the person sitting next to him/her (called the responder), and the responder (who knows about the $100 and the ground rules) has to accept the proposed division of the $100 (but not necessarily the money). In theory, the responder should accept any proposed amount, no matter how small, because he/she would be better off with even a cent, even if that meant the proposer kept $99.99. In fact, most people in the role of proposer offer between $40 and $50, and their proposals are almost always accepted. But some proposers offer very little, and the majority of responders reject any amount that is less than $20 even though turning down the money is not in their best interests from a purely rational economic standpoint.[15]

In mediations, the parties often turn down offers that would make them objectively better off than their alternatives (such as going to court) because the proposed division of available resources seems unfair, as measured by what the other party is getting. In the Ultimatum Game, responders punish ungenerous proposers but, in doing so, unavoidably punish themselves. In short, people are not ruled entirely by economic self-interest. When one of the parties in a mediation refuses a reasonable offer "on principle", this innate sense of fairness may be at work. (Interestingly, this phenomenon is not limited to humans; in experiments in which two dogs could see that one was receiving significantly more doggie treats as a reward for performing a task, the short-changed dog stopped performing.[16])

Fortunately, neuroscientists have found that there are other circuits in our brains that light up with pleasure when we cooperate (coexisting with the circuits that indicate pleasure when we best our opponents).[17] Mediators can reinforce the cooperative impulses by asking the parties whether they would feel good about a settlement in which each party had been equally accommodating. Mediators can also reinforce the view that fairness is unavoidably subjective, and the other side might have its own quite different view of what would be fair.

One of the major social psychology principles at work in conflict situations is the

---

13 See generally Dan Ariely, *Predictably Irrational* (2008); Jonah Lehrer, How We Decide (2009); Daniel Kahnemann, *Thinking, Fast and Slow* (2011); and Jonathan Haidt, *The Righteous Mind* (2012).

14 The discussion is this paragraph and the next two paragraphs first appeared in David Hoffman and Richard Wolman, "The Psychology of Mediation," 14 *Cardozo L Rev* 759, 795 (2013).

15 See Alan G Sanfey, James K Rilling, Jessica A Aronson, Leigh E Nystrom and Jonathan D Cohen, "The Neural Basis of Economic Decision-Making in the Ultimatum Game," 300 *Science* 1755 (2003).

16 See Friederike Range et al, "The Absence of Reward Induces Inequity Aversion in Dogs", 2008 *Proceedings of the National Academy of Sciences*.

17 See Louise Knapp, "Study: Brains Want to Cooperate", Wired (24 July 2002) (available at http://xrl.us/bpzsvm).

principle of reciprocity,[18] and it is deeply ingrained in us. Social scientists have begun to demonstrate that human evolution has played a role in reinforcing norms of fairness and reciprocity.[19] Accordingly, mediators may be swimming upstream when they try to persuade people to abandon their 'gut instinct' about what's fair, based on purely economic criteria of what is in their best interests.

A more promising approach to dealing with emotional reactions to conflict can be found in the Internal Family Systems (IFS) model pioneered by psychologist Richard Schwartz.[20] In that model, as applied to mediation, people are encouraged to explore those elements of their psyche that come to the fore in a negotiation – rather than treating the person's emotions as a unitary phenomenon. For example, each of us has a part of our psyche that fears being mistreated, perhaps harking back to an experience in the school playground of our youth. We may have another part that is good at managing our money, balancing our bank current account and making wise choices when we go shopping. There may be other, more impulsive, parts that lead us to make poor shopping choices. And there may be yet other parts that yearn for reconnection with family members with whom we are in conflict.

In the IFS model, people are encouraged to find an inner mediator (so-called 'self' energy, in the parlance of the model) to assist these various parts to act in harmony. One of the benefits of the IFS model is the recognition that there are no 'bad' parts – all of them serve us, or can be guided towards serving us, in productive ways in certain settings. For example, the part of us that fears mistreatment can by over-stimulated and hyperactive in some settings and thus stand in our way; but when it plays a more appropriate role in our internal system, it serves us by being vigilant and also noticing (altruistically) the mistreatment of others.

The goal of the IFS model is to help people become 'self-led'. The self in this model is that part of our psyche that is calm, curious, centred, and free of agenda other than healing. One of the metaphors that Schwartz uses in describing self energy is the conductor in an orchestra: all of the performers are needed but they need to be working in harmony, and if any one of them is hyperactive, or (worse) tries to take over conducting the orchestra, havoc will ensue.

One of the mediation techniques that can help people identify parts of their psyche and speak for them (rather than from those parts) is to ask people to write down the views of that part regarding settlement. So, for example, a mediation participant could be asked to write the advantages and disadvantages of a particular settlement from the vantage point of his/her wealth-maximising part. S/he could be asked to do the same exercise, on a separate page, from the vantage point of an angry part, and maybe one more page on behalf of a part that longs for reconnection. These are just examples (because the participants may have parts other than these that have been activated by the conflict), but the exercise has the following effect: the act of writing enables people to take a step back from their visceral reactions and to take time to

18 See generally Robert Cialdini, *Influence: The Psychology of Persuasion*, chapter 2 (1998).
19 See, eg, Martin Novak, "Five Rules for the Evolution of Cooperation", 314 *Science* 1560 (2006).
20 For an excellent discussion of the IFS model, see Richard Schwartz, *Introduction to the Internal Family Systems Model* (2001). See also David Hoffman, "Mediation, Multiple Minds, and Managing the Negotiation Within", 16 *Harv Negot L Rev* 297 (2011).

examine them. To use the parlance of Daniel Kahnemann's book *Thinking, Fast and Slow,*[21] writing helps people shift from highly emotional, fast-track 'System-1' thinking to the slower, more deliberate, and more rational patterns of 'System-2' thinking.

Of course, to elicit self energy and self-leadership in the people that mediators work with compels the mediator to be aware of, and manage, his/her own out-of-kilter parts. Mediating in a family business can be especially evocative for mediators because of parts of their psyche that developed in them as a result of their own family experiences.

8. Beyond the basics (2): styles of mediation

The scholarly and practice-oriented literature of mediation focuses on the following styles: facilitative, evaluative/directive, and transformative.[22] Although, as in any field of endeavour, there are purists who espouse a particular style of mediation and use no other, many mediators would describe their styles as eclectic. For example, some commercial mediators move from a facilitative style at the beginning of a mediation (as they are learning about the case and the parties and starting to build trust) to a more evaluative/directive style if the parties need some measure of pressure to prevent an impasse, while at the same time being alert for transformative moments that might in some cases lead to settlement.

8.1 Facilitative mediation

Mediators who use a facilitative style are not seeking to direct the outcome, but only to enable the parties to reach an outcome that meets their needs and goals.[23] These mediators resist answering the following types of questions from the parties (which are common):

- What do you think we should do?
- What do most people do?
- What would a court do?
- What do you think is fair?

Facilitative mediators believe that they are responsible for the effectiveness and integrity of the process, but the parties are responsible for the substantive outcome. A facilitative style of mediation is commonly seen in community mediation programmes, where the mediators come from a variety of professional backgrounds and there are fewer lawyers serving as mediators.

8.2 Evaluative/directive mediation

Evaluative/directive styles of mediation are commonly found among mediators who are former judges and, in some instances, lawyers.

An evaluative style of mediation can range from its starkest extreme, in which

21 Daniel Kahnemann, *Thinking, Fast and Slow* (2011).

22 This section is taken from David Hoffman, *Mediation: A Practice Guide for Mediators, Lawyers, and Other Professionals* (2013), sections 1.7.1–1.7.3.

23 See, eg, Leonard Riskin, "Understanding Mediators' Orientations, Strategies, and Techniques: A Grid for the Perplexed", 1 *Harv Negot L Rev* 7 (1996).

the mediator makes a prediction of what a court will do with the case or with a particular issue, to the more subtle end of the spectrum in which a mediator might ask probing questions designed to provide reality testing if the parties seem to be unduly optimistic about their likely outcome in court.

Directive mediators are more likely than facilitative mediators to help the parties generate options, formulate proposals, and even advocate for particular solutions.[24]

8.3 Transformative mediation

In 2004, mediators and scholars Robert A Baruch Bush and Joseph Folberg published the second edition of an influential book entitled *The Promise of Mediation: The Transformative Approach to Conflict*,[25] in which they argued that the goal of mediation should not be settlement but empowerment and recognition of the parties. They described their approach as transformative because the focus was on the power of the conflict resolution process to change the parties' perspectives, feelings about themselves, and feelings about the other parties.

Using a transformative style, mediators allow the parties to determine not only the outcome of the dispute but also the process. A significant number of mediators in the US, though far from a majority, have adopted this style of mediation, and the US Postal Service calls for mediators in its REDRESS mediation programme, which handles internal conflicts among employees, to use this technique. Many mediators find that even if this is not their orientation, there are transformative moments in some mediations – for example, moments in which a genuine and spontaneous apology reconnects the parties in a profound way.

9. Conflict as opportunity

Conflict is inevitable in any family business. Conflict fosters change, and any system in which conflict is suppressed may stagnate. Mary Parker Follett, an early negotiation theorist, said that "all polishing is accomplished through friction".[26] And US President John F Kennedy sounded a similar theme in his oft-quoted statement that "when written in Chinese, the word 'crisis' is composed of two characters. One represents danger and the other represents opportunity".[27]

Successful management of conflict is not inevitable and requires thoughtful choices. One option for family enterprises is to include mediation clauses in the company's operating agreements, requiring the use of mediation before any member of the enterprise pursues litigation.

10. Conclusion

When conflicts emerge in family businesses, the use of outside resources is sometimes needed, and this chapter has discussed some of the available options for such help, ranging from facilitators to mediators to family business consultants.

---

24 See, eg, Marjorie Corman Aaron and Dwight Golann, "Merits Barriers: Evaluation and Decision Analysis" in Dwight Golann (ed), *Mediating Legal Disputes: Effective Strategies for Neutrals and Advocates* (2009).

25 Revised edition published by Jossey-Bass in 2004.

26 Pauline Graham (ed), *Mary Parker Follett: Prophet of Management* (1995), p68.

27 Remarks at the Convocation of the United Negro College Fund, Indianapolis, Indiana, 12 April 1959.

Mediation is an underutilised, but highly effective, tool in resolving family business conflicts. It is a voluntary process that builds on the insights about interest-based bargaining that were developed in *Getting to Yes*, and adds tools such as active listening, reframing and private caucusing to repair relationships and generate sound business options.

Family business turnarounds: non-financial fixes are the key

Gerald Sherman
Pathway Advisors LLC

1. Introduction

I sat in a client's conference room when he called his advertising agency to ask that they pull the coming weekend's advertisement for his family's furniture and appliance store. Midway through the call he broke down in tears as he told the account manager to design an ad for the store's "going out of business sale". Having run the company for the last 30 years with his brother, they had just lost too much money. It was the end of the business their father started 48 years before. On another day, I sat around the table with members of the fifth and sixth generation of a 135-year-old manufacturing company when the decision was made to sell what remained of the family business. Decades of decline had taken their toll.

Both companies had enjoyed many years of success and had a significant presence in their respective markets. The appliance store was one of two iconic locally owned retailers in their mid-sized northeastern US city, and the manufacturer was just one of several major producers that served a highly specialised niche of replacement equipment for paper mills. Furthermore, the family members of both companies were recognised as smart, hard-working and good people.

So what went wrong? What if the founders had fully appreciated the depth of training the next generation would need to competently assume control? What if the families had found more effective ways to work together? What if the family members had recognised the need to prepare for major shifts in the nature of their industry? The questions were virtually endless.

Since 1983, about half of the 350 or so underperforming and financially troubled companies I've worked with have been family owned. They've ranged in size from US$5 million in annual sales to more than US$250 million; they have operated in scores of industries and spanned the United States. The degree of financial difficulty I've addressed has ranged from companies whose profits were declining and debt was increasing, to those facing heavy losses, severe cash flow shortfalls and the likelihood of insolvency.

Regardless of these circumstances, my viewpoint has always been that financial difficulties are symptomatic of much more fundamental issues. Furthermore, I've found that troubled family businesses almost invariably struggle with the same constellation of core non-financial challenges:

- family dynamics/dysfunction;
- a flawed chief executive officer (CEO);
- flawed decision-making processes;

- underdeveloped organisational and administrative practices; and
- underdeveloped family management practices.

Furthermore, I've seen that the most significant failing of many, if not most, family business turnaround efforts has been that these non-financial issues are often given relatively little, if any, real attention.

This chapter explores these five fundamental non-financial challenges in depth and will present strategies to initiate and foster a successful family business turnaround effort. Together with sufficient progress financially, every family that makes an effort to address these non-financial challenges can significantly enhance the potential for taking their troubled company and restoring its prospects for being a strong multi-generational asset.

2. Background

I grew up in a family business environment where my father and his brother had been partners in a distribution company for 10 years when I was born. While I wanted to join the business when I graduated from college, my father actually discouraged me. He believed the business was in a dying industry – shoe manufacturing in the US – and he told me he didn't want to see his son spending his days in dirty factories working as a salesman like he did. It took me many years to understand his wisdom about my future. It's also very important to note that when my father passed away, I learned that my uncle's family held a deep resentment towards him. I had no idea. The issue was that my father, a Russian immigrant and the youngest of eight children, was the family's first college graduate and he regularly demeaned his brother's ability in helping to manage the business. Looking back, I understand why our families rarely socialised.

Before graduate school, I worked for a large consulting firm that was focused on Fortune 500 and governmental clients, and I thrived on both the challenge and the variety. Then, after completing an MBA, I began my career as a commercial banker with the belief that the experience would be an excellent foundation for my future – and it was! During my six years in the industry, I became a specialist in lending to the weakest companies that still qualified for bank financing. Then, with the experience and contacts I had developed, I left and started a consulting practice that quickly became focused on helping underperforming and troubled companies.

As I developed my consulting skills, I had four formative experiences that shaped my beliefs about why a family business falls into trouble and helped me understand what strategies would be particularly important for a successful family business turnaround. These are as follows and are described further below:

- working extensively on site;
- working with a trained family clinician;
- working with behavioural assessment instruments; and
- developing a CEO database.

2.1 Working extensively on site

My substantial turnaround engagements often require me to spend the majority of my time on site – sometimes for more than a year. While I generally take on a number of responsibilities, two have been particularly meaningful. First, on many occasions I act as chairman of the 'executive committee', an *ad hoc* group of the senior managers responsible for every major functional area of the business: finance, marketing, sales, production, human resources etc. The CEO is always a member of the committee but typically cedes significant influence to me as chairman. On some occasions, when a defaulted bank insists, I become the chief restructuring officer and have virtually total control of the client. I also become the CEO's coach and mentor – to the degree he/she allows me to.

Coming from a background in commercial lending, where I was really on the outside looking in, this was the first time I had been down in the trenches. It was an enormous learning experience that allowed me to gain an understanding of both the families I worked with and their businesses. From my standpoint, I could not have gained these experiences in any other way. Being with these clients almost daily, I got to know them well and was able to observe their personalities, their professional strengths and weaknesses, their interactions with others and, typically, their family dynamics/dysfunction. My time with family member CEOs in particular has been invaluable.

2.2 Working with a trained family clinician

In 1991 I became chairman of one of these specially formed executive committees at a troubled company where the family was crippled by incessant conflict. For the two second-generation brothers and one brother-in-law who ran the business, heated battle was a regular event. The basic dynamic was easy to identify: the CEO and eldest brother always got what he wanted; his younger brother always supported him in the end, even if he outwardly disagreed; and the brother-in-law, who more often than not got it right as I saw it, was always overruled. Despite this, the brother-in-law was a fighter and refused to just give in easily. Needless to say, his persistence only made matters worse. As just one example of the challenges occurring in the business, I can highlight that while I was involved there was a pressing need to close unprofitable distribution centres; nonetheless, I was vehemently overridden by the two brothers despite both my role and the brother-in-law's well-founded objections.

Given this dynamic, there was little doubt in my mind that the company was going to fail. As a result, I found myself facing an ethical dilemma. Should I continue to take substantial fees while I believed I had little chance of being successful? Or, should I resign? While discussing the issue with several peers, one suggested that I contact a consulting group he knew that specialised in family business conflict resolution. The firm was one of the first to use a multidisciplinary methodology, and its underlying theory was simple: when working with a client where the family dynamics are highly problematic, two professionals are essential. The first needs to be a clinical professional trained in family dynamics and the second should be a business professional trained in management, financial and operational issues.

Eventually, I was able to bring one of the firm's clinicians into the case. Working together, we were able to help the family to both work together more effectively and stabilise the company financially. Did we fully resolve all of the family dysfunction?

Absolutely not! What we did accomplish, however, was to facilitate enough change in the family dynamics and management processes to allow for more-effective decisions to be made. As a result, the family stayed in business for another 15 years and then sold out successfully.

With the benefit of this experience, the clinician and I have worked together on about a dozen cases subsequently. We always begin by developing an extensive family history. The clinician focuses on developing a family history that examines the personalities, interpersonal relationships and significant events of the prior and current generations – for example, the divorce and remarriage of the founder, a feud between two prior-generation siblings or a debilitating illness of the current-generation's mother will sometimes have great significance with respect to the family's dysfunction. On a parallel track, I focus on:

- how the business was started;
- the personalities, strengths and weaknesses of the founding and successor generations (if any);
- the training of the founding and successor generations (if any);
- the evolution of the company's business activities;
- the evolution, or lack thereof, of the company's organisational, administrative and family management practices; and
- how successor generations (if any) were trained and selected.

This first step is central to working effectively with a family business because the issues that have to be addressed are always rooted in these histories, and the information they provide enables the clinician and me to develop significant insights into the family dynamics and management issues of the current generation. For example, the founder/CEO may have been a dogmatic and domineering personality with little concern about the thoughts or feelings of his siblings in the business. As a result, the successor generation may have had little, if any, exposure to the kind of constructive conversations that family members can have to resolve differences. Similarly, the founder/CEO may have been a driven salesperson with little interest in developing the rigorous administrative or family management practices that could have provided a sound foundation for successor generations to manage effectively.

Overall, my experiences working with a clinician have provided me with two critical business perspectives that are central to my work with financially troubled family businesses. First, I was able to observe that the inadequate organisational, administrative and family management practices of the current generation were typically rooted in the personalities, strengths and weaknesses of the prior and current-generation CEOs. Indeed, I was able to observe that the CEOs of troubled family businesses – most particularly the founders – primarily focus on selling and delivering their business's goods and services, and they pay significantly less attention to how the company is organised and administered. Secondly, I was able to recognise that I didn't have the training to help resolve significant family dysfunction. In saying this, I also need to make very clear my view of the clinician's goal when such a specialist works with me: the clinician's focus has to be helping the active family members become good business partners (not necessarily best friends). Given this, when I work with a troubled family business without the involvement of a clinician, while being very mindful of the impact of family dysfunction I focus my efforts largely on the critical financial- and management-driven issues that have to be resolved.

2.3 Working with behavioural assessment instruments

A behavioural assessment instrument is a highly sophisticated tool that can be used to develop insights about a prospective or current employee's personality traits and tendencies when working with others. Most typically, they're used for employee hiring and development purposes. Among the areas these tools can evaluate are self-awareness, leadership style, the ability to listen to and learn from others, decision-making processes, the ability to initiate and tolerate change, sales orientation and attention to detail.

Within the family business world, the behavioural assessment can help family members to:

- develop a better understanding of themselves;
- identify areas where additional support and training may help improve their job performance;
- develop a better understanding of one another; and
- develop ways to work together more effectively.

When a family is open to using these types of instrument, the insights I get invariably enhance my ability to be of help. However, even if I'm not using an assessment tool with a particular client, the understanding I gained by working with them always puts me in a better position to coach family members.

Several years ago, I found a particularly helpful assessment instrument that's built around the concept of emotional intelligence (known as 'EQ'). As succinctly described in the book *Emotional Intelligence 2.0*, EQ can be measured by looking at four behavioural characteristics as follows:

- *self-awareness:* the ability to accurately perceive your own emotions in the moment and understand your tendencies across situations;
- *self-management:* the ability to use your awareness of your emotions to stay flexible and direct your behaviour positively;
- *social awareness:* the ability to accurately pick up on the emotions in other people and understand what is truly going on with them; and
- *relationship management:* the ability to use the awareness of your own emotions and those of others to manage interactions positively.

The instrument to measure each of the four EQ components can be completed online in no more than 10 minutes, produces results virtually instantaneously and is made available to every purchaser of the book. Furthermore, the book provides strategies for improving weaknesses in each of the areas listed above and, for about US$20 in a hard-copy version, the instrument is accessible to all.

While extremely valuable to me when working with every active family member,

I've found the instrument particularly helpful when I'm working with the CEO. In virtually every instance, they're the dominant personality in the business and their behavioural characteristics – both strengths and weaknesses – have great significance with respect to the financial and non-financial issues being addressed. Furthermore, with even modest progress in several if not all of the EQ components, the CEO's effectiveness can be meaningfully improved. Conversely, little or no progress with any of these four components does not bode well.

2.4 Developing a CEO database

In 2009, I decided to compile a database in order to catalogue a large number of facts about 25 of the CEOs of underperforming and financially troubled family businesses I have worked with. I had no intention of developing statistically significant data; rather, my goal was to see whether my visceral observations about these CEOs would be confirmed.

The facts that I compiled for each CEO were as follows:

- their age at the time of their entry into the business;
- their age when they were named CEO;
- their highest level of education;
- if they attended, their major in college;
- the number of years they worked outside the family business prior to joining it;
- the highest level of responsibility they attained in a job prior to joining the family business;
- the average annual sales of the family business for the two years prior to experiencing significant financial difficulty;
- the number of years they worked in the family business before they became CEO;
- the area(s) of expertise they developed while working in the family business;
- the number of years they worked as CEO prior to the family business experiencing financial difficulty;
- the number of hours of outside professional education they participated in during the two years prior to experiencing financial difficulty;
- their participation in industry organisations;
- the generation number of the business they represented;
- the number of siblings they had in the business; and
- the number of family members they had in the business.

The facts detailed above that correlated most closely with experiencing financial difficulties were the number of years the CEO worked outside the business prior to joining, the level of responsibility attained in a job prior to joining the family business, and the number of hours of professional education participated in during the two years prior to experiencing financial difficulty. In other words, the CEOs of underperforming and troubled family businesses tended to lack both vital experience and an interest in improving their skills through professional education.

To that point, when I begin a new engagement, an initial priority is to conduct one-on-one interviews with each family member in the business. In these interviews,

I always ask how much time they have spent in the prior 24 months attending professional education programmes. Typically, the answer is none – and my most memorable answer by far was when a second-generation son answered, "I haven't attended any classes but I have read two business books over the past 25 years."

3. Core non-financial challenges

Each of the formative experiences discussed above has helped shape my beliefs about why the five core challenges listed in section 1 above are so common in troubled family businesses and why they have such significance. Furthermore, it's very clear that these core challenges feed on and exacerbate one another.

Set out in the remainder of this section is further discussion of these challenges.

3.1 Family dynamics/dysfunction

The *Psychology Dictionary* begins its definition of 'dysfunctional family' as "[a] family showing impaired communications and relationships", and in many respects this is the essence of the issue. And how can significant dysfunction in a family business be distinguished from the normal disagreements and challenges that even the strongest of families will encounter? In my experience, dysfunction becomes significant when it prevents the family from consistently considering, making and implementing business decisions based largely on the business issues at hand. As just two examples, an underperforming child or sibling might not be held accountable for – or even made aware of – how the quality of their work is viewed, or a family member may be paid a salary far in excess of what the job would pay a non-family member.

With the family businesses I've worked with, no more than 15–20% have displayed dysfunction very openly. Rather, what I've more typically observed is a dominant and flawed CEO (see section 3.2 below) who usually gets his/her way, rendering other family members disempowered and unable to contribute to the extent of their abilities. As a result, these family members hold resentments that fester and grow, and the business loses the potential benefit of their contributions.

(a) An illustrative example

Sandy was a self-made man and serial entrepreneur. His first venture was building a chain of 10 vehicle dealerships, and during that time he also built a substantial investment real-estate portfolio. Then, at the age of 64, he started a specialist vehicle manufacturing business and built it into a US$135-million company within 15 years. He ruled with an iron fist and was an unrepentant micromanager whose style I called 'management by butting in'. Given his dominance as the CEO, his son, daughter and two sons-in-law in the business, as well as senior-level non-family members, felt entirely disempowered. Much more often than not, they knew what should be done – or at least that more research and discussion was needed. Over time, however, the successor-generation family members became both afraid to buck Sandy and totally disheartened. The one occasion that they were actually able to act on their own beliefs was when Sandy was out for six months with a life-threatening illness. When he returned, though, he reversed virtually every major decision that had been made by them. In my professional opinion Sandy was wrong every time.

I was brought in by the company's bank to evaluate the business. My manufacturing expert quickly determined that, among other things, massive manufacturing inefficiencies were driving costs 4–5% above where they should have been. Sandy disputed this vehemently and had no interest in considering our findings. In fact, he accused me of presenting these findings only because I "wanted a five-year contract" to remedy the problem. Furthermore, during my presentation to the bank, I reported that the company's profitability issues could largely be solved by improving efficiencies. Sandy's follow-up comment at the meeting was to tell the bank I was wrong – exactly what they didn't want to hear. Sandy was smart enough to know that but was incapable of accepting someone else's opinion; and to make matters worse, he just couldn't keep his mouth shut.

Shortly thereafter, to my great surprise, Sandy convinced another bank to take over the company's loan. With my encouragement, albeit still amazingly, Sandy's son called the prospective new bank and asked them not to make the loan. He knew that the only chance he had of initiating change was to have the current bank continue to exert pressure. Wanting the business, the new bank wouldn't comply with the son's request.

Sandy was also a screamer and regularly abused his family by his words. At a meeting I attended shortly before the new bank came in, Sandy started to scream at me uncontrollably – and from my standpoint, irrationally. My response was to tell him that while his family might choose to tolerate his outbursts, I wouldn't. I walked out and never looked back. While somewhat extreme, this is a classic example of a highly flawed and inflexible CEO disempowering the family, to the great detriment of the business.

(b) Another example

My favourite story about the disempowerment of a family member involves the son of a dominant and entirely unethical father. The company was suffering from severe cash-flow shortfalls and the father's complaint was always, "If the vendors just worked with me, everything would be fine." After living with this situation for more than a year yet being unable to do anything about it, the son had had enough. He got up at a meeting and, in response to his father yet again complaining about vendor cooperation, he said: "Dad, your definition of 'vendors working with you' is that they sell you stuff and you don't pay for it." Once he said this, he resigned.

3.2 A flawed CEO

The CEO database discussed in section 2.4 helped to identify the lack of appropriate experience and training as an indicator of future financial difficulty. How does this lack of experience show itself? The answer is everywhere, although not typically all within the same company. Quite frequently, the lack of experience is reflected in weak administrative and family management practices. On many occasions however, other areas are impacted just as significantly if not more so.

For example, I recently worked with a third-generation CEO who took direct responsibility for managing the development of his business's first 'direct to the consumer' website. This was a crucial initiative because internet sales had captured more than 50% of the market for their products. After a US$4 million investment and four years of work, the site generated less than US$550,000 during its first year of operation – far less than was needed. There's no doubt in my mind that the most significant reason for this failure was the CEO's total lack of experience or training in website development and marketing. Would US$2.5 million in sales during the same period have saved the company, or at least bought it more time? At a 70% contribution margin, the answer is "yes". Unfortunately, with the CEO's lack of experience and expertise, the company was simply not in a position to succeed.

Even more than inexperience and a lack of training, the most salient aspect of the flawed CEOs with whom I've worked is their ineffective and sometimes destructive behavioural characteristics. Indeed, in my experience the flawed CEO, far more often than not, is the single most significant reason that the business gets into financial trouble. In fairness, the current-generation CEO's performance issues are invariably rooted in experience levels and behavioural characteristics of the preceding generation or generations of CEOs.

And what are these problematic behavioural characteristics? The ones I most typically observe include:

- an inability to understand the impact of their behaviour on others;
- an inability to really listen to others;
- inflexibility;
- an aversion to change;
- difficulty establishing constructive relationships with the entire senior management team;
- an inclination towards either rapid or extremely slow decision-making; and
- a lack of financial restraint.

I should also note that these destructive characteristics have been identified on numerous occasions by various behavioural assessment tools I've used.

3.3 Flawed decision-making processes

Ultimately, the direction of every business, family owned or otherwise, is driven in many if not most respects by the major decisions that are made. In financially troubled family companies, the decision-making process is invariably flawed – sometimes catastrophically so.

On an overview basis, there are five reasons:

- Family concerns often override fundamental business factors.
- A dominant CEO simply gets his/her way. Indeed, the more vehement the CEO's position, the worse the decision tends to be.
- Many times, decisions are made without adequate information. More often than not, this is largely because the family has never learned how to investigate issues thoroughly.
- "We've always done it this way" is often the basis for decisions.
- There is what I call 'the non-decision decision' or the 'inertial guidance system'.

For the most part, these issues are a reflection of both family dysfunction and the lack of accountability that most troubled family businesses are plagued by.

3.4 Underdeveloped organisational and administrative practices

'Organisational and administrative practices' are meant to encompass all of the structures, processes and policies that every business needs to effectively manage its activities. In popular parlance, the quality of a company's organisational and administrative practices determines its ability to execute.

With respect to family businesses, underdeveloped administrative practices are typically a direct and very significant reflection of the inadequacies in the CEO's training and experience. Furthermore, I have no doubt that an inability to execute decisions severely diminishes the results of even the best strategies. To that point, there was a fascinating study published several years ago by Professor Peter Boyle of the University of Texas.[1] Professor Boyle conducted research for the purpose of identifying key factors that lead to businesses experiencing financial difficulty. His two key findings were as follows:

- "Business failure correlated with the internal environment of a company more than its external environment."
- "Solutions to internal problems are generally administrative, not strategic."

Clearly, Professor Boyle drew a direct connection between a company's weakness in administrative practices and the eventuality of encountering financial difficulties. My experience is largely consistent with his findings, and the key underdeveloped organisational and administrative practices I regularly observe are as set out under the five headings in the remainder of this section.

(a) Developing and maintaining a clear organisation chart

As is generally known, an organisation chart is a common-sense document that details the authority structure and reporting relationships between the various functional groups of a business – executive management, sales and marketing, accounting, operations, etc. Without a well-thought-out and clearly communicated organisational structure, the only result is inefficiency and confusion – and particularly so with larger companies.

I will always remember the day that I met with the dozen customer service representatives who worked at a new client. Before I began the engagement, I had been told by Cyrus, the third-generation CEO, that customer service was a major organisational bottleneck. In fact, he told me that the problem was so bad that the company's salespeople didn't want to solicit new customers because they knew customer service would be inadequate.

Getting into the issue, I started by asking the reps a simple question: "Who do you report to?" Various team members named four different people as the supervisor of the department. Imagine the confusion! In particular, team members were given mixed messages about what their work priorities should be. That was their life.

Notably, Cyrus was a graduate of one of the most prestigious graduate business schools in his country and yet, he adamantly refused to prepare an organisation

1 Peter Boyle, "Turnaround Strategies for Troubled Companies", *Journal of Small Business Management*, July 1995.

chart. His employees believed he wanted to have ultimate control over everything and didn't want anyone else to have too much authority. With respect to customer service problems specifically, Cyrus knew that on average his reps managed about 30% less in sales volume than his competitor's did. Furthermore, he also knew that this was costing him close to US$250,000 a year for additional staff. Nonetheless, he would not address the central issue of the confused authority structure and the mixed messages it created.

(b) Developing and maintaining consistent internal communications processes

Referring back to the definition of family dysfunction in the Psychology Dictionary, it is clear that impaired communications are characteristic of a dysfunctional family and, similarly, my experience shows impaired communications are also indicative of distressed family business. In particular, while consistent communication is invaluable at every level of a business, it is crucially important among executive-level family members. What are the primary reasons why poor communications are so common in distressed family businesses? I see three: the entire family's inexperience with effective administrative practices; a flawed CEO's behavioural characteristics; and general family dysfunction.

Here is an example of how pervasive and destructive poor communication can be. Ralph was the CEO of a family business client of mine that had 15 stores throughout the northeastern United States. Shortly after I was engaged, I asked how often Ralph held meetings with the store managers, and the answer was never. And then, to my amazement, I was told that Ralph had stopped the practice many years prior because he felt that the managers ganged up on him to talk about the problems they were having. Could there be a worse way to address his store managers' issues?

(c) Enforcing accountability throughout the organisation

'Accountability' is the simple concept that every executive and lower-level employee is expected to do what they are supposed to do when they are supposed to do it. Being realistic, this can't always be the case; and when it is not, the executive or lower-level employee should report the delay to the appropriate party and commit to a new completion date. When this does not happen consistently and there are no consequences, a business cannot maximise its potential.

Kevin, a family member, was responsible for preparing new product catalogues every several years. These catalogues typically required an investment of US$400,000 to US$500,000, were prepared in order to present the company's new products and were considered a crucial piece of his company's ongoing success. His performance actually became a family joke – he was always three to four months late and substantially over budget. As a result, the company was continually behind its competition with the fresh offerings that their industry demanded. Nonetheless, Kevin's poor performance was tolerated – and he wasn't even pressured in any meaningful way to do better. The family just wasn't able to call him to task. As a result, over time, they lost millions of desperately needed sales.

(d) *Developing and maintaining effective planning systems*

There are two key aspects of business planning: short-term, most typically for a year, and longer-term, most typically for two to five years. For internal purposes, a one-year plan should first and foremost be financial in nature. The company may or may not undertake new initiatives during the year, but the cost, timing and capacity to pay for them has to be reduced to numbers.

Typically, these one-year plans have one or more of four basic failings in troubled family businesses:

- the plans simply don't exist in any meaningful way;
- the plans are poorly prepared;
- the plans are over-optimistic; and/or
- the plans are not adhered to.

As for a longer-term plan, the failures are simpler. They generally don't exist in any meaningful way.

(e) *Developing and maintaining a strong human resource management system*

Most of my troubled family business clients have had, at best, poorly prepared job descriptions and little to no formal review process. Furthermore, measurable goals and objectives for either employees or family members were not typically established. Thirdly, troubled family businesses tend to offer little to no training to help employees, or family members for that matter, improve their skill levels.

Nonetheless, a common complaint I receive from clients is that their employees don't perform satisfactorily. From my standpoint, it's illogical to think that an employee can perform to their full capability if they don't explicitly know what their tasks are, what their perceived weaknesses are and what their goals are – and, finally, when they are not provided with adequate training to develop their skills.

3.5 Underdeveloped family management practices

Countless articles have been written over many decades with titles such as "Why Family Businesses Fail". Reasons that are typically cited include poor succession planning, inadequate governance practices, insufficient training of successor generations, little accountability for family members working in the business, and different visions occurring between generations.

Given this, it's quite fair to look at underdeveloped family management practices as the root cause of many family business difficulties. Most significantly, from my standpoint these deficiencies often lead to a poor or even disastrous choice of a successor CEO. At the same time, a narrow focus on underdeveloped family management practices, such as poor succession planning or inadequate governance, will not lead to a successful turnaround. In fact, immediate attention must first be given to the other core turnaround challenges discussed above.

4. Areas not perceived as core turnaround challenges

4.1 Strategy – a special case

Referring again to Professor Boyle's study, he states: "Solutions to internal problems are generally administrative, not strategic." Accordingly, and while it is perhaps counterintuitive, Professor Boyle found that poor strategy does not correlate with business failure as closely as administrative weaknesses do. Put another way, the effective execution of a strategy is generally more important than the strategy itself. My experience is consistent with these findings.

One significant exception to this finding, however, has become crucial since the study was completed in 1995: specifically, when a company's industry is experiencing a major transition. For example, the internet transformed many industries, and the transition of some retail segments to 'big box' stores did the same. In those cases, a company must shift its strategy or risk ultimate failure. It is important to note that such a strategy shift can be either subtle or visibly extreme. For example, a family-owned hardware store close to where I live in the US has continued to thrive despite the advent of Home Depot. Why? The family that owns the business refocused itself into becoming the area leader in customer service. Outwardly, the store looked the same and no substantial changes were made in its product offerings. The "customer experience", however, was greatly enhanced. Speaking for myself, I go to Home Depot to buy a commodity-like item at a low price; but I will always go to this neighbourhood store if I need advice about the best product to solve a particular problem. In effect, the family is now selling both a product and a service; and while the customer pays more, they still see themselves as getting good value.

Conversely, Netflix has totally changed how it delivers movies and other video content. Ten years ago, it shipped DVDs to its customers; today, Netflix delivers through the internet. More importantly, it made the shift proactively and, as a result, continues to be a growing business with a strong outlook.

4.2 The economy

My simple analysis is that even in the worst of times, the failure rate of businesses is still relatively low. It's not as if 50%, or even 10%, of companies fail during a recession – even an extreme one. Furthermore, the owners' responsibility is to position their company with the financial cushion needed to withstand declines. Accordingly, economic cycles should be viewed as a management issue – and a far from insurmountable one.

I should also note that companies become troubled throughout the economic cycle, again pointing to management as a more critical issue.

4.3 Capital

Another study of interest was conducted by Dr Robert Lussier of Springfield College.[2]

---

2 Robert Lussier, "A Non-financial Business Success versus Failure Prediction Model", *Journal of Small Business Management*, January 1995.

Dr Lussier conducted his research for the purpose of determining whether a model could be developed that could predict business success or failure with an acceptable level of reliability. Interestingly, capital levels proved to be a less reliable predictor than seven other variables, including effective planning, sound record-keeping, sound financial controls and the use of outside professional advisers.

My experience is consistent with Professor Lussier's findings and my viewpoint is that ownership's responsibility is to manage the company in a manner that is consistent with its capital levels.

5. Driving the turnaround process

True turnaround efforts don't occur spontaneously. Rather, there are always one or several factors that create the impetus for major change. And what are these factors? As a practical matter, they are numerous and can develop internally, externally or both. For example, an unhappy bank, persistently weak earnings or losses, significant industry changes or the general dissatisfaction of a few (or even all) of the family members can all motivate action. Regardless, every successful family business turnaround effort requires a rock-solid commitment by all family members. That's because to be successful, this will eventually require many, if not all, family members to approve and/or accept necessary business decisions that are uncomfortable, undesirable or both.

Set out in the remainder of this section are the steps required to implement a comprehensive turnaround effort. As a practical matter, though, while these steps are presented in a linear fashion that might work well, generally they occur somewhat simultaneously and from time to time a critical issue requiring immediate attention will surface regardless of any clear order for addressing issues that had previously been established.

5.1 The first phase: establishing a framework for managing the turnaround process

(a) Step 1: designating a change agent or change agent group

Going hand in glove with the commitment to change, a steady, insightful and resolute turnaround leader (or 'change agent') is also an absolute requirement. However, when a family member (or a group of family members) takes on this role, the job becomes more complex and the likelihood for success is, accordingly, compromised. Most particularly, the role calls for a decisive, direct leader, and a family member's effectiveness will often be impacted by non-business considerations. Secondly, a family member's experience with turnarounds will typically be limited, often creating an unachievable learning curve. In those instances, the support of the company's public accountant, or an appropriate independent board member if there is one, may be very helpful.

Given the factors detailed above, the benefit of a turnaround professional is clear. However, the involvement of a family therapist as part of a 'change agent group' from the outset of a turnaround is not quite as simple. The reasons for this include the cost, the time demands that the pure business issues place on the family members, and the resistance that family members often have to addressing difficult interpersonal issues. Given these considerations, a family therapist is rarely engaged when a turnaround effort is initiated, regardless of whether they could make a significant impact.

(b) ***Step 2: establishing an effective communication structure***

A successful turnaround process requires regular working sessions with all of the key family members, and the participation of senior-level non-family executives is also essential. That's simply because the numerous issues arising will demand a healthy dialogue about alternatives, methods for implementing change, cost and personnel implications, etc. Ideally, these meetings should be held at least twice weekly when the process is initiated. Furthermore, in order to maximise their effectiveness the meetings must be given virtually 100% precedence over both day-to-day business and personal matters.

(c) ***Step 3: establishing ground rules for decision-making***

To be effective, a family business turnaround must be based on two fundamental ground rules for decision-making.

First, all family members have to agree that the preservation of the business is the top priority. This is not to say that individual and family considerations should be disregarded; rather, it means that when difficult business decisions are made that negatively affect family members, every realistic effort will be made to help these members move forward, both financially and professionally.

The second ground rule to establish is how key decisions will be made. On many occasions, this can be the single most difficult issue that the family will deal with. In particular, a minority stockholder or stockholder group may view the majority stockholder or stockholder group as being the underlying problem. At the same time, it is unlikely that the majority stockholder or stockholder group will relinquish control. While a buy-out may be considered in this type of situation, in the author's experience it is rarely a realistic option. At a minimum, it is vitally important for all parties to agree to make a sincere effort to reach a consensus. In practice – and particularly when family dysfunction is a significant issue – the development of a true consensus will take considerable effort and may be impossible. The turnaround consultant or consulting team will often play a key role in facilitating a resolution in such instances.

5.2 The second phase: enhancing the performance of senior executives

The fate of every business, whether family owned or not, is ultimately driven by its people. For a family business, where the selection of key executives is often limited to family members, the need to maximise their performance is particularly crucial. Given the foregoing, in many respects the enhancement of family member competence is at the heart of the turnaround effort.

At the same time, this is often the most difficult turnaround challenge to address because of the complex family dynamics and individual behavioural characteristics that are involved. It should also be noted that while the performance of a flawed family CEO has been cited as one of the core non-financial issues in an underperforming family business, it's best to address CEO performance in the broader context of examining the competencies of all family members and senior non-family executives. By doing so, the performance issues of all of the major contributors are addressed and the CEO doesn't feel singled out.

There are a number of approaches to address these issues, the most significant of which are twofold: open discussions on both a group and one-to-one basis; and the use of various testing and survey instruments, including behavioural testing tools, 360-degree surveys and company surveys. Here, one or several skilled professionals beyond the turnaround consultant can be particularly valuable. They may include a family therapist and an expert in the administration and interpretation of the various testing and survey instruments that might be used.

Even so, through this process it is likely that a number of very difficult discussions will occur, along with individual soul-searching. Ultimately, one or several family members may have to accept a change in their role and/or title and have their compensation reduced in order to maximise the benefits of the turnaround effort. Furthermore, many (if not all) of the family members may have to commit themselves to participation in outside training programmes as a part of the process. This is where the family's commitment to change, and the strength and capability of the change agent or change agent group, will be truly tested.

5.3 The third phase: addressing financial, organisational and administrative issues

(a) *Step 1: developing a financial plan*

Near-term cash flow shortfalls, creditor demands and the implementation of cost-cutting measures, etc have to be given priority during the early stages of a turnaround. Having got beyond these initial challenges, if it is believed that the company is viable on a longer-term basis the focus should move to restoring both positive cash flow and profitability as quickly as possible.

Typically, the time frame for accomplishing these goals should be three to 24 months, depending on the circumstances. As the foundation for this effort, a detailed monthly plan for the first 12 to 24 months must be developed. Within the plan, every critical aspect of the business – spanning staffing levels, locations or divisions, and the financial aspects of new strategies – must be reflected.

(b) *Step 2: developing an execution plan*

An execution plan identifies the key elements of how the financial plan will be implemented. Importantly, the development of this plan is central to the turnaround effort because it provides the platform for rigorously addressing two of the core non-financial turnaround challenges: the flawed CEO and the upgrading of organisational and administrative practices.

While these two areas will typically be worked on simultaneously, addressing the flawed CEO and his/her specific roles, responsibilities, strengths, weaknesses and training needs is the first priority. First and foremost, the CEO must be willing to engage in an open discussion and make every effort to listen to the concerns and suggestions of other family members and advisers. When the CEO is open to using them, tools such as the EQ assessment instrument, discussed previously in section 2.3, can help substantially. In addition to the insights that the instrument can provide, it can also take these discussions beyond the realm of simply debating what the CEO does or does not do. The goal of this effort should to be re-craft the CEO's job description so that it focuses on his/her strengths, clarifies responsibilities and provides the CEO with a training agenda designed to help improve performance to the fullest extent possible. On a worst-case basis, it could be decided that it would be best for the CEO to transition into an entirely new position or to exit the company; but this is an exception for obvious reasons.

As discussed previously, the organisational and administrative practices that typically have to be addressed are the following:

- *Developing and maintaining a clear organisation chart:* This is perhaps the most challenging task when addressing organisational and administrative practices. That is because the roles and responsibilities of all the family members other than the CEO must be considered. Ultimately, clear job descriptions for key managers at every level of the company have to be specified as the key part of the effort.
- *Creating sound decision-making processes:* The organisation chart will spell out day-to-day authorities. Outside of that, a separate governance process must be developed that details how decisions on particular types of issue get made.
- *Developing and maintaining consistent internal communications processes:* The key component of this process is the meeting structure. Specifically, there should be a clearly articulated process that details when meetings are held, who runs them and who attends them. In addition, the process for maintaining and distributing meeting minutes should be specified.
- *Enforcing accountability throughout the organisation:* As discussed previously, 'accountability' is the simple concept that every executive and lower-level employee complies with what is expected of them. 'Enforcement' considers the consequences when employees at all levels of the company fail to do that.
- *Developing and maintaining effective planning systems:* This involves the consistent development of one-year and two-to-five-year plans every year, and the monitoring of results against such plans.
- *Developing and maintaining strong human resource systems:* This entails working with the appropriate manager to maintain accurate job descriptions, individual goals and objectives, compensation systems and training programmes company-wide for all levels in the organisation, including family members.

5.4 The fourth phase: focusing on family-related issues

Even if a therapist has been present from the outset, it is virtually certain that significant family-related issues will remain after the business has been stabilised and profitability has been restored. If this is recognised as indeed the case, in order to create the best opportunity for long-term success the family will be well served by focusing its attention on remaining family-based issues that have the potential to compromise ongoing business success.

(a) ***Step 1: addressing family dysfunction***

As suggested earlier in the chapter, the goal of addressing family dysfunction is to position family members to both make business decisions based primarily on business considerations and be good business partners. Further, the hope is that, with the work needed to complete the first three phases of the turnaround process, at least some progress will also be made on family-based issues as a by-product. However, that typically does not turn out to be the case – and this is where the contribution of a family therapist can make all the difference.

(b) ***Step 2: addressing family management practices***

All of the key aspects of family management practices must be addressed, including sound succession planning, well-structured governance practices, the training of successor generations, the accountability of family members working in the business, and the development of a shared vision for the future across generations. The hope and expectation should be that, with the successes needed to get to this phase of the process, the family will be well equipped to have broad-ranging and productive discussions in these areas.

6. Conclusion

There are countless reasons why the saying "Rags to rags in three generations" is so commonplace – and so true. Nonetheless, a committed family-business turnaround effort has the potential to create significant, and sometimes positively life-altering, results. Will the process be as successful as the family might hope? In many cases, the answer will be "no"; but that is not the point. The important question here is whether sufficient progress is achieved to create a material difference.

In many cases, by communicating more effectively, developing sound plans and executing them well, the family's business performance will substantially improve. Furthermore, with true progress on the non-financial issues – dealing with a flawed CEO and other underperformers, family dysfunction, underdeveloped organisational and administrative practices or underdeveloped family management practices – the opportunity for lasting improvement is even greater. This is extremely hard work; but considering the benefits that could accrue for future generations, it is worth the time and effort.

Family enterprise guide to major mental illness

Eugene J Fierman
Commonwealth Medical Psychiatry Associates
Janet B Fierman
Sheehan Phinney Bass & Green PA

1. Introduction

Most families have members with mental illness and most businesses encounter issues relating to mental illness in their workforce. For family controlled enterprises, these issues present additional complexities and opportunities. It is critical for both the continuity of the enterprise and the health of the family that the family enterprise stakeholders understand how to identify, approach and manage major mental illnesses as it impacts the family enterprise.

Medical psychiatry is still a young discipline: mechanisms of action in major mental illnesses have yet to be defined and there are no definitive diagnostic tests. However, most major mental illnesses can be managed through diagnosis and treatment by a skilled psychiatrist, often combined with the help of a knowledgeable counsellor.

This chapter is a lay person's guide to identifying, diagnosing, treating and managing people with major mental illness. It is not exhaustive, complete or intended to direct the diagnosis, treatment or management of any particular person or case. It begins with advice on how to recognise common mental illnesses encountered in the workforce (and elsewhere) and how they might be handled, and it concludes with observations about the special strengths and unique challenges facing leaders of family controlled enterprises who encounter mental illness in their businesses.

2. Identifying mental illness as a potential issue

Significant changes in behaviour may indicate the onset or recurrence of illness. It is in everyone's interest – employer, co-workers, family members, the enterprise, advisers and the person at issue – that these changes are noticed and that mental illness, as well as somatic illness or other problems, be considered when trying to identify what is causing the changes.

It is significant if someone:

- starts losing his/her temper easily;
- becomes unusually irritable;
- seems distant;
- is talking to the point of incoherence;
- is very negative;
- becomes difficult to manage;

- is complaining that people are out to get him/her;
- is unreasonably frightened or suspicious;
- starts making mistakes or missing deadlines;
- can't finish projects;
- seems to be talking to him/herself;
- says things that don't make sense;
- has a serious drop in personal hygiene;
- has alcohol on his/her breath during time at work;
- has slurred speech;
- disappears periodically without explanation;
- is always short of money; or
- is spending unusual amounts of money.

When these 'red flag' behaviours are identified, the response of the person in question and the people around them is often denial. Reports or complaints are ignored or they are dismissed as inconsequential. When the person in question is a family member, the urge to overlook these behaviours and avoid family complications may be strong. Regardless of the source of information or especially if the person is a family member, those in authority should enquire further when learning of these behaviours.

Another common response is disciplinary action – taken on the assumption that the problem is lack of self-discipline, lack of will, laziness, weakness or other characteristics within the control of the person at issue. If the source of the behaviour is mental illness, however, disciplinary action will probably be ineffective and may well be counterproductive. In addition, in some countries applicable laws governing disabilities in the workplace may limit disciplinary options and/or mandate accommodation for persons with major mental illnesses.

When these behaviours appear in persons with authority (or even control), complexity of response increases. People around the person are often reluctant to identify the behaviour as symptomatic of illness out of respect, fear of a punitive response or concern that identification will be misattributed to interpersonal motives. The role of trusted advisers in these situations becomes critical. Trusted advisers (such as primary-care physicians and long-time family enterprise consultants and other professionals) generally have enough experience and emotional distance to analyse the changed behaviour and consider what steps are appropriate (such as consulting the family primary-care physician or psychiatrist). They are most likely to have the gravitas and credibility to overcome denial, dismissal, criticism and other emotional responses to the changed behaviour, and to convince the enterprise, family and workplace to move forward with appropriate steps.

Family enterprise advisers and colleagues may learn of 'red flag' behaviours from other family members, colleagues or co-workers. They will need to deal not only with the person at issue but also with the response(s) of others within the family enterprise and the family system.

3. Possible diagnoses

After realising that mental illness may be an issue, the first step is to understand that there are many forms of psychiatric disorders and, even today, diagnosis is as much an art as a science. The symptoms of different illnesses may overlap, and so proper medical diagnosis is the key to effective treatment and management.

The following is a brief description of some major forms of mental illness, their symptoms, presentation characteristics, present-day treatment and common obstacles to treatment. It is not exhaustive or technical, being designed to assist lay people in their general knowledge of the issues.

3.1 Depression

(a) Characteristics

Depression is the most common psychiatric disorder. It can and does occur at any age – from childhood to senior citizenship. It can have gradual or acute onset. It can be chronic or occur in acute episodes, or both (known as 'double depression'). Some depression is familial. Some is seasonal, often worsening in late autumn and winter. It may or may not be related to life events. It can have a wide range of severity and at times can carry a risk of suicide.

When the science is better understood, it should become easier to distinguish the illness of depression from related somatic and psychological conditions.

(b) Symptoms

Symptoms of depression include:

- a depressed mood;
- pessimism;
- feelings of hopelessness, helplessness or worthlessness;
- sleep disturbance (particularly with early morning awakening);
- irritability;
- difficulty concentrating;
- suicidal ideation;
- decreased appetite/weight loss;
- somatic concerns;
- social withdrawal; and
- a lack of initiative or motivation.

Some of these symptoms are clearer indicators of depression than others and, generally speaking, depressions do not include all these symptoms. However, depression should be considered when a group of symptoms is present, particularly when combined with behavioural impacts.

(c) Impacts

Depression has behavioural impacts, such as missed deadlines, excessive or obsessive worry about small matters, pessimism about results, misreading of the environment, hesitancy about taking opportunities, overestimation of liabilities and threats, or a fixation on a single idea or concern (rumination). Difficulty concentrating is not always seen as a symptom of depression but can be one of the more distressing symptoms as the individual cannot exert mental control of ruminations.

It is difficult for depressed persons to control these behaviours when they are caused by their illness. Criticism or instructions to change are likely to make the depressed person defensive and/or to cause them to conceal their symptoms.

(d) *Treatment*

Antidepressants can be quite effective in reducing/eliminating major symptoms. The most common medications prescribed these days are serotonin-specific reuptake inhibitors (SSRIs). Some depressions respond better to tricyclics (an older and less commonly prescribed class of medication). Electric shock therapy is a tool of last resort, but when indicated can be successful. Cognitive therapy can help to challenge false assumptions. Psychotherapy may be helpful in understanding the impact of depression and how it has affected the patient's life course. Hospitalisation or partial hospitalisation may be needed in situations of suicide risk or extreme dysfunction.

(e) *Obstacles to treatment*

Depressed people may fail to identify their need for help, fail to obtain help or resist help for a variety of reasons. They may have concerns that are realistic, such as social stigma or medication side effects; but these concerns may be out of proportion to the reality of their situation. Their inaction may be a natural consequence of the stress she/he is undergoing – inertia is a common part of the illness's demotivating symptom. Feelings of hopelessness may make the effort seem fruitless.

Acute onset depressions tend to be more noticeable to third parties than chronic depressions, and thus more likely to lead to treatment. Chronic depressions may be seen as the 'normal' state of the person and go untreated, with damaging long-term consequences to the depressed person, his/her family, his/her work performance and the family enterprise.

3.2 Bipolar disorder

(a) *Characteristics*

Bipolar disorder is characterised by extreme mood states, with prolonged periods (many weeks or months) of mood extremes ranging from elevated mood (mania) to severe depression. It can be hard to diagnose when it presents only its depressive side, and no clear diagnosis can be made until both extremes occur. It can have acute onset, or first present itself as chronic depression. Onset can occur at many ages, most commonly in young adulthood. Mania may appear as euphoria, increased energy, hostility, impulsiveness, unusually high levels of spending, excessive talking, risk taking and paranoia.

Bipolar depressions can be extremely long and extremely withdrawn. Significant mania is often detected and treated as it is clearly outside the realm of usual experience. Less severe swings of mood can go undetected and untreated as they often border on normal states. For example, a mildly manic (termed 'hypomanic') bipolar person can appear (and be) funny, creative and energetic; a chronically depressed bipolar person can appear to be subdued and asocial.

(b) *Symptoms*

The symptoms of bipolar illness are both mania and depression.

Bipolar mania exhibits symptoms including some of the following: impulsiveness, impaired judgement, increased energy, less need for sleep, hyperactivity, humorousness, irritability, aggressiveness, combativeness, delusions and excessive talking. Often, bipolar patients, when manic, make rash or imprudent decisions, putting themselves at increased risk of physical harm because of misjudgement. A manic person might spend unusually large amounts of money and take unrealistic financial risks, creating financial risks to him/herself and others. Onset can be gradual or may appear as a switch-like process.

Bipolar depression is similar to unipolar depression, but tends to manifest itself in increased sleep (rather than trouble sleeping). It also tends to have slowed motor activity and thought ('psychomotor retardation'), and extreme social withdrawal (long periods in the home or in bed). It can sometimes last for years.

(c) *Impacts*

Bipolar mania can cause misuse of funds, excessive or inappropriate speech, rash decisions, erratic behaviour and misjudgements, and so mania can create serious exposure to financial and other types of liability. A bipolar manic person's aggressiveness and irritability can adversely affect workplace and personal relationships, as well as reputation and effectiveness with other entities.

The impacts of bipolar depression are similar to those described in unipolar depression: absence from work, missed deadlines, overestimation of risks and obstacles, and reluctance to act.

(d) *Treatment*

Mood stabilisers are currently the primary medications used for the treatment and prevention of mood swings. Major tranquillisers may be needed for episodes of acute mania and can also be used as alternative mood stabilisers. Antidepressants, used judiciously and in combination with mood stabilisers, can be helpful in treating bipolar depression (with a watchful eye in case they induce a switch to mania).

Hospitalisation may be indicated for severe mania, which carries a risk of significant harm – involuntary hospitalisation may be needed in cases of extreme risk. Hospitalisation for depression may be indicated for starting treatment, although admissions in such circumstances are currently quite short in duration. Psychotherapy can be helpful to understand the condition and its impact on a person's life and relationships, as well as to understand underlying psychological issues that may impair function.

(e) *Obstacles to treatment*

When manic, a person feels subjectively quite well and does not see the need for treatment, even when symptoms are extreme. Hence third parties (such as family members, law enforcement officers or the courts) may become involved in treatment decisions.

The obstacles to treatment for bipolar depression are the same as those listed under unipolar depression. Since bipolar depressions can involve extremely low energy and motivation, an inability to mobilise oneself to accept treatment is common.

3.3 Alcohol abuse disorder

Alcohol abuse is widespread in many societies without regard to money, class, race or ethnicity. Its impacts on families, businesses and the economy are heavy and well documented around the world.

However difficult it may be to identify, treat, manage and discuss, family members, their advisers and their businesses should undertake that effort. Laws vary from country to country, but most jurisdictions recognise the impact of liquor on behaviour and regulate its use in situations such as driving a car or operating machinery.

(a) Characteristics

Alcohol abuse disorder is characterised by use of alcohol that is not objectively under control and within appropriate parameters. Overuse and/or frequent intoxication can be quite recognisable, but the disorder may also not be clearly apparent. Abuse may take the form of binges or be continual.

There may be a familial susceptibility toward abuse, possibly related to the way alcohol is metabolised in the body. Those that can 'hold their liquor' may be at greater risk to addiction. Denial is extremely common and self-reported use often underestimates or conceals use entirely.

(b) Symptoms

The most obvious symptoms are hidden bottles of alcohol, alcohol consumption early in the day, and a smell of alcohol in inappropriate environments such as work or professional settings. Unexplained absences and inconsistent functioning may indicate that there is a problem of intoxication – whether continual or intermittent. Acute intoxication causes disinhibition, with behaviour that can be harmful to the intoxicated person, other people and business.

Depression is quite common among those suffering from alcohol abuse, either co-occurring with or as a consequence of overuse. People with this symptom often use more alcohol to mask their depression.

(c) Impacts

Misuse and chronic use of alcohol can cause impaired judgement on business decisions and relationships within and external to the family enterprise. Alcohol abuse may cause inconsistent work performance and/or attendance, as well as disrupted family, social and work relationships. Alcohol overuse can cause multiple physical medical consequences, including liver disease, cognitive impairment, gastro-intestinal problems, insomnia and sexual dysfunction. Alcoholism bears an increased risk of suicide.

(d) ***Treatment***

Treatment is difficult and relapse is common. For acute alcohol poisoning, emergency treatment may be needed. Brief hospitalisation for detoxification can help with the physical addiction, but is not sufficient for long-term treatment. Some medication treatments can help with cravings. Other medical treatments are aversive. However, medication is rarely definitive.

Treatment of co-occurring depression can be important. Twelve-step programmes are very useful by establishing a culture of sobriety. Residential treatment programmes may also be helpful for those who have frequent relapses, can afford the cost of such programmes and agree to participate. Al-Anon or Alcoholics Anonymous can be an important resource for families if groups are available locally.

(e) ***Obstacles to treatment***

In most countries, alcohol is a legal substance, used openly in many settings and socially accepted, so it may be difficult to discern when use becomes overuse. Denial is extremely common and makes acceptance of treatment difficult.

3.4 Substance abuse disorder

Substance abuse disorder is similar to alcohol abuse disorder, discussed in section 3.3 above – but with some significant differences. Mostly obviously, there are many chemical substances involved and the substances used are generally not used openly or with widespread societal approval. Substance abuse often involves violations of the local laws.

(a) ***Characteristics***

Substance abuse is the use of substances when such use is out of control. Some substances, such as the opiates (heroin, morphine, oxycodone etc), are highly addictive and rapidly addicting. Others (such as cocaine and other stimulants) become addictive less quickly and casual use is more common. The substances may be entirely illegal and only obtainable through illegal gateways; or they may be obtainable legally by prescription and misused by the prescription holder or sold illegally. Illegality makes substance use much more expensive and riskier than alcohol use.

(b) ***Symptoms***

The symptoms vary by substance. Stimulant intoxication may cause symptoms similar to mania: hyperactivity, talkativeness, irritability, lack of sleep. Intoxication with hallucinogenic substances or designer drugs may cause psychosis-like symptoms. Depressants such as opiates may cause disinhibition, social isolation, and antisocial behaviour occurring in order to pay the high cost of the habit, including theft from family, friends and/or the family business. Erratic behaviour is a further symptom of substance misuse.

(c) ***Impacts***

The costs of substance usage create an increased need for money, financial duress and a risk of mismanagement (or theft) of funds. Use of the substances can result in erratic work performance, loss of focus, unexplained absences, interpersonal issues and generally a lack of transparency regarding behaviour. Illegal activities can jeopardise a business and business relationships.

(d) *Treatment*

Treatment is difficult and relapse is common. Opioid addiction has a particularly high rate of multiple relapse. As with treatment for alcoholism, hospitalisation may be needed for detoxification from addiction or the management of temporary psychosis, but it is not sufficient for long-term treatment.

For some substances, medication may assist in addressing symptoms and there are a range of therapeutic options. For opiate use disorder, other opiates can be useful to prevent cravings and block the 'high' of opiate use. Here, too, residential treatment programmes may be helpful for those who have frequent relapses, can afford such programmes and agree to participate.

Narcotics Anonymous can help to maintain long-term abstinence. Again, family support groups can be extremely helpful to both individual family members and the enterprise.

(e) *Obstacles to treatment*

Denial and secretiveness/deception are common and prevent addicts from seeking or accepting help. Opiate addiction particularly can be very hard to treat and has limited success rates.

3.5 Psychotic disorders: schizophrenia and later-life psychoses

(a) *Characteristics*

Psychosis is a disorder of thinking. In all likelihood it is a symptom produced by a number of distinct biophysical disorders.

Schizophrenia is the most common disorder, with psychosis as a symptom. It is not a 'split personality' (a real but entirely different and rarer disorder), but a disorder of thinking. Approximately 1% of the population is afflicted with schizophrenia. Thoughts are bizarre and can be paranoid and persecutory. Onset of schizophrenia most often occurs in adolescence and is quite often disabling.

There are also later-life psychoses, which usually occur from a person's forties onward. Such psychoses can be quite severe and often have a depressive component. Although many people with psychotic disorders have clear symptoms and presentation, some have more mild and encapsulated symptoms and can appear outwardly unremarkable, if perhaps somewhat odd or limited.

(b) *Symptoms*

Psychotic people can have delusions (often of persecution), hallucinations (usually auditory in the form of voices in the head), ideas that random events refer to self (eg, the TV talking directly to the person rather than a wider audience). Other symptoms are a dishevelled appearance, inattention to hygiene and an inability to concentrate and complete tasks. Better-functioning individuals may work, but appear unusually restricted and limited or have odd ideas/thinking and difficulty in relationships.

(c) ***Impacts***

Psychoses are often disabling conditions. Early onset may cause lifelong disability. Such individuals will manage to work only infrequently, and then in simple jobs. The family, its advisers and its business need both to address issues of long-term management and provision for the family member (as with other disabled family members) and strategies to manage such family members within the family enterprise. Late-onset psychoses can be particularly problematic for the family enterprise if involving a principal, or person with significant responsibilities.

(d) ***Treatment***

Antipsychotic medication can be quite helpful in controlling symptoms but is not curative. Hospitalisation may be needed at times, as well as participation in other psychiatric rehabilitation services. Social services can help with daily life issues. Government assistance or private disability insurance may be available, but long-term planning for suitable support will be needed.

(e) ***Obstacles to treatment***

Psychotic individuals often have limited insight into their condition and often refuse treatment. Legal proceedings to arrange hospitalisation and treatment with anti-psychotic medication involve legal requirements that vary from jurisdiction to jurisdiction. Individuals with major business responsibilities, afflicted with later-life psychosis, may deny that a problem exists and use their position of power to thwart efforts to manage and treat the illness.

3.6 Anxiety disorders

(a) ***Characteristics***

The term 'anxiety disorders' covers a group of disorders in which the predominant symptoms are a degree of anxiety that is outside the realm of everyday anxiety and that has marked effects in a person's functioning. Others close to such individuals are often asked to accommodate themselves to symptoms that seem objectively irrational. There is a good deal of overlap/co-occurrence between anxiety and depressive disorders.

(b) ***Symptoms***

Below are symptoms of a few forms of anxiety disorders.

Obsessive compulsive disorder (OCD): is marked by unusually repetitive behaviour and thought patterns that are over and above neatness or orderliness and not within the control of the individual. Obsessions and compulsions intrude on a person's behaviour and time in a way that may seem irrational to others. Examples include repetitive behaviours (such as checking the gas or locks multiple times), handwashing rituals (such as counting, or performing a series of behaviours before an action) and intrusive or unwanted thoughts. The individual often knows that the obsessions and compulsions are irrational. Infrequently, there is an overlap between OCD and psychotic symptoms.

Panic and agoraphobia: Panic attacks are marked by intense feelings of panic occurring spontaneously and unpredictably. They are marked by extreme anxiety, shortness of breath, rapid pulse, sweating or light-headedness. The individual may be fearful that he or she is having a heart attack and seek help in emergency rooms.

Agoraphobia is usually a consequence of untreated panic. Such individuals will retreat to the safety of their home environment. While they are able to function within the home, they may be unable to leave the home independently. This condition can be quite severe, with people sometimes staying at home for months or even years at a time.

Performance anxiety: This is a relatively benign condition in which a person experiences symptoms of anxiety only in the context of activities such as public speaking or acting.

(c) Impacts

OCD reduces efficiency in the workplace because of the sufferer's inflexibility; it also impacts personal relationships and may have an impact on the morale of supervisees and co-workers. Individuals with severe agoraphobia and panic may be disabled and unable to perform in the workplace – they may reasonably considered disabled and may apply for disability benefits. Less severe cases may impact attendance when symptoms are more severe and may cause interruption at the workplace in the event of acute panic. Performance anxiety can inhibit workers/leaders from freely giving speeches to large gatherings of employees and clients.

(d) Treatment

OCD can be difficult to treat. High-dose antidepressant medications are approved for the treatment of OCD and may be effective, particularly if administered over a long period of time and if combined with behavioural treatments such as cognitive behavioural therapy and exposure therapy.

Panic disorder can usually be readily treated with anti-anxiety or antidepressant medication. Psychotherapy and cognitive therapy can be helpful in readjusting to life without panic if successfully treated. Agoraphobia can improve with the treatment of panic, but often requires a more concerted effort with home-based treatment, staged exposure to the outside world, cognitive therapy and support.

Performance anxiety can often be readily treated with beta blockers, which take away physical symptoms such as rapid heartbeat and sweating, or anti-anxiety medications, which can promote a feeling of calm. For chronic anxiety, a gradual re-exposure to presentations may make sense.

(e) *Obstacles to treatment*

OCD and agoraphobia can be difficult to treat and the nature of the disorder tends to make the sufferer avoid treatment. For other anxiety disorders, social stigma is always an issue; but the sufferer's discomfort and availability of treatment may make them more accepting of treatment, especially for acute episodes of panic or performance anxiety.

3.7 Trauma and post-traumatic stress disorder

Although these two conditions are technically anxiety disorders, post-traumatic stress disorder (PTSD) and other trauma disorders are very distinct from others in that category and hence are treated separately here. They are perhaps the best example of how life's circumstances can produce biological change.

(a) *Characteristics*

Although there are traumas in life, major trauma is outside the range of usual experience and includes such events as assault (sexual or otherwise), sexual trauma, military trauma, witnessing violence, natural disasters and life-threatening experiences. These traumas produce similar symptoms, which may occur in a delayed fashion – sometimes years after the traumatic event(s). PTSD and trauma are severely disruptive of a person's relationships, ability to trust and quality of life. Severely traumatised individuals can be quite disabled.

(b) *Symptoms*

Full-blown PTSD can have symptoms such as flashbacks and the reliving of traumatic events, easy startling and increased arousal, emotional numbing, feeling disconnected (known as 'dissociation'), traumatic nightmares and sleep disturbance, avoidance of issues and difficulty concentrating. Persons who have experienced significant trauma may not meet the full criteria for PTSD but may have many of the symptoms and be adversely impacted by traumatic memories.

Many victims of past trauma exhibit symptoms that are similar to 'borderline personality disorder', such as neediness, emotional volatility and lack of trust. Without identification of the traumatic origin of symptoms, such persons may not receive appropriate treatment – being subjected to rigid limit-setting and demands for self-control (which are ineffective and often counterproductive) rather than thoughtfulness, patience, encouragement and medication.

(c) *Impacts*

Traumatised victims generally have disturbed and inconsistent relationships, overly emotional and erratic responses to stress (as perceived by others), over-predicting threat in the present, and difficulty accepting supervision or guidance. Undiagnosed, they can be difficult to manage.

(d) *Treatment*

PTSD can be helped with medication to help with associated depression, anxiety, impulse control difficulties, sleep disturbance and traumatic nightmares. Cognitive therapy can help to address the need for a reordering of one's cognitions concerning the nature of threat and stress. Psychotherapy and group treatment, often over the long term, can help to integrate traumatic experience and improve interpersonal relationships.

(e) ***Obstacles to treatment***

Severe PTSD can be disabling and preclude consistent work performance. Persons with traumatic disorders have often had experiences that impede trust and collaboration and may be perceived (and be) erratic, overly emotional and defensive, making them very difficult to work with. Limit-setting responses may exacerbate the disorder and the resultant difficulties.

3.8 Alzheimer's disease and other dementias

(a) ***Characteristics***

The most common characteristic of dementia is a decline in cognitive capacity, most often seen in older individuals. Onset can be insidious and early signs may be hard to detect, or attributed to depression or 'normal ageing'. (Note that, conversely, depression is often undiagnosed in the elderly and treated as 'normal ageing' or dementia.) Early dementia can occur in individuals in their fifties and can be particularly hard to detect in the early stages.

(b) ***Symptoms***

Symptoms of dementia include significant memory loss, disorientation to time or place, difficulty with problem solving, apathy, social withdrawal, changes in mood and personality, difficulty performing previously familiar tasks, and perceptual changes. The condition progresses with time but the pace of progression is variable.

There are different forms of dementia, which can be identified by neurological and neuropsychological testing; but the symptoms and impact of the various forms are usually the same. Identification of dementia in its early stages is helpful to patients, their family and associates, as well as for necessary planning.

(c) ***Impacts***

Dementia, even in its early stages, impacts judgement, planning, attendance and performance within both the workplace and other organised settings. However, the cause of such deficits are sometimes not initially appreciated by the person involved and/or those around him/her – out of embarrassment or other reasons the person and those around him/her may deny the existence of the deficits. Whatever the reasons, the longer that action is delayed, the greater the likelihood of risk to the person, his/her family and the family enterprise, particularly where the demented person has authority or control within the enterprise.

As dementia reaches its later stages, diagnosis becomes clearer and action is imperative. Persons with more advanced dementia are unable to function in the enterprise, and if they do they may cause irreparable harm to the enterprise and/or the family.

(d) ***Treatment***

Medications are available that may slow progression of dementia, but there is no definitive treatment. Significant (and expensive) support may be needed in the later stages of the disease, including institutional placement.

(e) ***Obstacles to treatment***

There are no known treatments for dementia. The early stages can be hard to detect and the individual does not perceive or accept the existence of problems. In the absence of advanced directives, interventions can be complex.

3.9 Personality disorders

(a) ***Characteristics***

The term 'personality disorders' describes a broad category of maladaptive personality traits that diagnostically have been grouped in clusters: odd or eccentric; having overly emotional, demanding or unpredictable behaviour; or having anxious or fearful thinking or behaviour. These traits often describe behaviours that cross a spectrum from 'disorder' to 'normal' without clear dividing lines (eg, from avoidant personality to shyness). At other times the traits describe behaviours that range across a spectrum of full-blown disorder (eg, from schizoid personality to psychosis).

In subsections (b)–(e) below, only an antisocial personality disorder is discussed because this disorder can have a highly destructive impact on a family enterprise or the family itself.

(b) ***Symptoms***

People with antisocial personality disorders exhibit all or some of the following symptoms: exploitative behaviour, recklessness, irresponsibility, impulsivity, deceitfulness, a tendency towards violence, lack of empathy, lack of intimacy, callousness, and skill at manipulation. In relation to the last in the list, because they are often skilled manipulators and superficially charming and personable, they may be highly successful at masking their symptoms to further their interests.

(c) ***Impacts***

These are individuals who put their own interests above the interests of others or of any organisation, including the family enterprise (or others supported by the family enterprise). Criminal behaviour is possible. Risky behaviour and lack of empathy can at the very least damage relationships, impair the reputation of a business and inflict serious financial and human harm.

(d) ***Treatment***

There is currently no known medical treatment for the antisocial personality. Management should focus on identification of the disorder, containment of behaviours (perhaps through positive and negative reinforcement) and protective measures to prevent harm to others and the enterprise.

(e) *Obstacles to treatment*

Such individuals do not readily accept treatment, since they cannot see their actions as problematic or themselves as needing change. Given an ability to present superficially as engaging or sincere, it may take time for others to identify symptoms and appreciate the nature of their deceptiveness.

3.10 Attention deficit hyperactivity disorder

(a) *Characteristics*

Attention deficit hyperactivity disorder (ADHD) impairs function and impacts interpersonal relationships. It should not be confused or conflated with a desire for improved performance at work (or school) by individuals without significant deficits in concentration. It may occur as extreme distractibility or inability to focus, with or without hyperactivity. Symptoms usually are recognised first in childhood; in adults, it may be co-morbid with alcohol or substance abuse disorder.

(b) *Symptoms*

The most common symptoms of ADHD are a difficulty with maintaining attention to tasks, difficulty with organisation, and unusual sensitivity to extraneous stimulation. The patient may be characterised as easily distracted, avoiding tasks requiring prolonged concentration, with forgetfulness, lateness, losing things, inattention to detail, impulsivity, fidgeting, restlessness, irritability and trouble coping with stress.

(c) *Impacts*

Impacts comprise erratic behaviour and decision-making, poor follow-through, lack of attention to detail, procrastination, and difficult interaction with co-workers.

(d) *Treatment*

Stimulant medication can be very helpful in decreasing the core symptoms. However, where there is alcohol or substance abuse, it may be contraindicated.

(e) *Obstacles to treatment*

ADHD is difficult to diagnose definitively and often overlaps with other psychiatric issues. For example, depression causes poor concentration and alcohol/substance abuse can impair function globally in similar ways. Premature or unnecessary use of stimulants may mask these other psychiatric issues.

3.11 Autism spectrum disorders

These disorders are not discussed here. They are characterised by dysfunction in social communication/interaction and by repetitive behaviour or interests. These disorders, when severe. are diagnosed in early childhood and consequently do not generally impact a family enterprise except as regards management of the condition.

4. Managing people with major mental illness

The management of people with major mental illness is an enormous field, which cannot be addressed in this chapter. However, we set out below some general advice to help with understanding the management process in different contexts. It should not, however, be taken as advice in any particular case.

4.1 Dealing with the acutely ill

A person with significant disturbance in mood, thought or cognition, which significantly interferes with function and a sense of well-being, is acutely ill. Diagnoses include somatic illnesses that might present with psychiatric symptoms as well as mental illnesses. Examples of such somatic illnesses include: neurological conditions such as seizures and brain tumours; endocrine disorders such as thyroid or adrenal disease; diabetes; and acute infections such as pneumonia. The ill, their family and their advisers should get prompt, good-quality diagnosis and treatment, including an initial assessment that includes consideration of potential somatic causes for the observed behaviours.

There is a range of options for handling the acutely mentally ill. So long as the person is not too agitated or out of touch with reality, the first approach is to try to talk to the person with the goal of having him/her voluntarily seek or accept treatment. Such a conversation should be calm, low-key and direct, containing no hint of value judgement, threat or accusation and using simple, declarative statements. Beating around the bush is confusing and often counterproductive. Express concern in general terms such as "I am worried about you." Expect the person to be defensive and push back on concern. It may be helpful to objectify the symptoms observed – for example, "You seem unable to concentrate on work," or "You are talking a lot about suicide." Reassure the person that you are bringing this up because you want to try to help and not in order to be critical. If the person is a family member, it may be helpful to tie the observations to events: "Remember that, last week, you could not find your way home," or "Since your wife died, you don't leave the house much." For non-family members, reference to personal issues may be too intrusive.

The second option is to bring in family, advisers and/or third parties to help talk to the acutely ill person. The same approach to conversation should apply. Avoid threats, accusations or judgements; express concern and a desire to help. Appeal to their healthy self ("You are such an independent person – your inability to go to work shows you are not doing well."). See whether the person will agree to accept help.

If the person who is ill will not accept that he or she needs help, or if there are significant concerns about that person's potential response to a personal approach (such as reactive use of authority), family or advisers may want to seek trained advice on handling the situation. The person's primary-care physician or treating physician is the most obvious choice for such a consultation. In many jurisdictions, physicians are under legal or professional constraints that make them unable or reluctant to provide information without their patient's consent. However, those constraints should not prevent them from receiving information and using it in treating the patient. The goal is the alleviation of suffering.

If the person in question is extremely agitated, out of touch or presents a threat of danger to him/herself or others, that person needs to be treated on an emergency basis. First, see whether he or she will go voluntarily by whatever means seems to work. Involuntary means of obtaining treatment are a last resort, but sometimes the only option available. In emergency situations, professionals may be less constrained by confidentiality concerns in order to ensure a person's safety.

4.2 Managing the chronically ill

The keys to managing the chronically mentally ill are:

- identifying and obtaining good treatment providers;
- managing the environment for the chronically ill, including their family systems; and
- accepting the illness as a reality that is likely to require long-term, perhaps lifelong, treatment and management.

That said, each illness is different and each person is different, so this discussion is necessarily confined to some general outlines.

Good treatment and treatment teams are critical to the management of the chronically mentally ill. The treatment team generally includes a primary-care physician, a psychiatrist for medical/psychiatric treatment and a psychotherapist for help with insight, dealing with life's stresses, and reality checks. Social workers can provide both psychotherapy and case management to mobilise resources as needed. Counsellors can be brought in to help family members accept, understand and manage both the treatment and the person with illness. Good treatment is hard to identify, particularly for lay people dealing with a problematic illness. It is helpful to listen, analyse information and, if the information does not make sense, obtain another opinion.

Very often, the family members and family systems of the chronically ill have primary responsibility for care and management of the patient. The overarching task for the family providers is to guard against denial and wishful thinking, which may provide emotional solace but which may ultimately prove to be counterproductive and even destructive. Maintaining a balanced, structured approach to the provision of care is very helpful to all involved.

Be practical. For example:

- Pay bills directly to vendors (landlord, utility providers, treatment providers, tax authorities), to avoid the family member who is needing care having to do so. This ensures that the family member's money is used appropriately – if not, it adds unnecessary disruption to the family relationships. Don't pay credit card bills except in small, controlled amounts.
- Triage all information received. Respond to objective evidence. Self-reported information may be the result of impaired insight, misperceived realities or poor judgement, rather than misreporting. With addicts and antisocial personalities, self-reports may be deliberately deceptive.
- Use third-party managers for the management of treatment/support and of financial matters (assets, income) if financially feasible. This approach

simplifies family relationships and objectifies key decisions. Oversee such third-party managers and, as noted above, seek second opinions and alternative advice when 'red flags' pop up.

When/if remissions occur, family members and advisers should use the opportunity to work with the chronically ill person on the systems that are needed to manage the illness. For example, that is the time to obtain consents needed for access to health, treatment, financial and similar information. It is the time to discuss the management and treatment of a recurrence, should one arise, and to agree on the warning signs of recurrence that should trigger permission to bring up the possibility of recurrence. It may take more than one cycle of remission and recurrence for the ill family member to recognise the need for these procedures. Persevere.

Perhaps the hardest task for family caregivers is avoiding guilt or personalisation of the behaviour of the mentally ill. Try not to take unfounded accusations or personal attacks to heart – accept them as symptoms and make decisions without factoring them into the equation. Defensive or apologetic responses are unlikely to be useful. In addition, despite best efforts, stressed caregivers may act in ways that are punitive, judgemental or emotional. Accept the frailties of the well as well as the problems of the ill.

5. The family enterprise and members with disabilities

Family enterprises have unique opportunities and abilities to provide care and support for disabled stakeholders in their systems, whether members of the family, in-laws, outside owners, valued employees or others. Options range from special trusts for the disabled to employment accommodation by a family controlled business. The key is an understanding of the nature of the stakeholder's disability (characteristics, symptoms, impact), some integration in treatment of the disabling condition and use of trusted advisers in managing the systems put in place.

Work can be helpful for those with major mental illnesses. It can provide structure, social contact, financial support and self-esteem. Employers in the US (and elsewhere) are required to make "reasonable" accommodation of persons with disabilities, including mental disabilities, so long as the accommodation needed does not interfere with the business. However, family enterprises often have the financial means and governance abilities to make accommodations and implement structures that reach far beyond those available in other enterprises. One family created a computer business that was able to employ a severely autistic child. Another retained a family member as an officer of a major business after mid-life onset of bipolar disorder, implementing some internal checks and balances for protection of the enterprise. A third created an advisory board position for a founder with early-stage dementia.

Family members and advisers, when considering possible roles for the disabled in the family enterprise, should first consider the best interests of the enterprise, its constituent businesses and its various stakeholders. These interests may be strikingly different from those of a chronically ill family member (and his/her nuclear family).

In analysing the nature of the disabled person's illness, it is key to get objective opinions and advice from experts most likely to be trusted within the family system. It is also helpful to get appropriate advice on whether, what, how and how much to disclose to, and discuss with, other stakeholders in the system.

Family enterprises and their owners also can provide financial support for disabled family members outside the employment realm. For example, families can create for, or apportion to, the care of a disabled member a special class of ownership interest in one or more companies, providing income without control. In many jurisdictions, families can create private trusts for the care of the disabled, preferably managed by trusted advisers. In such ways, the family can ensure continuity of care without regard to employability.

For obvious reasons, family controlled enterprises may well be more committed to accommodating the needs of individual family members suffering mental illness than national or local laws require, or even than best practice in modern business indicates. Such accommodations are most likely to arise in companies where the culture of the controlling family constitutes the basis of the corporate culture of the enterprise. Such enhanced accommodations may not only assist in the management of, or recovery from, mental illness by a family member engaged in the family controlled enterprise, but also may encourage widespread expansion of such accommodations into company-wide state-of-the-art programmes. Such leadership across a family controlled firm in the treatment of mental illness may well provide new models of treatment for a much broader universe of companies and other institutions.

6. Conclusion

It is in the interests of all, from the individual level to the societal level, for mental illness to be promptly identified, properly diagnosed, appropriately treated and well managed. Unfortunately, it may be difficult to identify optimal treatment, because the science of mental illness is still too undeveloped and inexact – good treatment is hard to find, hard for lay people to identify and can be costly. Furthermore, stigma (overt and covert) is pervasive and serves as an obstacle to obtaining care.

There are many obstacles to care among individuals, families, communities and society generally. Thoughtful, well-informed analysis and consideration of objective evidence are the best tools available to overcome such obstacles and to provide suitable care for those with mental health problems in family controlled businesses.

Assessing going-concern risk in family enterprises

Patricia A Frishkoff
Leadership In Family Enterprise LLC

1. Introduction

The assumption that a firm is a going concern underlies financial reporting for a considerable portion of the world's enterprises. It presumes that a company will continue normal business operations into the future, and it can be used to prompt stakeholders in enterprises controlled by families to ask whether that particular family enterprise is likely to survive.

This chapter takes a hard look at the process of assessing a family enterprise's capacity for being a going concern. It challenges responsibility for making going-concern assessments and typical circumstances in which the evaluation might be used. Moreover, the author proposes that recent financial reporting requirements, whose responsibility lies first with management and then with the firm's public accountants, fail to address factors prevalent in family enterprises that threaten their ability to continue, but that rest outside the scope of observation detailed by mandates governing both the accounting profession and management. The chapter concludes with indications of additional observations needed by managers of family enterprises, advisers and researchers in the field.

2. Accounting standards in the United States and internationally

Financial reporting is the language that communicates information about the financial condition and operating results of the company, and that has been the primary evidence used in the past to assess whether an enterprise will continue normal business operations. Specifically, this information includes:

- the firm's financial position: balance sheet and statement of net position;
- the results of operations: statements of revenue and expenses, changes in the net position, statement of comprehensive income, etc; and
- disclosures: footnotes explaining the above and adding further information or explanations.

The US Government does not directly set accounting standards by statute. However, the US Securities and Exchange Commission (SEC) requires that US standards be followed in financial reporting by publicly traded companies. The Financial Accounting Standards Board (FASB) publishes accounting guidelines

* This chapter is an update to a 1992 article published in *Family Business Review*, the academic journal of the Family Firm Institute, an international association].

applicable to publicly traded companies in the US. These standards are termed the 'Generally Accepted Accounting Principles' (GAAP) and they are practised by Certified Public Accountants (CPAs).

Although not mandated (because the enterprises are privately owned, and often are not audited), "many private companies make the decision to use GAAP-based accounting".[1] Table 1 indicates the various stakeholders/constituents interested in financial reporting requirements.

Table 1: Who uses GAAP in the private company space?

Preparer community	User community	Auditing community	Legal community
Private companies	Institutions that lend to private companies	The big audit firms	Law firms and attorneys that represent private companies
Private companies that intend to go public	Investors – private equity, venture capital, angel investors	Audit firms that predominately or exclusively serve private companies	
	Government lenders	Smaller audit firms	

Source: Financial Accounting Foundation

Looking wider than the US, the International Accounting Standards Board (IASB) publishes International Financial Reporting Standards (IFRS), which are becoming the global standard for the preparation of public company financial statements. In most countries outside the US, the users are termed Certified Accountants (CAs).

Within both GAAP and IFRS the concept of 'going concern' is crucial for preparing financial statements. Attesting to the going-concern assumption validates the methods of asset valuation, depreciation and amortisation. If liquidation of the company is likely, this assumption is not valid – in other words, it is not reasonable to assume the business will continue operating in the near future and should be viewed as such. If that were subsequently found to be the case, asset values would most likely be reduced.

2.1 New GAAP requirements related to going concern

Between GAAP and IFRS, the time frame used in evaluating going concern differs.

1 Financial Accounting Foundation, "The Importance of Generally Accepted Accounting Principles for Private Companies", available at www.accountingfoundation.org/jsp/Foundation/Page/FAFBridgePage&cid=1176164539633#section_2.

Accounting in IFRS is for a period defined as 'the foreseeable future'. However, in GAAP the going-concern period is generally 12 months. Changes to GAAP in 2014 have impacted which 12-month period is relevant to this issue, changing both responsibility for and timing related to making the judgement as to whether an enterprise is a going concern.

A new FASB requirement related to going concern describes how entities should assess their ability to meet their obligations and sets requirements about how this information should be communicated.[2] Until passage of this new requirement in 2014, assessment for going concern in this context was solely related to the audit function under the American Association of Certified Public Accountants (AICPA) Auditing Standards Board (ASB) Statement of Auditing Standards (SAS) No 59.

Key aspects of the 2014 changes are as follows:

- Management, not auditors, are mandated to assess going concern.[3]
- Going concern is associated with GAAP, making it applicable to all businesses when financial statements are issued annually and on an interim basis (not just those that are audited).
- The definition of the time frame is a look-forward period of one year from the financial statement issuance date (which is always later than the published date of the statements).
- If it is probable that an entity will be unable to meet its obligations, then incremental 'substantial doubt' disclosure is required if the doubt is not mitigated by management's plans. A special pronouncement defines 'substantial doubt'. Even then, there is a disclosure requirement when an initially identified substantial doubt is alleviated by management plans.
- The new standards apply to all entitles for the first annual period ending after 16 December 2016, and interim periods thereafter.

As clearly pointed out by PricewaterhouseCoopers (PwC), "FASB requires *management* to assess a company's ability to continue as a going concern and to provide related footnote disclosures in certain circumstances. Before this standard, there was minimal guidance in US GAAP specific to going concern." (author's emphasis).[4] Moreover, PwC explains that the emergence of substantial doubt is the trigger for footnote disclosure, and that SEC registrants must make the determination quarterly – other firms must do so if they issue interim statements.

Large accounting firms such as PwC and KPMG recognise that companies (ie, the accounting firms' clients) will need to implement processes to assess risk, and controls to mitigate those risks when they become substantial. New models of risk analysis will be needed for consideration of:

- conditional and unconditional obligations;

---

2 See the FASB Accounting Standards Update 2014–15, entitled "Disclosures of Uncertainties about an Entity's Ability to Continue as a Going Concern", available at www.fasb.org. See also KPMG, "FASB Issues Going Concern Standard", *Defining Issues* 14–40, August 2014.

3 See Dugan Lopatka, "Management Not Auditors Mandated To Assess Going Concern Issues", available at www.duganlopatka.com/articles/business-articles/accounting/605-going-concern.

4 PwC, "In depth: A look at current financial reporting issues", *Footnote*, 23 September 2014.

- funds necessary to maintain operations; and
- other adverse conditions:
  - negative trends;
  - internal matters;
  - dividend or owner compensation reductions;
  - disposals of substantial assets;
  - legal proceedings;
  - loss of key client or supplier;
  - loss of franchise, licence or patent; and
  - an inability to meet a distributorship agreement.

If the measured risk raises substantial doubt (as specifically defined), then mandates require management to reconsider its plans and their mitigating impact.

As early as 2009, the Australian Institute of Company Directors (AICD) raised concern about going-concern reporting, because of an environment in which "Australian companies ... were experiencing the impact of difficult or uncertain economic conditions."[5]

2.2 Defining 'management'

The Australian publication referred to at the end of the previous section, 2.1, directly addresses a critical question: given that management is responsible for assessing going-concern status, who is the management in a company? The Australian publication refers specifically to 'directors'. A formal board of directors is required for publicly held companies, in Australia and generally throughout the world; however, no such mandate exists in the US for non-public companies, although GAAP may be used by such companies. The circumstances under which such procedures might be selected include those where:

- the company intends to go public;
- the company is up for sale;
- distributorship or franchise agreement requirements apply; or
- lenders' or outside investors' requests apply.

The UK Financial Reporting Council (FRC) updated the UK Corporate Governance Code (hereinafter the Code) in 2014 with changes, including some relating to going concern. "The changes to the Code are designed to strengthen the focus of companies and investors in the longer term and the sustainability of value creation."[6] The revised Code promotes the inclusion of a 'viability statement' in the strategic report to investors, aimed at providing an improved and forward-looking assessment of long-term solvency and liquidity.

This brings us to the issue of formal boards of directors. No clear data identifies what portion of private companies have a formal 'board of directors', defined as a

5 AICD, "The guide for directors from Australia going concern issues in financial reporting", 2009, available at www.auasb.gov.au/admin/file/content102/c3/going_concern_issues_in_financial_reporting.pdf.

6 *The Accountant* magazine, 18 September 2014.

governing board with at least one outside director. Only publicly held businesses need report on board membership. When questioned, many owners will indicate that they have a board of directors when what they actually have might simply be a group of family members or friends who meet irregularly on an informal basis. What this statement usually means is that they either have family meetings, or that the terms 'family council' and 'board of directors' are in this context intermeshed or confused.

If there is a formal board of directors, that board fulfils the role of 'management' and is responsible for assessing the going-concern status of the family business. But, what happens if there is no formal board? 'Management' might then consist of a team of managers – possibly with some non-family members or possibly just one family leader – taking all the key decisions. In either case, checks and balances are lost, given that management that assesses going concern comprises the same group of people who make operating decisions, including the operating decisions that may have placed the company at risk of no longer being a going concern. The higher the level of family involvement in managing a family controlled company, the more intertwined are the goals for the business and the needs of the family.

3. Risks unique to family enterprises

Another major problem exists in assessing the state of going concern. Within current guidelines under both GAAP and IFRS, most characteristics relate to data measured by prescribed methods or through commonly employed footnote disclosure.

Family enterprises present a unique set of risks that fall outside any previously presented by accounting firms under their audit function. The revised GAAP guidelines are so new that fresh checklists have yet to be made publicly available. However, this author believes that the management bodies of firms, and their accountants, would be reluctant to disclose many of the risks inherent in family enterprises because they are very difficult to measure and because owner–managers don't want to disclose or even acknowledge that such risks exist.

The remainder of this section 3 considers risks unique to family enterprises.

3.1 Use of a checklist to assess risk

Auditors have long used checklists to conduct their assessments of financial reports, including evaluations of what is a going concern. However, with this new FASB requirement affecting GAAP, responsibility has been shifted to management, and need for the assessments extends beyond firms for which audits are conducted.

In my 1992 article I constructed a list of warning signs of risk that are unique to family businesses, and this has now been completely revised. It is intended as an assessment tool to be used by managers of family businesses (especially boards of directors or principal owners), by families (through family councils), and by advisers to family businesses who are helping those businesses transition to the next generation. I have divided the assessment questions using a strategic scheme developed by Dr Dennis Jaffe (see section 3.2 below). The list itself is given as Table 2 in section 3.3 below.

3.2 The Jaffe model

Dr Dennis Jaffe is a leading educator in the field of family business. His 2005 article entitled "Strategic Planning for the Family Business" defines a model for how financial planners (broadly defined) "can help the family business survive into subsequent generations, by using a two-dimensional planning process: the family council and the business board of directors".[7] He further states in that article:

The family council comprises the actual members of the family, including in some cases in-laws, young adults and family members not directly involved in the business. The family council's task is to develop a new generation of family members, regulate their involvement in the business, and align the business with the family's plans. ... The council expresses the will of the family in relation to its business.

The task of the board of directors, composed of family members, and perhaps key employees and independent directors, is to look at the business independently from the family. The board should focus on such strategic planning needs as succession governance and capital needs. It may need to challenge family needs and set limits on such things as pay and income distribution ... The planning process must deal with business realities ... This is achieved by convening a proactive business board of directors that represents the needs of the business.... The board ... is responsible for oversight and development of the business.

Statistics gathered by the Family Firm Institute[8] suggest that many family businesses do not survive from one generation to the next. Jaffe points to a key reason for such failures as principally twofold: the ways that family considerations can overwhelm business realities; and their consequent lack of focus on the need for business renewal. With these failures at the core of his evaluation, Jaffe recommends that financial advisers assist clients with discussions and decisions related to:

- *business renewal:* this involves reigniting the engine of growth to begin a new upturn for the enterprise;
- *generational development and succession governance:* this combines guidelines for involvement and choice of next-generation leaders; and
- *family harmony:* I use the term 'family glue' – those strong positive feelings that nudge the family to behave in ways that help them stick together. Inherent in this concept is the family working together to define what aspects of being both a business and a family they share – in other words, what really matters to them all.

Jaffe addresses the quest for family harmony within the role of the family council:

Planning is not a natural function for a family. Family members spend a lot of time bumping up against each other, and rather than plan, they try to find a fast way to restore family harmony. They develop habits of avoiding issues, denying problems, and keeping secrets from one another. If an issue is controversial or upsetting, families often learn not to talk about it, or to talk with everyone but the person in question.

---

7 Dennis T Jaffe, "Strategic Planning for the Family in Business", *Journal of Financial Planning*, March 2005, available via www.journalfb.net.

8 Website available at www.ffi.org.

He recommends that advisers assist in establishing the process of family meetings, and preparing statements and policies that define the family's mission, values, guidelines and policies – all as means of lessening conflict. Working with the GAAP 2014 guidelines relating to going concern, it is my conclusion that Jaffe's recommendations should become requirements.

3.3 A checklist of early warning signs of risk

As stated in sections 3.1 and 3.2 above, I have constructed a checklist of early warning signs of significant risk emerging within family businesses, and this checklist is largely based on the model created by Dr Dennis Jaffe. The checklist is set out in Table 2.

Table 2: Going-concern risk warning signs in a family enterprise

Generational development and succession governance (category G)		
G1	S	Is there a recorded history of the family business(es) that could guide future decisions?
G2	S	Does the senior generation want to perpetuate the family business into the next generation?
G3	S	Is there a written transition plan for the business(es)?
G4	O	Are there written rules of involvement that define conditions necessary to become a family-member employee in the business?
G5	O	Is there a named successor–manager (or successors) included in written documents such as a transition plan or franchise or distributorship agreements?
G6	O	Has a family member been named as the successor?
G7	O	How old is the intended successor(s)?
G8	S	Has the successor(s) completed advanced education related to operations of the family business(es)?
G9	O	Has the successor(s) worked at least two years in a management position outside of the family business?
G10	S	Is the next generation passionate about the family business?

continued on next page

Generational development and succession governance (category G)		
G11	O	Is there key-person life insurance on individuals with substantial holdings?
G12	S	Is the next generation sufficiently experienced and skilled to meet the challenges of business today and in the future?
G13	O	Do principal owners have personal financial statements prepared on an annual basis?
G14	S	Is there a buy–sell agreement that defines who can own, and what would happen in case of death, divorce or permanent disability?
G15	O	Do owners of large portions of the family business have formal documents that specify where that ownership goes upon their death?
G16	O	Have ownership transfer documents been reviewed and updated within the last three years?
G17	O	Has a recent valuation determined the pricing in the buy–sell agreement?
G18	O	Upon the death of key owners, will there be a majority owner (or owners) who controls the family business(es)?
G19	O	Are financial statements, ownership intentions and other wishes of founder/key owners shared with their heirs?
G20	S	Could ownership become a source of conflict for this family for reasons other than the split of proportions?
G21	S	If the key owners were to die, could the family afford to pay necessary estate taxes without jeopardising the business?
G22	S	Can the senior generation financially afford to retire?
G23	S	Will the senior generation be willing to relinquish control?
G24	S	Is the senior generation actively teaching the younger generation?
G25	S	Does the ownership plan provide opportunities for those not working in the business(es)?

continued on next page

Family harmony (category H)		
H1	S	Does the family hold regular family meetings?
H2	S	Is the family business a place where the family shares good times together?
H3	S	When conflict occurs, is it brought into the open and resolved quickly?
H4	O	Do family members share stories about the business?
H5	S	Are family members willing to work to perpetuate the family business(es) for themselves and others?
H6	S	Can the family discuss business issues without becoming entrenched in family roles and old patterns?
H7	S	Do family members listen to one another, respectfully?
H8	O	Does the family have a family council, to represent the family's position in relation to the business(es)?
H9	S	Is family conflict impairing business practices and operations?
H10	S	Are family members granted concessions or treated in a differential manner so that business operations, liquidity and/or morale are affected?
H11	S	Can the next generation get along running the family business(es) together?
H12	S	Does the family use advisers or consultants to assist in maintaining harmony?
Business renewal (category R)		
R1	O	How old is the founder or leader in the senior generation?
R2	S	How good is the health of the founder or key leader?
R3	S	If the founder or key leader were to die today, could the business(es) be effectively managed?

continued on next page

Business renewal (category R)		
R4	O	Does the plan for the future preserve a viable business structure and operation?
R5	S	Do the family business(es) create enough cash flow to support all employees and retirees?
R6	S	Are family members comfortable having personal guarantees on business loans?
R7	S	Are there options in terms of product, industry, customer base, etc that could allow for business continuation if core production were no longer viable?
R8	O	Does the business have a formal, functioning board of directors that makes key strategic decisions?
R9	O	Are there non-family members on the board of directors?
R10	O	Are principal owners covered by long-term-care insurance?
R11	S	Are all family members covered by health insurance?
R12	S	Is there sufficient insurance of all types to cover risks that could jeopardise the business(es) or greatly diminish personal wealth?
R13	O	Are important papers stored in a secure place known to key family members or their representatives?
R14	S	Are owners clear about the circumstances in which they would sell the business(es)?

Code: S = subjective assessment; O = objective assessment.

Note: This checklist includes questions from two sources where Frishkoff served as sole or co-author: (1) Patricia A Frishkoff, "Farm Succession Risk Management Checklist Online", Austin Family Business Program, Oregon State University, 2009 (funded by the US Department of Agriculture); and (2) Michael A Schaefer and Patricia A Frishkoff, "Evaluation of Auditor's Going-Concern Risk in Family Businesses", Family Business Review, *Family Firm Institute, 1992. Additional questions have been added to those extracted from the articles. Categories for the checklist are based on a model developed by Dr Dennis Jaffe as set out in "Strategic Planning for the Family in Business",* Journal of Financial Planning, *March 2005.*

4. Assessing going concern

Ultimately, management of the family enterprise must prepare data and a report, for its certified (public) accountants, to assist in the accountants' assessment of going concern. When assessment of going concern results in an evaluation of reasonable doubt, a plan must be developed by management to mitigate the circumstances that place the enterprise at risk, and certified (public) accountants must evaluate that plan.

I recommend that work with the checklist first be undertaken by individuals who are, or who are considered, part of management. The next step would be to undertake a review of these checklists, with group meetings to compare responses and develop a report. The next required user of the report is the accounting firm, which will employ a typical order of practice, usually consisting of having junior practitioners review the situation, followed by the partner on the engagement.

If there are shortfalls relating to going concern (the author expects that some aspects would be lacking in almost every enterprise), then management would work with the engaged accounting firm to develop a plan that mitigates the situation. I recommend that a meeting of management, family council and accounting firm deal with the shortfalls and define the plan. Integrating management's plan with objectives set forth by the family council could help to refine policies that affect family involvement in the enterprise and lessen situations that place the business at risk.

The effects of a plan in a family enterprise have a broad reach – to owners and managers, to employees, to the family, and to the community and industry within which the enterprise functions. Other advisers could add value to the analysis by adding their perspectives about the warning signs to the information gathered by management. Such advisers might include:

- an estate planner (lawyer)
- a family wealth adviser;
- a clinically trained adviser dealing specifically with addictions or other mental health issues;[9] or
- a general family-business adviser.

5. Conclusion

Many family enterprises fail to have a formal, written transition plan. The absence of a comprehensive plan such as this is a primary cause of failure of an enterprise. While the new GAAP requirements in the US might cause family enterprises to take on additional work and cost, this mandate could enhance the importance that owners and family members place on transition plans. Moreover, the mandate has global applicability.

---

9 For further information on this topic, see the chapter by EJ Fierman and JB Fierman in Part III of this publication, entitled "Family enterprise guide to major mental illness".

Special issues in strategic planning in family controlled enterprises

Julian E Lange
Babson College

1. Introduction

Strategic planning should be an important part of business strategy development for every company and organisation. There is an old adage that warns us, "If you don't know where you're going, any road will do." If a business's leaders truly do not know where their company is headed, they run the risk of missing opportunities and being forced to deal with problems that could have been anticipated and avoided.

At its simplest level, strategic planning helps company decision makers choose the best path into an uncertain future. It is about documenting the current state of the company, analysing how it got there, envisioning possible desirable future states of the business, and suggesting courses of action that will enable the company to get to the desirable future.

All businesses will benefit from having an overview of the direction in which they are heading. For family controlled businesses, there are important additional reasons to plan, including consideration of how factors affecting the family interact with business strategies and how a family business can leverage family factors to create a win–win for both the business and the family.

2. Strategic planning as a process

It has been said that the only constant in business is change. It follows that the recognition that change is inevitable and ongoing is a key component in the development of business strategy. The anticipation of changes in the market, in the desires and demands of customers, in the actions of competitors and in the overall business environment is crucial in order for businesses to survive and prosper. An important implication of constant change is that strategic planning for businesses in general and family businesses in particular is of necessity an ongoing process.

The product of strategic planning is too often considered simply a report that summarises an analysis of the state of the business and the delineation of possible paths forward. But such a report, however detailed, is by itself incomplete. Rather, the most important product of strategic planning is the establishment of an ongoing strategic planning process itself. Given the pace of change in the overall business environment, it is important that the strategic planning process results in the creation of a framework for envisioning and analysing possible future directions for the business and incorporating the key factors affecting the business going forward. It is particularly important to recognise that the key factors that have enabled the success of the business in the past may well be (and probably will be) different in the future, and the strategic planning process must be set up to take this into account.

3. Resistance to strategic planning in family businesses

Despite its benefits, strategic planning can encounter considerable resistance in some family controlled enterprises. This is not as surprising as it may seem at first glance for a number of reasons.

First, many founders of family businesses are entrepreneurs who started their businesses without formal business education or business plans, instead using their instincts and 'gut feelings' to identify opportunities and build their companies. They will often question why they shouldn't simply continue to do that. In addition, planning also involves a continuing commitment of time, people and resources, which the business's initial management might believe could be better used elsewhere in the firm to build revenues and profitability. Moreover, founding entrepreneurs will often be sceptical about a process that they anticipate will add constraints to their ability to act quickly to develop and take advantage of new opportunities.

Perhaps most important, strategic planning may be perceived by current company management as leading to a reduction of their control of the business by granting significant influence over of the future direction of the firm to a strategic planning committee or a consultant whose analysis and conclusions are not predictable in advance and might possibly run counter to the judgements of current management.

4. The key contributions of strategic planning

Despite possible misgivings about planning, as cited in section 3 above, it is important that company decision makers and members of the family shareholder control group understand that the benefits of strategic planning far exceed the costs. Not to plan implies moving into the future with a short-term outlook and without an overview of the business's longer-term opportunities and challenges. Not planning can lead to a lack of focus and direction, unnecessary mistakes and missed opportunities.

It is also important to note that planning does not have to inhibit or constrain executive action. Rather, as elaborated below, a dynamic planning process will provide a context and framework with which the business's leaders can generate and evaluate new ideas and approaches, and thus enable the application of entrepreneurial techniques to the creation and enhancement of value for the business and the family.

Planning does not need to result in the loss of control for the current leaders of the business or constrain their entrepreneurial spirit. Since an important output of the planning process is the identification and analysis of alternative courses of action for the future direction and growth of the firm, strategic planning can in fact lead to the pursuit of exciting new opportunities that might not otherwise be identified, and to the suggestion of new ways for business managers and family members to follow their entrepreneurial instincts and create significant value for the firm and the family.

4.1 Planning as a key process for family businesses

Strategic planning is especially crucial for family controlled enterprises because of the dynamic interaction of business issues and family issues in family firms. For all companies, it is a difficult and formidable task to coordinate the strategic, competitive, operational and growth-related issues involved in leading the business into the future. When a company is controlled by a family shareholder group, family considerations and issues must be taken into account as well, and strategic planning becomes a more complex task in order to best serve the interests of both the business and the family.

When business and family objectives are working in concert, the combination can be very powerful in building value for both the business and the family; but when business and family objectives and actions are in conflict, the challenges are often magnified and more difficult to overcome. It is important that managers of family controlled firms are able to anticipate and act not only upon sets of potential opportunities but also upon the challenges that might emerge. This is because strategic planning can play a very important part in addressing these issues by providing a framework and process to guide company managers in their decision-making.

5. Components of a family business strategic planning process

At this point we turn our attention to how strategic planning is accomplished for a family controlled enterprise. As previously noted, one of the key characteristics of family businesses is the simultaneous presence of what we might call strictly business issues (such as products, markets, competition and industry growth) and family issues (such as the roles of family members in management, succession planning, governance, and family culture and values). Strategic planning can help company decision makers maximise the advantages that families bring to the business while identifying, anticipating and proposing solutions to problems and areas of conflict that may arise.

We present in the remainder of this section an overview of the main components of the strategic planning process as applied to family controlled enterprises. We first discuss strategic planning as applied to business issues, both in the current time frame and in possible future scenarios. We then broaden our analysis to include family issues and their impact on the business. The outcome of all this work needs to result in a set of feasible recommendations for the future of the business, together with associated metrics, which (once accepted) can be formulated into a detailed plan.

While there are many variations in strategic planning frameworks, we take the approach that the ultimate objective of strategic planning is to guide company decision makers in creating value for company stakeholders. Accordingly, we adopt an overall framework that can be used by investors and entrepreneurs alike to focus on the main components of a business that lead to value creation. This includes the following major steps, each of which is described further below:

- assessment of the current state of the business – which examines (among other things – see section 5.1 below) the business's objectives, products and

services, customers, competition, financials, technology, success factors and competitive advantage;
- envisioning the future of the business – which focuses on development of a view of future alternative scenarios for the business;
- assessment of the impact of family issues; and
- documenting recommendations, metrics and deliverables.

5.1 Assessment of the current state of the business

In order to plan for the future, it is useful to consider the state of the business today and in so doing also gain perspective on how the firm reached this point. Preparing an executive summary of the business is a logical starting point for analysing the current state of the business. The executive summary describes the important component parts of the business and ultimately answers the question as to why the firm is a good business to invest in and grow. Put another way, the executive summary provides a case for how value is being created in the business and how it will be created in the future. The executive summary will include a brief and focused description of the following items:

- *Objectives and goals:* What overall goals are the business's stakeholders trying to achieve? How is success measured? Has the company achieved its goals to date?
- *Products and services:* What products and services does the business offer to its customers? What are the main products' characteristics? Are the products and services sold to businesses or directly to the ultimate consumer – ie, is this a business-to-business (B2B) or a business-to-consumer (B2C) type of business? How have the products and services that are being offered changed over time?
- *Customers:* Who are the customers? Why do they buy the firm's products or use the firm's services?
- *Customer value proposition:* Probably the most important component of a company's business strategy is to identify and understand the customer. It is imperative to keep in mind that the customer is at the heart of the business, and without customers there is no business. The customer value proposition addresses this crucial business–customer relationship. Simply put, the customer value proposition provides an answer to the overall question: What do customers get and what do they pay or give up to get it? In answering this question, the customer value proposition examines important additional questions, including the following:
  - Does the product or service solve a significant problem for customers?
  - Are customers willing to pay to solve that problem and alleviate that pain?
  - Are there other significant benefits for customers, such as a fast and reliable service or access to cutting edge technology?
  - Is the product or service relatively new and untested, implying that customers are taking a risk that it might not work as intended?
  - Is there a compelling reason for customers to act now rather than do nothing and postpone the purchase decision?

  - Does the business delight its customers; and if it doesn't, how can it accomplish that?
- *Market size, segments, and dynamics:* How big is the market? What are the market segments and the characteristics of the different segments? Is the market growing, static, or declining?
- *Competition:* Who are the competitors and what are their product or service offerings? Is competition local, regional, national or international? What are the main dimensions of competition – eg, quality, service, convenience, price etc? Are there barriers to entering and exiting the market or do competitors enter and exit the market with relative ease?
- *Management team:* Who are the key people in the business? What are their attributes, such as previous industry experience, training, current role in the business and attitudes towards risk? What are the individual skill sets of the team members, and are those skill sets complementary? Are members of the management team able to operate effectively in situations involving uncertainty and ambiguity?
- *Economics of the business and financials:* Describe the economics of the business, including the important drivers of revenues and costs?. What do the cash flows and profits look like, and what is the break-even point for different market segments and for the business overall? Does the business make money at an adequate level for stakeholders – or, put differently, has the business been a good investment for stakeholders to date, and is it expected to be a good investment going forward?
- *Distribution strategy:* How do the products and services reach customers? Who are the business's partners, if any, in the distribution process? Which actors are essential in making the distribution process work well?
- *Overall business context:* How is the business affected by the state of the economy? For example, do sales of the business's products and services vary to a greater or lesser degree than variations in the overall economy? Are the products and services of the business affected by government environmental regulations? Does the business compete in markets characterised by easy entry and exit, or does the business dominate its markets or face dominant competitors? In what ways is the overall business climate in which the company operates likely to change, and how can decision makers best position the firm to remain competitive and create value from such possible changes?
- *Success factors:* What have been the most important reasons for the business's success to date and what is its distinctive competitive advantage? For example, is success in the marketplace due to a superior product and outstanding product quality, an efficient distribution network and logistics, fast and responsive customer service, a cost advantage, efficient and effective sales and support staff, a wide range of products to meet customers' needs, barriers to entry for competitors, technological superiority or other factors? Alternatively, if the business has faced challenges and difficulties, what are the reasons underlying the business's substandard performance? How can

periodic monitoring of the key success factor measures be utilised to identify opportunities and overcome challenges? Since the past key success factors and competitive advantage may change in the future, how should the business strategy going forward be adjusted to reflect this possibility?

- *Competitive advantage:* The concept of competitive advantage is closely related to the company's success factors. Indeed, the analysis of success factors leads logically to the articulation of the company's competitive advantage. So, what combination of factors has made the company successful to date? As pointed out in the previous bullet item, it is important to consider whether these success factors will continue to support the company's competitive advantage in the future.

5.2 Envisioning the future of the business

After analysing the current state of the business, the next step of the strategic planning process is to project the current situation into the future. It is necessary to develop possible alternative scenarios, taking into account company objectives, present and likely future company resources (including human, physical and financial resources, as well as intellectual property assets) and the competitive landscape. A useful analytical tool for this part of the strategic planning process is the SWOT analysis – delineating the company's strengths and weaknesses as well as its opportunities and the competitive threats that it faces.

The SWOT analysis can shed light on new opportunities that can be developed by the company and the generation of scenarios to exploit these opportunities. In like manner, possible threats can be identified and scenarios to deal with them can be analysed. The emphasis in this part of the strategic planning process is to explore the implications of changing some of the assumptions in the analysis in the previous step (see section 5.1 above) and projecting the likely outcomes resulting from the changed assumptions.

It is important to note that scenarios for the short, medium, and long term should be developed in order to fully analyse future possibilities. After articulating the scenarios, the most promising ones will then be compared, along with the implications of pursuing them.

5.3 Assessment of the impact of family issues

The third step is to introduce family issues into the planning process. Unfortunately, this step is often omitted by management teams of family controlled enterprises and even by the consultants they might have retained to assist their enterprises in the planning process. As noted previously, family factors can add complications to the business, but they can also result in additional opportunities compared with non-family controlled businesses.

Our task at this point in the strategic planning process is to determine how our previous analysis needs to be adjusted to take account of these additional opportunities and challenges. Depending upon the particular business and the culture, relationships and history of the family that controls it, the family issues will vary. A detailed analysis of how those variables impact individual companies lies beyond the scope of this chapter;[1] but certain family issues are common to many family controlled enterprises and we explore these briefly as an example of factors that will necessitate the adjustment of the strategic plan.

Such factors include the following:

- *Family objectives and culture* – Family objectives may be different from, and in conflict with, business objectives and be influenced by the family culture. The strategic plan must be adjusted to take such differences into account. The issue of value creation is a good illustration of this point. For example, from whose point of view is value being maximised: that of family shareholders; non-family shareholders, if any; family members who work in the business; family members who don't work in the business; employees; customers? In addition, how should value be measured – for example, just according to monetary value or other metrics used by financial analysts; or should the value of the family controlled enterprise include the addition of non-monetary considerations, such as enhancing the company's brand, improving working conditions for company employees, or creating value for the wider community by improving the environment and furthering corporate social responsibility?
- *Transmission of entrepreneurial passion and the founder's values* – Continuing in the tradition of the founder is important to many family companies, often long after the founder is no longer directly involved in the management of the company. The selection of alternative scenarios for growing the business in the future will need to reflect the fact that some scenarios may be in keeping with the founder's values and entrepreneurial passion and some may not, and this reality may lead to conflict in charting the company's future course.
- *Transition of authority in the family* – Clear lines of authority and responsibility are important in effective management. As the business moves into the future and leadership of the business changes, the planning process is an important aid to addressing this issue in a way that maintains continuity of the founding family/founder's vision, while at the same time providing opportunities for the next generation of leaders. For example, the plan can include a scenario that uses the European model of a non-executive chairperson, thus giving stature to the company founder while transferring authority to the next generation. Selection of an effective governance model is important for all enterprises, but the reality of the situation relating to family control of the enterprise may lead to a preference for one model over another.
- *Succession planning in the family and in the business* – Succession planning is important for all businesses. It is a key task for current management and boards of directors, and some would say it is the most important task. For

---

1 Nonetheless, see the chapter by Everett Moitoza, entitled "Culture and ethnicity in family enterprises", in Part I of this publication; and the chapter by Shari Wyner Narva entitled "The power of family" in Richard L Narva, *Family Enterprises: How to Build Growth, Family Control and Family Harmony*, Globe Law and Business, 2015.

family businesses, this task has the added complication that family members have relationships both inside and outside the business. Additionally, company managers need to have the right skill sets for the jobs they perform. This can sometimes lead to conflicts over who is best suited to assume specific leadership roles. Let's take the example of planning for the next chief executive officer (CEO) of the business. If it turns out that the middle sibling in a family has skills more appropriate to becoming the next CEO than the oldest sibling, this can create adverse consequences for the business and the family. The strategic planning process can help to resolve such conflicts by establishing consensus around what qualifications in the next CEO are best suited to support a thriving future for the company.

It is important to incorporate resolution of these and other family issues into the strategic planning process for any family controlled enterprise. These issues can clearly impact both the analysis of the current state of the business and the generation and evaluation of future business scenarios. They will add another level of realism to the strategic planning process that the family shareholder control group will demand (either explicitly or tacitly), and further an important objective of planning – ie, that the strategic planning process will enable decision-making and the comparison of alternative scenarios to be based on objective analysis in which the assumptions are clear and transparent.

5.4 Documenting recommendations, metrics and deliverables

After all of the analysis described in sections 5.1–5.3 has been completed, it is necessary to document the recommendations being made as the way for the business to move forward. These recommendations, once accepted (with or without modification) by the decision makers in the business and the family, will form the basis of a detailed plan for the future of the business.

Together with any recommendations put forward, there should be deliverables specified that arise from those recommendations. And for such deliverables there should be milestones and other metrics specified, as a means of measuring progress against the plan.

6. Implementation of an ongoing strategic planning process

The ultimate goal of the strategic planning process is to guide key decision makers in planning for the future of the company by enabling them to analyse alternative future scenarios, make choices among them, develop metrics, milestones and deliverables, and take actions to bring about the desired future. It cannot be overemphasised that, in order to derive the most benefit from strategic planning, it must be an ongoing continual process that is made an integral part of not only management's toolkit but also the toolkits of the board of directors and the owners, all of whom must ratify the planning decisions made by management.

It is often useful to obtain a consultant to lead the strategic planning process. An experienced consultant can prepare a plan of action, facilitate the strategic planning process, and provide useful feedback. Skilled consultants can also take the role of an unbiased objective observer and facilitate the gaining support for difficult decisions. However, it is crucial to note that while all competent strategy advisers are fluent in the language of business, an adviser on strategic planning must also have the facility to learn the dialect of the family controlled enterprise that he or she is advising if the engagement is truly going to add value to the client.

A practical implementation plan for a strategic planning process would include the following steps:

- Obtain the commitment and support of the CEO and key family and non-family decision makers for the implementation of a strategic planning process.
- Have the CEO appoint a strategic planning committee.
- Secure commitments from the top management team and key family and non-family managers to participate in the process.
- Conduct the meetings offsite, and at approximately monthly intervals.
- Select subcommittees made up of people with differing skill sets and experience in different functions in the company.
- Assign responsibility for analytical tasks to subcommittee members.
- Prepare and circulate detailed agendas for each meeting, indicating what topics will be discussed and which preparation materials need to be read prior to each meeting.
- Obtain a facilitator for each meeting to make sure there is a productive and free-flowing discussion.
- Obtain regular written feedback from participants about what they think is valuable in the sessions, what isn't and their suggested changes.
- Have participants prepare a final report summarising the essential parts of a strategic plan.
- Before concluding the planning sessions, make sure to implement a follow-on continuation process for strategic planning, detailing its objectives, who the participants will be, the milestones and the deliverables.

It should be noted that an ongoing strategic planning process for a family business provides continuing education for participants and useful feedback for the management team and the family.

7. Conclusion

The main points arising from this consideration of strategic planning in a family controlled business can be summarised as follows:

- Strategic planning is an essential tool to help company decision makers choose the best path into an uncertain future.
- Change is the only constant in business, and strategic planning enables key decision makers to anticipate changes in the business and its environment, and to take appropriate actions to create value.
- For a family business, strategic planning enables the coordination of business issues and family issues so that they are working in concert rather than in opposition.

- Facilitating value creation for stakeholders is the overall objective of strategic planning, and the choices as to which stakeholders should receive what value must be made by key family and management decision makers.
- The strategic plan and strategic planning should not be confused with one another. To be most effective, strategic planning needs to be an ongoing process, not simply a static report prepared at a particular point in time. It is important to keep in mind that the purpose of the process is to help decision makers make decisions and take action.
- An ongoing strategic planning process for a family business provides continuing education for participants and useful feedback for the management team and the family.

Mindfulness and the management of family business stress

Thomas Hubler
Hubler for Business Families Inc

1. Stress in a family business

If you are worried about stress, STOP; worrying only makes it worse. Stress causes deterioration in everything, from your heart to your arteries to your gums to your immune system. Good stress can be as draining as bad stress. Stress kills brains cells. Failing to manage stress can kill you.

Yet it is hard to imagine any career setting that can engender as much stress as working in an enterprise controlled by one's own family. Research estimates workplace stress costs for US businesses at between $50 billion and $150 billion annually in worker health issues and lost productivity. Thus, stress carries high financial, physical and psychological costs that can be doubly punishing in a family business.

Take a look at this list of common family-business stress triggers:

- death of an entrepreneur/owner;
- business decline;
- management turmoil;
- firing of a family member;
- avoiding discussion of critical, emotionally powerful issues arising in either the family or the business;
- erosion of family rituals (eg, family holidays) as a result of business differences; and
- impact of wealth and entitlement on the next generation.

And this is just the beginning of a long list of stressful situations that are a part of being involved in a family business.

When a person works in a family business system, work and life stresses can have a profound personal impact. In my practice as an adviser to family controlled companies, I help family businesses learn to balance business and family obligations by keeping certain aspects separate, by learning to communicate authentically and by setting goals together. Even in difficult situations, business families have demonstrated that they can draw new boundaries and overcome rough circumstances, not just to survive hard times but also to thrive as both a business and family.

What many consider normal day-to-day family issues can produce stress that goes unmanaged if unacknowledged. Two examples illustrate this painful reality (where I have changed client names and details to protect their privacy):

- **Case 1:** Larry is the patriarch of the Mattison family business, Sento. He does not realise that he is the cause of a critical problem in this family firm. He recruited his son-in-law, Tim, into the family business, telling him, "I would like you take over my job." Tim left a successful position with a Fortune 500 company thinking he would be the next president of Sento. Years went by, and Tim still was not promoted to the top spot. Larry defended the decision by saying, "All I meant was that I wanted Tim to take responsibility for my sales account." In the meantime, Jen (Larry's daughter and Tim's wife) is upset with her father about the confusion he created and how he has mistreated her husband, Tim.

  In addition, Larry is struggling to let go of power, to create a management succession plan, and to develop a financial exit strategy for himself and his wife. This aggregation of difficult business and financial challenges has raised Larry's stress level, exacerbating the negative impact he has had on family relationships. Some would call these situations simply 'misunderstandings' or 'issues' that should be readily resolved. Maybe so. But in the meantime, everyone in the Mattison family is suffering under the stress.
- **Case 2:** To save taxes, John, the owner of the Stephens family business, was told by his financial adviser to transfer 2,000 shares of stock into a family limited partnership with his three adult children: Ron, the oldest; Jerry, in the middle; and Philip, the youngest. The idea was that the three sons would eventually receive the value of the company in stock. John is general partner and holds the voting control of the company, while the sons are limited partners in the venture. John found the stock transfer experience enormously stressful. Then things got worse.

  Jerry and Philip work in the business but Ron has his own career outside the family firm. Jerry is the company's general manager, and he recently fired Philip (his younger brother) as he had different expectations of Philip's role in the company. Philip thought he and his oldest brother Ron were equals, not only as limited partners and also as brothers, but also as business leaders. Philip had helped the company succeed until he was fired, and he resented his older brothers and his father; he felt they ignored him and treated him unfairly. Philip questioned Jerry's lifestyle and the compensation he received from the business. Philip also felt that Ron was abusing his position as a family member to run personal items through the family firm's accounting department for payment. All of these actions contributed to a breakdown in the communication among family managers and piled massive stress on the family.

Stress produced deep divides. Sources of stress can come from inside a person as well as from the outside world, because our attitudes or perceptions may produce a stressful view of the world. A person may have unrealistic expectations or live with fear, uncertainty, perfectionism and/or low self-esteem. But few people can lower their stress until they recognise their own triggers.

Look at this brief list developed by Minnesota's Mayo Clinic. Are you experiencing any of these stresses in your family business?

- I'm impatient with details.

- I make things happen.
- I think most people seem to work too slowly.
- I work long hours.
- I have tight deadlines.
- I need to talk in front of colleagues.
- I have a lot of responsibility.
- I work based on efficiency and vision.
- I am hard on myself when I make a mistake.
- I have been told I "have a lot of energy".
- I have overcome many hardships.

These are all symptoms of stress and burnout – and by now this chapter itself may be stressing you out as you read it. Let's take a look at how so-called 'mindfulness' can help you manage stress in your family business.

2. Mindfulness

When your brain perceives you are under threat, your body's stress response kicks in. These perceptions of threat don't have to be an encounter with a mugger or fear of losing your job; subjective situations of almost any nature can trigger stress whenever the brain senses an imbalance of resources. Anything can cause you and your family business to feel stress – for example, lack of control, lack of meaning in life or work, or fear of the unknown. Stress is the friction between actual events and how one subjectively perceives those events.

Sometimes circumstances can't be changed, but we must learn to control our perceptions of and responses to stressful situations. This resilience is not simply an ability to bounce back, but a conscious technique called 'attention training'. To understand this technique we must first look at how our brains process stress.

2.1 How the brain processes stress

According to Amit Sood, a Mayo Clinic professor of medicine, our brains operate in two functional modes, 'focused' and 'default', where:

- in focused mode we react to novel occurrences with an 'undistracted presence' (ie, we are 'in the moment'). It could be fight or flight, pleasurable, meaningful, or some immediate experience in the external world; and
- in default mode, the brain wanders and creates manifestations of the external world. This is the inner focus of our thoughts and reflections. Excessive internalisation can create stress, anxiety, depression and even attention deficit disorder.

The mind focuses on three primary aspects: threat, pleasure and novelty. In the modern world it might surprise you that threat is the primary focus, although threat exists most often only in the mind. Fear of being eaten by sabre-toothed tigers has receded greatly, even as fear of failure in business has become rampant. But it is manifested by hurts and regrets from the past, as well as desires and fears for the future.

Professor Sood says that this brooding creates 'attention black holes' in the mind, which take away the experience of joy and reduce bodily energy. To combat these attention black holes, he proposes that we use a technique called 'attention training' in order to direct our attention outward, to others, so that we can experience joy, happiness and fulfilment.

2.2 How to employ attention training

It's all too simple to say that attention training is a state of mind. Yet it essentially is. To perform this attention training, Professor Sood suggests three actions:

- *Joyful attention* – Begin each day, even before you get out of bed, by expressing gratitude for the special people in your life such as spouse, children, parents and friends. From that early moment, be conscious so that when you return home from work you treat your family as if you are meeting them after a long period of absence.
- *Kind attention* – Practise caring and being kind, either directly or indirectly, to the first 20 or 30 people you encounter each day. You can express this attention silently with a kindly look, or orally with a kind word.
- *Self-monitored intention* – Become aware of how you interpret events and activities as they occur. Recognise that you are viewing these through your 'normal lens', which has been created by family and society and which induces prejudice, constrains your interpretation and causes stress. Instead, begin viewing life through the lenses of compassion, acceptance, acknowledgement of a higher power, forgiveness and gratitude.

Let's understand how forgiveness, compassion and gratitude, which are the three most important lenses, can alter your perceptions about what occurs in your family business.

(a) Forgiveness

To be wronged is nothing, unless you continue to remember it. (Confucius)

In the flow of life, it is certain that individuals in a family business will anger, offend or upset another family member. It frequently happens with people we love because we share such a special bond. The participants and leaders in successful family businesses whom I encounter have learned to forgive each other and create a new beginning in their relationships. Business (and household) families who do not practise forgiveness stay mired in past hurts and negativity. This stance damages everyone: transgressor, victim and other family members.

It is your choice to forgive someone who wrongs you; you do it voluntarily. In fact, I suggest that a person cannot move forward until he or she forgives. And when you forgive, you relieve your own suffering and stress. Forgiveness leads to a healthier life, improves relationships and releases you from the negatives of the past.

Forgiveness provides a feeling of peace. As Khaled Hosseini writes in his book *The Kite Runner*,[1] forgiveness occurs "not with the fanfare of epiphany, but with pain

1 Bloomsbury Paperbacks, 2011 (first published by Riverhead Books in 2003).

gathering its things, packing up, and slipping away unannounced in the middle of the night". When you forgive, you take responsibility for how you feel, which allows you to give and receive more love from the important people in your life. It re-energises relationships.

To reach the peace that forgiveness provides, you must begin with an open heart. You feel vulnerable and, at the same time, courageous. "The weak can never forgive," said Mahatma Gandhi, "Forgiveness is the attribute of the strong." That is why it is important to recognises that you are doing this for yourself; you forgive as a way to heal and make your own life. You have compassion for yourself. You also have compassion for the person who caused the hurt. You chose to forgive – the perpetrator cannot successfully demand it. This is another reason why forgiveness comes from strength, not from weakness. You learn to forgive gracefully to reduce the burden on the person you forgive. The idea is similar to the philosophy of Alcoholics Anonymous, to not harm others in any way.

A final important aspect of forgiveness is that it is polite acceptance of life's imperfections. It comes from gratitude rather than expectation. Through forgiveness, we learn to understand and appreciate the blessings we receive, broaden our world view, and live life with greater ease. As my teacher Professor Sood said, "Since you didn't write the script, there is no reason to think you should be able to edit it."

We must learn to accept the many things in our lives that we cannot control. This lifelong endeavour requires regular, conscious practice. Living a life of forgiveness is a gift to yourself that resonates inside yourself even as it radiates to others. As activist and author Maya Angelou put it, "I've learned that people will forget what you said, people will forget what you did, but people will never forget how you made them feel."[2]

Practising forgiveness in your family business is crucial, both to enable a business to thrive and individuals to grow. Getting past conflict between family members can sometimes mean the difference between passing the legacy down another generation or having to close or sell the business and its legacy of family endeavour. Forgiveness is the feeling that ever expands and never reduces. It ennobles you and renounces anger on those who wronged you. It just might be the most powerful prescription for bettering your family business and our world.

(b) Compassion

Love and compassion are necessities, not luxuries. Without them, humanity cannot survive. (14th Dalai Lama)[3]

Chinese rulers of antiquity knew that compassion brings true inner peace. The so-called 'golden rule' of "do unto others as you would have others do onto you," originated in early Chinese rituals, but versions of the same rule exist in the major world religions, including Christianity ("Love your neighbour as yourself") and Islam

---

2 As quoted in Bob Kelly, *Worth Repeating: More Than 5,000 Classic and Contemporary Quotes*, Kregel Academic & Professional, 2003, p263.

3 Dalai Lama XIV and Howard C Cutler, *The Art of Happiness*, Easton Press, 1998.

("Not one of you can be a believer unless he desires for his neighbour what he desires for himself").

Human beings have always known that when life seems tough, home can be a place where they find love, compassion and warmth. Because it is within our family that we feel reassured and that we are most likely to find someone who understands and cares how we feel, compassion is a crucial element that makes up a strong and united family business. The compassion we witness and experience in our home inspires us to be more compassionate to others, ultimately strengthening the family business by establishing deep relationships within and outside the company – including with stakeholders such as customers, employees and vendors.

Compassion happens when you personally acknowledge and understand a suffering person. This kindness arises by validating the other person's experience – as Plato said, "Be kind, for everyone you meet is fighting a harder battle." Acknowledging the other person's battle brings you closer to their situation, validates their experience and creates peace in yourself. Like gratitude, love and forgiveness, compassion heals all that it touches. It radiates out as it resonates within. Compassion is a universal quality so often forgotten in the small moments of life. We underestimate the power of a smile, a kind word or a moment taken to listen. These are qualities each of us can consciously develop and strengthen.

Make compassion as natural as breathing. Bring your inner sense of love, forgiveness and acceptance to each greeting, each time. You can do these things directly or silently. Scientists say this practice stimulates the prefrontal lobes of your brain that generate compassion and inner peace. In other words, by regularly practising compassion – acknowledging and validating others – you are physically and emotionally improving your own well-being.

A final yet important aspect of compassion is service to others. I believe this is a learned behaviour. Serving others must be practised to become instinctive. Mother Teresa committed her life to treating India's poor with compassion and love. She said, "I would rather make mistakes in kindness and compassion than work miracles in unkindness and hardship." In that statement you can recognise how committed she was to acknowledging the suffering of others. You feel her courage to place herself in situations where she lived with compassion, gave of herself and undoubtedly drew resolve from that effort.

Each of us has opportunities every day to express compassion. We can serve by volunteering for our communities, schools or charities. We can serve our families by supporting ageing parents and grandparents. We can serve each other by conducting our lives with compassion in order to validate others.

Mother Teresa also said, "If we have no peace, it is because we have forgotten that we belong to each other." Understanding and practising compassion brings the realisation that we are all one people. The human race is our family tree, where compassion nurtures its growth, extends its branches, and flowers its existence. For, as Jamaican musician, Bob Marley sang, "One love, one heart, one destiny." It is the basis of morality.

(c) Gratitude

Gratitude is not only the greatest of virtues, but the parent of all others. (Cicero)

Gratitude is a spontaneous emotion, but not simply an emotional response; it is a choice we make. It is our readiness to express appreciation. Gratitude grows as we develop the ability to recognise the good in our lives. Gratitude is how we remember kindness such as cherished interactions in our family, the compassionate acts of strangers and everyday blessings. How often do you consciously consider that life is a gift, employment is a gift, beloved family and friends are gifts? This recognises the basis for gratitude.

Within the family business it is often easy to forgo expressions of gratitude. Family members have lived together and known each other their entire lives. This fact of life makes gratitude seem either unnecessary or like an added chore between relationships. However, the health of the family business and relationships among its stakeholders can become damaged or weakened without the element of gratitude to alleviate the stresses of everyday life.

It is easy to slip into negative thoughts and wander darkly in our minds (demonstrating the attention black holes described in section 2.1 above). Gratitude is the antidote to such stress-generating meanderings. As French author Alphonse Karr wrote in *A Tour Around My Garden*,[4] "Some people grumble that roses have thorns; I am grateful that thorns have roses." When we worry or imagine catastrophic outcomes or focus on past hurts or regrets, such negativity separates us from recognising the blessings in our lives. This is not just regretful, it is personally damaging. "You pay in your distress and in your need," writes Khalil Gibran in *The Prophet*.[5] "Would that you might pray also in the fullness of your joy and in the days of your abundance."

A developed sense of gratitude provides significant personal benefits, such as reduced stress and anxiety, enhanced health, an appreciation of one's own talents and gifts, and the clarity to live a most purposeful life. A strong sense of gratitude not only increases your personal happiness but also improves your personal relationships, helps protect you against adverse life experiences, and (scientists say) improves your productivity and even your sleep.

Gratitude is natural and can arise like a laugh in some situations. However, every person also has the ability to increase gratitude. The process is intentional. It is made simple by being mindful. It costs nothing and takes little time. You can increase gratitude by taking walks in nature or by activities like gardening that build your appreciation for nature's bounty. You can augment an intention for gratitude by being kind to people you meet during the day. It becomes especially important to treat family members and loved ones with love, care, and respect. We extend our expression of gratitude by serving others and through philanthropy. Service is on the outside, like prayer is on the inside. Gratitude is the intentional habit of recognising our blessings in how we live and serve others.

---

4 A gardening book first published in 1859.

5 A book of prose poetry that was first published (in the US) in 1923 by Alfred A Knopf.

3. Conclusion

The content of section 2.1 above may all sound too spiritual, too fluffy or too vague, but since I have enrolled and completed Professor Sood's programme I have noticed that I have become a calmer, gentler self. I am more even-keeled and able to manage the ups and downs in my life. Practising Professor Sood's three steps contained within attention training can help transform your life, and your family business to be a more stress-free, happier and fulfilling place by investing your attention in others.

In my practice, I have seen how the individuals in both the Mattison and Stephens families (see the case studies in section 1 above) redirected their lives and dramatically reduced their stress by investing in others. The Mattisons, paralysed by negativity and family business issues, learned to collaborate and come to workable solutions. Larry has created a financial exit strategy for himself and mended fences with his daughter and his son-in-law Tim. In addition, Larry has assisted in creating a meaningful role in the company for Tim, and family relationships have never been better. The members of the Stephens family have put into practice joyful and kind attention, but they have taken longer to resolve their differences. While the circumstances are now much less volatile, they have yet to fully resolve their business differences. The brothers are still upset with each other but their relationships have strengthened. The entire family has applied the experience to produce successful family gatherings at their lakeside cabin.

Stress is a killer. It is everywhere and only gets worse if individuals fail to recognise it. Anyone can do a lot to improve his or her own life, family life and even the vitality of a family business by practising attention training and focusing on others with compassion, acceptance, forgiveness and gratitude. This might sound too simple, but if you practise these simple actions I am confident that you will begin to respond to the world differently and stress will become much less present in your life and family business.

Afterword

Richard L Narva
Narva & Company LLC

Most people have a straightforward vision of the perfect family business. First, they hope for a continued strengthening of the company's financial and market position so that it can support the lifestyle and needs of the family members, from generation to generation. Secondly, they wish for family harmony.

But life gets in the way. Sometimes family members' short-term or individual needs can overwhelm the needs of the business. In other cases, family members strongly disagree on the strategic direction, or even on the day-to-day management, of the business. These family conflicts, when acted out on the stage of the family controlled enterprise, can seem insurmountable. As an unfortunate consequence – almost by default – many families end up in one of two places.

In one scenario, a family sells out and creates a pool of financial assets, infinitely divisible and generally free from controversy among family members. Those family members who are astute financially may thrive; others may dissipate their assets quickly. But the non-financial legacy of the family's enterprise begins to erode on the day the sale is closed. In the other scenario, the family devolves into a 'lifestyle company', in which all decisions are driven by the requirement to provide for the family's lifestyle needs. Similar to selling out, this alternative is a terminal position. Eventually the money is gone because the business exists only to finance family needs – it is no longer a vital enterprise independent of, albeit controlled by, the family. Unless a business continually strives to build as strong a competitive position as possible in its core marketplace, it will wither and die, much to the detriment of the lifestyle it was meant to support.

What both the family seeks and the business needs, are:

- continuity of family control and leadership, with adherence to core values;
- improved family harmony; and
- continual reinvention of business strategies and tactics.

To achieve these three core objectives, families need a roadmap (and usually a guide) through a process I call 'continuity planning', a holistic planning-and-implementation process encompassing at least seven independent, concurrent planning activities led by several different primary professional advisers.

This book is intended as the second part of such a roadmap and guide for family firms, begun with the publication of *Family Enterprise: How to Build Growth, Family Control and Family Harmony*.[1] My first collection of essays was emphatically not

---

1 Edited by Richard L Narva and published by Globe Law and Business, March 2015.

intended as a panacea for the ills of family firms or the pains experienced by their stakeholders. Rather, it comprises a collection of essays that were written and edited to provide the architecture for continuing family controlled enterprises.

This second collection is intended to provide sustenance for those stakeholders committed to the core objectives presented in the title to the first book, namely how to build growth, family control and family harmony. The readership for this book, as with its predecessor, is intended to be the owners, directors, managers of and advisers to family controlled enterprises and the families that control them. It assumes that such enterprises have been launched – or at least renewed – expressly as family controlled businesses, or as other enterprises such as foundations, investment vehicles, family offices etc. It addresses ongoing issues facing both family shareholder control groups and the enterprises they control – issues that surface in ongoing, mature and successful endeavours.

But the foundational premise remains the same: unless stakeholders in these enterprises integrate a commitment to family and to concurrent continuing efforts to measure material decisions against the core values and culture of the enterprise (which has, in most cases, been sourced by the enterprise from the founding family), there is little chance of sustaining such companies as family controlled enterprises.

When I was a United States Coast Guard deck watch officer on a buoy tender enforcing fisheries laws against an armada of trawlers from the fishing fleets of the Eastern bloc, I internalised the answer that members of the smallest of the armed forces gave to the frequent (and frequently dismissive) question, "What is the Coast Guard?" The answer I was taught was, "The Coast Guard is the hard core around which the Navy forms in time of war!"

In this same vein, the family is the hard core around which the culture, values and vision of an enduring competitive business enterprise controlled by a family are formed. Without acknowledging, internalising and measuring key decisions against this hard core, it is well nigh impossible to sustain a family firm against the normal dissonance that emerges across generations of families and the consistent challenges faced by the enterprises they control. As Tolstoy wrote in *Anna Karenina*: "All happy families resemble each other. But each unhappy family is unhappy in its own way." While families who control vital growing enterprises may encounter unhappiness (even sustained periods of unhappiness), adjusted for the particular culture from which the family emerges, there can often be in the endeavour of sustaining the family firm a common cause around which the family forms in times of difficulty – whether based in family conflicts or business conflicts. This reality raises the question as to what tools exist to help family controlled enterprise stakeholders manage such difficulties and continue to endure as a successful enterprise.

In the beginning, when I solicited and edited the first book of essays, I endeavoured to use the metaphor of smoked fish, or at least how eating herring early in life correlates with enjoying this very particular food as an appetiser – a *forshpeis* as my Eastern European-born grandparents would call it. To continue this culinary metaphor from my own culture of origin, this second volume should be understood as the cholent, the meat casserole prepared on Friday afternoons and left in the oven to cook slowly, for consumption as the Sabbath meal. As cholent sustained families across Eastern Europe for centuries, it is my hope that the enduring wisdom of the experts who have contributed chapters to this publication will aid families from across the globe to sustain the enterprises they have founded – and thereby all the stakeholders they support: employees, customers, communities, management and owners.

About the authors

Emily F Abrams
Adviser, Narva & Company LLC
eabrams@narvaandcompany.com

Emily Abrams is an adviser and a member of Narva & Company LLC's multidisciplinary leadership team. She has been helping family controlled enterprises for nearly 20 years to prepare members of the next generation for leadership roles in family governance, successful careers in the family enterprise, or for philanthropic activities that align with the family's core values. Emily also specialises in creating effective corporate governance processes and protocols and in assessing and recruiting candidates uniquely fit for councils of advisers and boards of directors of family controlled enterprises.

Emily is an active member of many professional and charitable organisations, including The Boston Club, which supports executive and professional women to achieve significant and visible leadership roles. She holds a degree in English and Art History from Simmons College in Boston. Emily spent her early career in teaching and designing programmes for art museum education.

George P Bukuras
Founder, Milestone Business Advisors LLC
george.bukuras@milestoneba.com

George Bukuras's professional training began at what is now PwC, before he entered the private practice of law where he was a co-founding partner of Lapping & Bukuras LLP, a boutique business law firm in Boston. In his professional capacity, he has assisted clients with business matters and transactions in numerous industries ranging from food services to heavy manufacturing.

During his career as an operating executive, Mr Bukuras has held positions in virtually all of the functional aspects of management, including chief financial officer, chief operating officer and chief executive officer of family-owned enterprises, and general counsel and chief compliance officer at a major private-equity-owned multinational manufacturing entity.

After leaving his own family business, Mr Bukuras founded Milestone Business Advisors LLC, a general management firm that helps middle-market businesses and their owners navigate the developmental stages of growth.

Mr Bukuras is an attorney and certified public accountant, earning his bachelor's degree in business administration from Suffolk University in Boston, Massachusetts, and his JD from Suffolk University Law School.

Christian W Dame
Principal, Interim Executive Solutions LLC
CDame@InterimExecutive.Solutions

Christian Dame is a change management leader with more than 40 years of government, business and non-profit experience in planning, management and organisational consulting. He has been an independent consultant since 1986, founding three companies (the latest being

Interim Executive Solutions LLC) and consulting for organisations in the fields of interim executive leadership, turnaround management and organisational transition.

For many years Mr Dame was involved in implementing large-scale change. Later he joined a successful consulting firm for family businesses facing leadership transitions and, paired with a highly experienced family therapist, his team assisted a variety of northeastern US closely held businesses, addressing complex and challenging organisational and ownership transition issues. Subsequently, Mr Dame used the experience he had gained in order to assist non-profits in some of the same leadership and organisational challenges.

Mr Dame graduated from Duke University, and earned a master's degree in city planning from Harvard Graduate School of Design.

Eugene J Fierman
Medical psychiatrist, Commonwealth Medical Psychiatry Associates
efierman@massmed.org

Gene Fierman is a medical psychiatrist with 45 years of clinical experience helping individuals with major mental illness and their families. Throughout his career he has focused on the medical treatment of major psychiatric disorders in adult patients and on counselling for the mentally ill and their families. Until his retirement at the end of 2015, he worked with physicians, psychologists, social workers and therapists to provide quality care tailored to patients' illness, culture and life situation. He continues to work as a psychiatric consultant in the Social Security Administration disability programme and supervises psychiatric resident physicians in the Harvard Longwood Psychiatric Residency programme in Boston, Massachusetts.

Dr Fierman earned his undergraduate degree at Columbia University and his medical degree at New York University. He received his psychiatric training at St Elizabeth's Hospital in Washington DC and the Massachusetts Mental Health Center in Boston. He is a past president of the Massachusetts Psychiatric Society.

Janet B Fierman
Shareholder, Sheehan Phinney Bass & Green PA
jfierman@sheehan.com

Janet Fierman is an equity owner of Sheehan Phinney, a law firm based in New England in the United States. She specialises in privately owned and family controlled enterprises. She founded, developed and managed her own law firm for 25 years before merging part of it into Sheehan Phinney in 2008 and liquidating the balance. Throughout her legal career, Ms Fierman has acted as outside general counsel to privately owned and family controlled businesses in many industry areas, including real estate, construction, life sciences, biotechnology, manufacturing, marketing and consulting. She has helped many of her clients to create and implement governance systems and transition plans tailored to their industry, business, family culture and demographics.

Ms Fierman has a JD law degree from Boston University as well as a master's degree in international affairs from Columbia University. She is a trained mediator.

Patricia A Frishkoff
Consultant, Leadership In Family Enterprise LLC
patosu@prodigy.net

Patricia Frishkoff founded and directed the Austin Family Business Program (AFBP) at Oregon State University, and served as professor of accounting, until her retirement in 2002. She was the inaugural holder of the AE Coleman Chair in Family Business. The AFBP celebrated its 30th anniversary in the third quarter of 2015.

Dr Frishkoff is a fellow of the Family Firm Institute and served on its board of directors as one of its early treasurers. She held both CPA and CMA certificates in accounting during her active teaching in that academic field. She has published many scholarly and practical articles in both accounting and family business, and continues to teach, consult, write and mentor in the latter field.

Robert Goodman
Founder, RGoodman Associates LLC
bob@rgoodmanassociates.com

Robert Goodman is the founder of RGoodman Associates, an organisational effectiveness consulting firm that specialises in helping leaders and teams to reach high performance. He has more than 30 years of professional experience in leadership and team development, primarily in the pharmaceutical, biotech, education and healthcare sectors. He coaches executives at all levels, including board chairs, CEOs and other senior staff. He has also worked with founders and senior leaders of family-owned and family-managed enterprises. Before founding his present company, Mr Goodman maintained a clinical psychology practice for 16 years and was owner/operator of a food retail business.

In addition to overseeing and operating RGoodman Associates, Mr Goodman is a clinical instructor in the Department of Psychiatry at Harvard Medical School and is on the faculty of the EdLD doctoral programme at the Harvard Graduate School of Education. He is a clinical associate at McLean Hospital in Belmont, Massachusetts, senior associate at Minds at Work, a *pro bono* senior leadership coach at the Foundation for International Leadership Coaching and a master coach supervisor in the executive coaching certification programme at William James College in Boston. Mr Goodman has degrees from both Rutgers University and Harvard University.

David A Hoffman
Founding member, Boston Law Collaborative LLC
dhoffman@BostonLawCollaborative.com

David Hoffman is a mediator, arbitrator, attorney and the founding member of Boston Law Collaborative. He teaches courses on mediation, collaborative law and legal ethics at Harvard Law School, where he is the John H Watson Jr Lecturer on Law. He is past chair of the American Bar Association (ABA) section on dispute resolution and is a distinguished fellow in the International Academy of Mediators. He has received a number of awards for his dispute resolution work, including the Lifetime Achievement Award from the American College of Civil Trial Mediators and the D'Alemberte–Raven Award from the ABA.

Mr Hoffman has published three books and numerous articles on law and dispute resolution. He is a graduate *summa cum laude* of Princeton University and obtained a master's degree in American studies from Cornell University. He gained his JD *magna cum laude* from Harvard Law School and while there was an editor of the *Harvard Law Review.*

Thomas Hubler
President, Hubler for Business Families Inc
tomh@thehublergroup.com

Tom Hubler, president of Hubler for Business Families and a founding member of the Family Firm Institute, integrates the notion of spirit in his work with family businesses. As a national expert with 40 years of experience in working with families, he purposefully designs innovative transitions for his client families.

Mr Hubler has been an adjunct instructor for the University of St Thomas, where he co-taught a class on family business management for 10 years. He currently serves the community through his work on the board and executive committee of Catholic Charities of St Paul and Minneapolis.

Julian E Lange
Governor Craig R Benson Professor of Entrepreneurship and Public Policy, and associate professor, Entrepreneurship Division, Babson College
langej@babson.edu

Julian Lange is the Governor Craig R Benson Professor of Entrepreneurship and Public Policy and an associate professor in the Entrepreneurship Division at Babson College, Massachusetts, where he teaches MBA, executive and undergraduate courses in entrepreneurship. He previously served as the Dean's Visiting Professor of Entrepreneurship at Princeton University in the School of Engineering and Applied Science and as an assistant professor of finance at Harvard Business School.

Dr Lange has considerable experience as an entrepreneur, having been CEO of Software Arts, the company that created VisiCalc®, the first electronic spreadsheet. In addition, he has more than 25 years' experience advising clients ranging from *Fortune Global 500* companies to start-ups and mid-sized businesses, and including private and public companies and family controlled enterprises. He has served on boards of private-sector firms and public agencies and has extensive experience developing and teaching in executive education programmes in the United States and internationally. He has also previously served as the Adviser on Entrepreneurship to Governor Craig Benson of New Hampshire and as chair of the governor's Task Force on Entrepreneurship.

Dr Lange's commentary on entrepreneurial topics has appeared through national and international media coverage, including in such publications as *The Wall Street Journal*, *The New York Times*, *Money* and *USA Today*. Dr Lange is a graduate *magna cum laude* of Princeton University; he also holds an MBA from Harvard Business School and a PhD in economics from Harvard University.

Ann Lindsey
Principal, Lindsey Leadership Consulting
Ann@LindseyLeadershipConsulting.com

Ann Lindsey is the principal of Lindsey Leadership Consulting, specialising in leadership development for organisations and individuals; she also serves as an adviser to Narva & Company LLC. She has focused her consulting work within private- and public-sector organisations in manufacturing, technology and public services, and has built up more than 25 years of consulting experience, having advised firms such as General Motors, Quantum Chemical Corporation, Malden Mills Industries and the NASA Space Center, as well as family-owned businesses.

Prior to establishing Lindsey Leadership Consulting, Ms Lindsey was a founder and principal of GLS Consulting and a professor of management at Simmons Graduate School of Management. In both the MBA and the executive development programmes there, she helped develop and expand the organisational behaviour courses that were part of the founding philosophy of the school. Ms Lindsey holds an MBA degree.

Greg McCann
Principal, McCann & Associates
greg@gregmccannspeaks.com

Greg McCann is the founder, principal and leader of McCann & Associates, a national family-enterprise consulting firm that creates workshops, consults, publishes and innovates on issues of importance to family enterprises. As an author, educator, coach, consultant and speaker, he works with family enterprises in the areas of transition, leadership, communication and conflict resolution, with a special emphasis on helping the next generation. He has coached leaders and executives for nearly 20 years and is certified in leadership agility and the Myers–Briggs Type Indicator. He is a JD and (inactive) CPA.

As a professor and founder of Stetson University's Family Enterprise Center, Mr McCann led the effort to create its award-winning internationally acclaimed programme; he has also redesigned Stetson's Executive MBA course with greater emphasis on leadership as a practice. Mr McCann has authored two books (*When Your Parents Sign the Paychecks* and *Who Do You Think You Are? Aligning Your Character and Reputation*), along with dozens of articles.

Daisy E Medici
Director, GenSpring Family Offices
Daisy.Medici@GenSpring.com

Daisy Medici is the managing director of governance and education at GenSpring Family Offices, focusing her time on developing and administering tools and processes designed to help families increase the likelihood of sustaining wealth over generations. She came to GenSpring with extensive experience in the field of family business, having served as a partner at The Roseview Group and as managing director of Genus Resources.

Ms Medici holds a master of science degree from Simmons College in Boston, Massachusetts, is a certified administrator of the Myers–Briggs Type Indicator® and has been an active member of the Family Firm Institute for many years.

Everett Moitoza
Principal, Moitoza Consulting
moitoza@comcast.net

Everett Moitoza has provided business consulting and executive coaching to family enterprises, partnerships, professional service firms, CEOs and closely held small to medium-sized companies for more than 25 years. His work has focused on providing innovative management consultation in a significant variety of industries on topics such as organisational assessment and development, organisational transitions and succession planning, conflict management, strategic planning, and executive team building and training for today's owners and executives.

Dr Moitoza has a doctorate in psychology from Boston University, an MBA from Southern New Hampshire University, a master's in behavioural science from Bridgewater University, Massachusetts, and a bachelor's degree in music from Berklee College of Music in Boston. He has taught graduate-level courses at Harvard University, Boston University Northeastern University and Lesley University. He is currently a professional sponsor of the University of New Hampshire's Center for Family Business.

Dr Moitoza has delivered numerous speeches and presentations to national, regional and local business and professional organisations – his opinions, perspectives and formulations regarding family business family and organisational issues and solutions are sought frequently and published by business and news media internationally. At present he is conducting research on the experience and management of conflict in family businesses and partnerships.

Richard L Narva
Founder and senior adviser, Narva & Company LLC
rnarva@narvaandcompany.com

Richard Narva leads a multidisciplinary team of advisers helping family controlled enterprises preserve their values and vision while addressing organisational, strategic, governance and human capital issues. He has been a member of the Massachusetts Bar since 1975 and practised corporate law (specialising in mergers and acquisitions) before succeeding his father as president of Morton Shoe Companies Inc, becoming the third generation in his family to head this US Stock Exchange-listed firm founded by his grandfather in 1921.

Mr Narva has been elected to the boards of directors of both public and private family controlled businesses and currently serves on the councils of advisers of several family controlled companies and as a trustee of a trust for the benefit of the family shareholder group that controls a global retail company. He is the author and editor of numerous publications on the general theme of improving the governance of family controlled enterprises. His book, *Family Enterprises: How to Build Growth, Family Control and Family Harmony*, was published in March 2015.

Mr Narva earned his AB from Brown University and a JD from Boston University School of Law. He lives in Boston.

Roger Patkin
Founder and principal, Next Generation Group
roger@nextgenerationgroup.net

Roger Patkin is the founder and principal of Next Generation Group, a consultancy dedicated to empowering enterprising families and their next-generation leaders to succeed in the 21st century. Prior to forming the consultancy, he was president and CEO of Autopart International, his third-generation family business that was acquired by Advance Auto Parts in 2005. He led the company both before and after the sale, and he currently serves as a board director and adviser.

Mr Patkin teaches entrepreneurial leadership at Tufts University and lectures on international business and family business at other Boston-area universities. He also advises social-impact entrepreneurs, and is a trustee of the Carroll School in Lincoln, Massachusetts. He received his BA degree in psychology and philosophy from Tufts University and his JD from the Boston University School of Law.

Gerald Sherman
Managing member, Pathway Advisors LLC
gsherman@pathway-advisors.com

Gerry Sherman has been involved with family businesses for his entire life. His father and uncle had started a distribution company several years before he was born and he fondly remembers playing at the office on Saturday mornings. After completing an MBA degree, he began his career as a commercial lending officer at a major US bank and six years later, in 1983, he started a business consulting practice. Since that time has worked with nearly 200 financially troubled family-owned companies. On many of those occasions he has been partnered by a family business psychologist to help ensure that the challenges faced by both the business and the family of the client were addressed.

Mr Sherman has spoken on his specialism to various groups, including the Family Firm Institute, the Turnaround Management Association and a number of university-based family business institutes. His articles on family business have appeared in *Family Business* magazine, the *Journal of Corporate Renewal and Commercial Lending Review.*

Louis Turchetta
CEO and founder, Strategic Psychological Services
lturchetta@spsri.com

Louis Turchetta is the founder and president of Strategic Psychological Services, a full-service multidisciplinary practice offering comprehensive behavioural health services. In addition, he is a member of Narva & Company LLC's multidisciplinary advisory team, where he helps family ownership groups and business partnerships to address relationship issues between and within generations, navigate business change and avoid emotional minefields that can undermine sound business decisions.

Dr Turchetta received a doctorate in psychology from Boston University. He is licensed as a psychologist in Massachusetts and Rhode Island, and is a long-standing member of the National Register of Health Insurance Providers in Psychology. He has been active in governance of the American Psychological Association (APA), as well as the Rhode Island Psychological Association for more than 25 years. He is currently a member of Division 13 (Consulting Psychology), Division 16 (School Psychology) and Division 42 (Independent Practice) of the APA.

Anna Xia
Principal, Market Ignition Group & Advisory LLC
annax@marketignition.com

Anna Xia is the founder and principal of Market Ignition Group & Advisory LLC, a firm that provides strategic intercultural consulting services to public and private enterprises in the United States and Europe. As a member of her family-owned business in Shanghai, China, she works on the introduction of innovative medical devices into the greater China market. Ms Xia has close to 20 years' experience in global strategic marketing and business development. When an executive working for several global financial institutions (including Wells Fargo, RBS and Citigroup), she led various marketing disciplines and worked closely with domestic and international staff.

Ms Xia was born in China. She attended Shanghai University there and Cesar Ritz College in Switzerland for her undergraduate degrees, and obtained a master's degree in business administration from Mississippi State University in the United States. She also received executive certifications from MIT in innovation and strategy and in management and leadership.